RAC

Gentlemen, It's Been My Pleasure

Four Decades in the Indiana Legislature

10-25-03

Wada —
Book does not do justice
to Ed, Curt & David.

Larry

Senator Lawrence M. Borst, D.V.M.

Guild Press Emmis Books

Dedicated to:

My wife, Eldoris, who urged me on,

And to

My father, Lawrence, who at 100 years of age is as interested in the outcome of this effort as I,

And to

Five grandsons: Adam, Brandon, Alex, Eric and Andrew

Contents

Foreword

I have been told: "You have stories to tell; you should write a book." I rather imagine that most everyone of any age, or of any accomplishment, has had that statement applied to them. Easier said than done.

My wife, Ellie, began urging me to write something years ago. Simply because I could type, she felt there would be no problem. Once I bought a computer, for some reason, she reasoned that the machine was at least a word-processor and could be easily managed.

Even Jerry Denbo, a state representative from French Lick, flattered me by telling me to write some of my political experiences down for others to read.

Carolyn Schott had been my administrative assistant in the Senate Finance Committee office for twenty-seven years and had saved every scrap of paper having to do with the day-to-day operations of the office. Without this, and my own files full of material to jog and to validate my memory, this book would never have been written.

I began the book. Struggled through fifty or more pages. Not having ever worked on a computer, much of my attention was being diverted from writing to the more mundane task of making the electronic gadget actually work. I lost pages of script. I had to learn to indent. Three months into the project I determined how to number the pages. *Windows XP for Dummies* was not easy for me to master. The Gateway manual was more gobbledygook than help.

The first efforts were not readable. The final effort may not be great but makes much more sense than did the beginning prose.

I knew what I wanted to write. I wanted to tell the story of the Republican Action Committee beginning and formation, its first campaigns, and the people that made up the textbook effort. Keith Bulen made the RAC what it was, and his brief chairmanship of the Marion County Republican party left a lasting impression on the GOP for thirty or more years. He knew talent and attracted the best. The book needed to tell that story.

I was also there when Uni-Gov was first thought of, researched, planned and formulated. Without this consolidation of government and its implementation by Mayor Lugar, downtown Indianapolis might today be desolate rows of empty buildings. Indianapolis' vibrant downtown is no accident and can trace its revival to that new form of government.

Ed Lewis needed to be written about. I, however, certainly did not do the man justice. Ed, a funny, shrewd man with all kinds of talents is a hidden icon in Indiana politics.

My seatmate in the Indiana Senate, Senator Jim Merritt, had written a book that had been published. One day I sought his counsel on how to write a book. I had no idea if what I was trying to write would be interesting to anyone in the world. Lo and behold, he wondered if I would mind if he showed the pages to someone in the publishing business.

Nancy Niblack Baxter read the abbreviated manuscript that weekend and called me to say that there were "possibilities."

Under her encouragement I did continue the task. After two rewrites by Nancy and me, she turned me over to Lawrence (Bo) Conner for another rewrite. I now know what it is like to completely redo a book. His help salvaged the effort.

Input and encouragement from Jim Biddinger, Pat Sullivan and Judith Essex were appreciated.

All in all, I would recommend my legislative and political experiences to most everyone.

I have learned that "one person can make a difference."

chapter 1

Barber Shop Politics

I was sitting in a barber chair having my hair cut, listening to the conversations that surrounded me in the five-chair shop. It became apparent that the shop owner, Everett Newlon, was more than a barber. From the questions and the kidding that went on, I realized that Everett had something to do with the Republican Party in Perry Township of Marion County.

On a later visit to Newlon's shop on Madison Avenue I asked him how one became a precinct committeeman. Several months later I got my answer. He called to ask if I would be interested in being appointed committeeman in the precinct where I lived, which was in Perry Township's Rosedale Hills subdivision. I said yes and Newlon, who was the ward chairman, said he would take care of the paperwork.

It was the first step in a political life that has lasted more than forty years. I was thirty-four when I got the offer in late 1961. At that time, I had been a veterinarian on the Southside of Indianapolis for seven years. I had a wife and three children and I was completely unschooled in politics. Politically naïve you could say.

This review of the four decades of politics that followed those first halting steps is an attempt to recall some of the highs and lows of those years; to record some of its significant achievements, and to tell about many of the interesting, even fascinating, people who made our government work, however imperfectly, in Indiana during the second half of the twentieth century.

It was a rocky beginning for me. What I didn't know when I agreed to being appointed committeeman was that the incumbent committeewoman, Geneva Smith, had not resigned, and moreover was a close ally and personal friend of H. Dale Brown, the Marion County Republican Chairman. There was obviously controversy in the Republican Party. Everett either didn't like Geneva or thought she was not doing an adequate job. It made me the proverbial "babe in the woods" when I stumbled into that political hotbed.

At the first ward meeting that I attended, I had thought that I would be welcomed by all of the other committeemen in the township and be privy to all manner of inside information. Not so. I was close to scrapping what I had thought would be a promising start in the political arena. But Mrs. Smith either resigned or just quit; I never found out how the outcome was determined. So, I was instructed to file for the elective office of precinct committeeman and was told I would be on the ballot in 1962. I was also told that I was to oversee the polling place in the primary election. Fortunately, Denise Andrews, the vice-committeewoman, guided me through the first step of running a precinct and conducting a primary election. She showed me how to open the old type of mechanical voting machine, how to crank it up, and how to read the back of that clunky monster the evening before the poll was to open.

It was all part of a learning process that would in a few years take me to the Indiana General Assembly where I have been something of a fixture for nearly forty years. It is a place where I have seen the best and worst of state and local politics.

But the first primary was not my introduction to the governmental process. Two years earlier, Joe Davis, owner of an insurance business and a member of the Perry Township School Board, had come to my Shelby Street Animal Clinic and asked if I would be interested in being appointed to the Second Perry Township School Building Corporation.

The township was in need of a second junior high school and it was to be built on south Keystone Avenue. I accepted the appointment and was elected president of the corporation. A school building corporation is a legal Indiana entity that is allowed to borrow money by issuing bonds to finance construction of a new school facility, which is then leased back to the school district. Harry Harman, a staunch Republican and a longtime legislative lobbyist for the commercial bus industry, was the corporation attorney who guided the new members.

The First Perry Township Building Corporation had built the new Southport High School and a couple of grade schools several years before. The five members of the new Second Building Corporation met on a regular basis with the members of the Perry School Board to develop plans for the new school. We corporation members had a lot to learn.

Fleck, Quebe and Reid Associates were the architects, engineers and construction managers selected to oversee the planning and construction of the school building. John Fleck, an outstanding architect, later was appointed by Governor Orr to supervise the remodeling of the Indiana Statehouse and to oversee all of the new construction in the Statehouse campus additions. Bill Quebe, a graduate of Southport High School and a resident of the township, was the engineer of the firm.

In planning for the school we discovered that the building and construction restrictions set up by the Indiana legislature were stifling. Hallways were required to be a certain width, ceilings a certain height, bathrooms a certain style and configuration. Air conditioning for a new school was nearly impossible. In one instance, the legislature had decreed the number of square feet of window space in each of the buildings, regardless of whether or not the new building was to be air-conditioned.

The size of the gymnasium was not restricted. The capacity of the Southport High School gym, built by the First Perry School Building Corporation, was for 7,200 people. Not the largest in the state but still listed in the top ten of the largest high school gymnasiums in Indiana.

We decided that the new school should have an auditorium, something that all of the other Perry township schools lacked.

After the first public hearing, our board knew that several of the more rabid and active taxpayers were opposed to the whole idea of a new school as being unnecessary and too costly. This being so, we surmised that they surely would not agree to an auditorium. We tried to explain that an auditorium would be beneficial to the school and would be available for use by the community at large. No go.

We, as members of the building corporation, concocted a diversionary tactic. Knowing that Southport High School had a very small, undersized, swimming facility, we had the architect make detailed plans for a regulation-sized swimming and diving pool for the proposed Keystone Avenue building. When these plans were presented the anti outcry was loud and outraged. The opponent's negative oratory shifted from elimination of the auditorium to stopping the swimming pool. So, what is now Southport Middle School was built with an auditorium, but was only plumbed for a swimming facility.

During those many months spent with the Perry School Board I had listened to the dos and don'ts for constructing a new school building, and generally, all of the do's and don'ts regarding education in general. I gradually began to realize that all of these rules and regulations that had to be addressed had been legislated by the Indiana General Assembly. I became convinced that if the opportunity arose, I could be more effective by serving in the legislature, rather than serving on a school board. During the construction of the new school, I was given the opportunity to serve out the term of office of a member of the Perry School Board who had resigned, but I declined the appointment.

Over the years, I have developed a pat speech for those who ask how and why I entered politics. I tell them that I was at a phase of my life where someone was taking a slice out of the money that I had worked for; where someone was transporting my children to a school and was keeping them for six or seven hours a day, and where someone was making laws that affected my everyday life. If government was spending my money, educating my children, and making laws that altered my life, I needed to become interested in the government that had a great deal of control over so many of the aspects of my life. So now, after my "barbershop nomination," I was at least a part of "government."

I thought that becoming a precinct committeeman would be an opportunity to become a minor insider and possibly have an effect on the system. Today, after having been in almost every position in organizational politics— committeeman, vice-committeeman, ward chairman, township chairman, assistant county chairman, and delegate to state and national conventions— I still feel, as I did in the sixties, that the position of precinct committeeman is the most important position in organizational politics. Some may feel with political messages saturating television, mail-boxes and electronic phone banks that the role of the committeeman has been diminished. I say that pounding on the pavement and knocking on doors still wins elections.

I believe that since the primary election is the most important election we have, it is in the primary election where the committeeman exhibits his value to the political structure. The committeeman makes the primary a success, or not a success, for the party. He or she is the one who identifies the registered and unregistered voters. The committeeman knows who and where his voters live. The voter is asked by his precinct committeeman to vote in the primary and is asked to vote for the party candidates. He or she opens and checks the voting apparatus and polling site the night before the elections; gets up at 4:30 in the morning, opens the polls, displays the political signs, makes sure that the Precinct Election Board and party workers are fed and catered to, hands out the literature, makes the telephone calls, and stays in the polling place until the votes have been tallied and the machines have been secured. A good committeeman can sway any primary election, regardless of the party he or she represents.

In 1962 Walter Andrews, the husband of my vice-committeeman Denise Andrews, was one of the Republican primary candidates for Marion County Commissioner. Our precinct went all out campaigning for him. Perry 19 may have been the only precinct in Marion County where the incumbent, Louis Ping, did not win. Though Walter never really had a chance to win overall, I came to understand the potential of a dedicated committeeman that primary day when Walter carried the precinct.

The precinct I served was beginning to show signs of change.

The heart and soul of the Democrat Party was on the southside of Indianapolis. Fountain Square and Garfield Park were Democrat strongholds. But the sons and daughters of the southside population, graduating from Manual and Sacred Heart high schools, became more educated than their parents, got steady jobs, moved south of the city, built houses of their own, assumed a mortgage, paid property taxes and developed a tendency to vote Republican.

Sometimes we, the precinct level people in politics, worked together. During my tenure as precinct committeeman I came to know Flossie Beghtel who owned the Rosedale Dairy, and her attorney friend and business partner, Sheldon Key. Both were solid Democrats. These were the people that a person with a problem sought out in order to obtain an audience with an elected Democrat official. Flossie was a friend of Philip L. Bayt, a supporter of Bayt's Democrat faction that was so dominant in Marion County politics. My backyard neighbor, Flossie's son Rex, was the Democrat precinct committeeman in the Rosedale Hills development when I was first appointed Republican committeeman. His wife, Agnes, did the legwork and she and I would compare our polls to determine who declared for which party. This was not exactly the way those things were supposed to be done, but then, we did not have to waste our time on someone who had purposely given out the wrong information.

The elections in our small world of Rosedale Hills were spirited and hotly contested. A few years later, Tony Maio, then the Democrat County Chairman, became the Democrat precinct committeeman in our area. His wife, Ernestine, did the work. She was good, thorough and tough. The precinct was growing. David Finney, a former Democrat mayor of Beech Grove, along with dozens of others became a resident in the Rosedale Hills subdivision.

The Republicans in those days used the wagon book system on election days. It was an organizational technique used by the precinct workers to identify which "friendly" voter had voted and which of the other "friendlies" needed a telephone call to remind them to vote. This precinct action worked well enough so that everyone that we thought should vote Republican was cajoled and reminded enough that they would finally go to Longacre Park to vote. The Rosedale precinct voted Republican, despite the heavy hitters from the other side.

I also came to know about election day inspectors. My inspector for all of the elections was Frank Spencer, a lawyer who read all of the footnotes and every reference of any decision that he researched. A deputy prosecutor, Frank was assigned to do the research for the most difficult cases by the prosecutor. Frank stuck to the rules of the election, opening the polls exactly at six AM and closing the polls at exactly six PM. Despite our pleadings, Frank would not bend an inch. He would never open and count the absentee ballots during the day, as was routinely done in other precincts, until after the polls had closed and the machines had been read, all according to election law. As a result, the precinct would be the last precinct to report its results, and Frank would be about the last to bring the official documents to the County Clerk's office late on election night. Frank's integrity was such that even the Democrat county chairman had no complaint. Rosedale Hills arguably had the most honest and legally correct election in all of Marion County.

During that summer of 1962, the Republican organizational structure was finally determined, and barber Everett Newlon was officially back in good standing. I suppose that I had never thought about the men and women who were barbers. I had never considered that anyone who was a barber could be an outstanding economic success. Most barbers talked about going fishing or hunting or drinking. None talked about stocks and bonds and other opportunities to succeed financially in life the way he did.

That same summer, Everett and his wife, Doris, asked Eldoris and me to have a drink with them. I was embarrassed then and am still embarrassed these many years later to have almost turned down this invitation because I didn't want to ride in a junky car and have a beer at one of the local pubs. How we stereotype people. I told my wife to expect the worst. At first I was speechless, and then over apologetic when Everett pulled into our driveway in a brand new Cadillac. We had drinks and dinner at the Columbia Club on Monument Circle. The Newlons obviously were in a higher economic stratum than the Borsts. A lesson to be learned. Titles and workplaces are not the criteria for judging people.

In the 1962 Marion County primary many citizens filed for the political contests. There were thirty-eight Republican candidates for the eleven Indiana House seats and forty-two Democrat filings for the same spots. Since those days, courts have ordered single member legislative districts, which has been a major deterrent to interesting the general public to seek elective office. The smaller districts, rather than the entire county, tend to restrict the geographical pool of potential candidates. Challenging a single member district incumbent, rather than a group of at-large candidates, also discourages likely candidates.

For the fall general election, Noble Pearcy was designated as Perry Township Republican campaign coordinator, assisted by Bill Byrum, Nelson Swift, Martha Burnett and Geneva Smith. For the most part, the Republican Party was the victor in the 1962 fall elections. The party worked extremely hard and was most effective in obtaining that victory.

Those legislative candidates elected in the fall of 1962 served in the infamous 101-day special session of 1963, which enacted the first two cents of the Indiana sales tax and also raised other taxes. Lieutenant Governor Richard Ristine cast the deciding, tie-breaking Senate vote in favor of the sales tax that concluded the marathon session.

Ristine's Democrat opponent for governor used photos of his "yea" vote in Ristine's unsuccessful campaign for governor in 1964.

I had become a member of the Downtown Lions Club, which met once each week at noon in the Claypool Hotel. It was the second largest of all of the Lions Clubs in the United States, with over a hundred members attending the weekly meetings. Donald Bruce, a local broadcaster later elected to Congress from Indianapolis in 1961, and Fred Heckman, a radio newscaster, gave a news update each meeting. Cornelius Reed was the Tail Twister, extracting ten or fifteen dollars a week out of the crowd, at a quarter or fifty cents a head. The leadership of the club was dynamic. Roscoe Stovall, George Gabel, Rex Campbell and Bob Beckman, Sr. had all been presidents of the club and each made sure that the members stayed active and attended the weekly meetings on a regular basis. Very few of the members were from the Southside.

Being a member of the club exposed me to a different cross section of the people in the county. Many of the local CEOs and civic leaders were members. Roc Stovall, more active than anyone else, was the owner of several successful laundromats in Marion County. He was a battle-tested veteran of World War II and a Purple Heart recipient. His energy was boundless. After serving as president of the Downtown Lions Club, he organized the Greater Indianapolis Information, Inc. designed to become the cheerleader for the city of Indianapolis. Roc spent his own money on this creation, funding the logos, office space, letterheads, cards and the complete works. After Roc found out that I had been president of Greater Southside, Inc., he recruited me and assigned me several tasks for the new organization. One of these was to organize a contest seeking entries which would submit ideas for a design of a flag for the city of Indianapolis. The winner would receive a fifty dollar government bond, with second place a twenty-five dollar bond. Roc served as one judge and appointed Wilbur Peat as the other judge to make the final selection. Wilbur qualified as being a member of Downtown Lions and he was also the director of the John Herron School of Art.

More than a dozen flag ideas were submitted. The winning design is still the official flag of the city of Indianapolis. The flag, done in red, white, and blue was entered by Roger Gohls, a student at John Herron. It depicted the city as being in the crossroads of America. Once the flag design was selected, it was up to me, as the committee chairman, to have the winning idea made into an actual flag and make sure that the new flag would be flying from all of the central city flagpoles.

I approached Eli Lilly & Co. because it had the tallest and most central flagpole downtown. Would they fly the new flag? I was referred to Eli Lilly himself. I had never met the man. He and I left his office and climbed some stairs to the roof of the Lilly headquarters on McCarty Street and surveyed the situation to see if the flag would work up there. It would. Eli Lilly & Co. became the first non-governmental entity to fly the official flag of the city of Indianapolis.

I always marveled that such a mundane decision as flying a flag on a rooftop would be made by the big boss himself. Long-time Lilly employees, when hearing of the trek to the roof, were not surprised and said, "That's the way it is at Lilly's." The only other occasion that I ever spoke directly with Mr. Lilly was when I suggested that he leave a portion of his vast fortune to the state of Indiana for the establishment of an autonomous facility for higher education in Indianapolis that would be named Eli Lilly University. The offer was politely declined.

Following the adoption of a resolution by the Indianapolis City Council designating the selected design as the "official flag," I presented a flag to Indianapolis Mayor Albert Losche. The mayor arranged for an acceptance breakfast ceremony, complete with dignitaries and the ROTC color guard from Manual High School.

Excess energy and some good press during the days of Greater Indianapolis Information stimulated Roc Stovall to think that he should enter the political arena. The mayoralty race in 1963 seemed to be a perfect spot for his ambitions. The main problem in Roc's political analysis was that Dale Brown, the Republican County Chairman, thought that Clarence Drayer would make a better Republican nominee. Charles Applegate, an avowed anti-organization candidate, had already announced his candidacy. Roc thought that if the other two candidates split their vote, he might just be the one to be selected by the organization screening committee. Roc recruited me and others from the Downtown Lions Club to help him contact committeemen on his behalf. I spent a lot of time with him and Robert Mathews (later a state GOP Chairman and friend of mine) and others learning about campaign strategy in Stovall's unsuccessful quest.

Roc published an eight-page "newspaper" hailing his past and announcing a ten-point action agenda for the city of Indianapolis. He mostly spent his own money; campaign contributions for the Stovall for Mayor race were scant. Some of his political techniques were well in advance of their time. For $1,200 he purchased a list of the precinct committee people from the Marion County Central Committee. The list included names and addresses, but no telephone numbers. Dale Brown was not about to help a candidate that he did not like.

Bill Leak was a possible fourth candidate for mayor in that election. Bill's campaign was not that dynamic, spending less than one hundred dollars on his campaign.

The slating convention overwhelmingly selected Clarence Drayer. Roc Stovall was appointed to a minor post on the Drayer for Mayor Committee. Drayer went on to secure the GOP nomination by out-polling Charles Applegate, the only other GOP candidate who stayed in the race beyond the slating convention. John Barton, the Democrat nominee, won the fall election, defeating Drayer and independent candidate Sam Unger.

In that same election, Elton Geshwiler, another Democrat, won re-election as mayor of Beech Grove by eighty-five votes. Every four years since, the Republicans seemed to have a chance to elect a mayor in Beech Grove, but it never happened, with our candidates almost always losing by a very slight margin.

chapter   2

The Beginning as a Candidate

And where was I, the aspiring politician, while all of this was going on? It appeared I had arrived. At least I was no longer being ignored.

My entry into precinct politics had been a flop. I had been appointed as a Republican committeeman under suspicious circumstances and then was allowed to be a candidate for that position. The year before, my name had been submitted for a position as officer for the Perry GOP Club. Not only did I not win, but also my name was not considered because of a lack of a second. Somehow in 1964 the political tide turned. The previous fall I had been appointed as a member of the Clarence Drayer for Mayor Committee. Now, I was also asked to submit my name for the presidency of the Perry Township Republican Club. My nomination was seconded and there were no other nominations. Evidently, I had become a "good guy."

And so, for a variety of reasons, few of them valid, I toyed with the idea of becoming a candidate for one of the nominations from Marion County for the Indiana House of Representatives. I believed I had a few credentials. I had been the secretary-treasurer of the Indiana Veterinary Medical Association for a number of years, and in that capacity, I had attended several sessions of the general assembly, focusing on issues affecting the veterinary profession. I had attended House and Senate committee meetings and had met several of the out-of-county legislators. I felt that I could work the legislative schedule into my private and business life, because being a legislator at that time was only a sixty-one day job every twenty-four months. Also, the statehouse was less than twenty minutes from the animal clinic.

And I really was intrigued by the challenge of one man "making a difference."

So, I decided to be serious about it.

The Southside of Marion County was underrepresented. Leo Kriner had been the last Republican to have served in the House, and that had been many years earlier. Carroll Dennis, a former Democrat House member, was a friend and a client, and he encouraged me to run. Prosecutor Noble Pearcy and Sheriff Bob Fields said that I could count on their support.

I did file for consideration. I knew that only a few of those Republicans who had served in the 1963 session were about to seek re-election. Heavyweights such as Speaker Richard Guthrie and L. Keith Bulen were tired out by the regular and special sessions and did not want to immediately begin campaigning for another term. Other incumbents were fearful that having voted for the sales tax would be a detriment to a candidacy in 1964.

The evening before the slating convention, key members of the Republican Party and all of the GOP ward chairmen were given a "Sunshine Slate," which was delivered to my home by someone that I had never seen, late in the evening after the sun had set. The deliverer was in a hurry to carry out the secret mission. Even though he denied responsibility, Dale Brown was the originator of the slate of "favored" candidates, and masterminded the covert delivery system. As a candidate, my name was on the slate that was delivered to me. Dale was always ingenious. Although there were fifteen vacancies to be filled, the "Sunshine Slate" listed only ten names. In this way, Brown could say there was no dictatorial policy and the delegates were free to choose whoever they wanted. I also found out that Brown was smart enough to distribute more than one list of names and that the ten names delivered to me were not the same ten delivered to other Republicans around the county. Dale covered all the bases and endorsed twice the complement for vacancies.

Under the Brown regime, a prospective legislative candidate was required to officially file for the office with the secretary of state in order to be considered for slating, thus producing a large number of candidates that competed all the way to slating. The Republican Action Committee, which was formed later, discouraged a candidate from filing before a slating convention. The RAC method winnowed out the opposition, and then the official slated candidates were the only candidates that might officially file for the primary.

For the 1964 Republican primary, therefore, there were sixty-four individuals who sought one of the fifteen Marion County at-Large slots for the Indiana House of Representatives; in addition twenty-four filed for the four Senate positions. Five people filed for U. S. Congress. Not all of those filing did submit their names for consideration at the slating convention. Once again, the Marion County GOP machine was under attack. E. Allen Hunter, the incumbent Marion County treasurer, and attorney Donald Tabbert formed what they called the Victory Committee. This committee filed its own competitive full slate of nominees.

The members of the Victory Committee were conservative and committed to the election of Barry Goldwater for the presidency of the United States. The Victory Committee did not strive to overthrow the county GOP chairman and opposed very few precinct committeemen. Still, the full slate of candidates the Victory Committee announced was a first for those opposing Dale Brown. Normally, only a few disgruntled or idealistic souls banded together to seek a nomination in opposition to the central committee candidate.

Many were the candidates; varied were the issues. I was part of a group of candidates going to innumerable local meetings. It was not unusual to have three or four candidate meetings scheduled for the same evening somewhere in Marion County. The order in which a candidate spoke was determined by the order in which he or she arrived and signed in at the meeting place. When the candidates for the county offices and those running for Congress were added to the ninety avowed legislative candidates, the number of candidates seeking to speak at each of the meetings numbered well over 100. Most would show up at each of the nightly meetings, and speeches were usually limited to two minutes.

Many speakers. Few listeners. Sometimes only three or four people were in attendance. Whoever was chairing the meeting had the option of simply introducing the candidates or allowing every candidate to orate to the best of his or her ability in such a sparse setting.

Tex Black would thunder. Charles Bosma would explain his vote on the sales tax in 1963. Tommie Caito proudly announced that he was an exceptional Italian because he was the only one in his family who was Republican. Wally Cox talked Butler basketball. Jim Cummings wanted to balance the ticket as an African-American. Jane Hunt Davis was erudite. Fred Ewry was logical. Kenny Greenwood was the most dignified. Rosemary Adams Huffman gave everyone in the audience a rosemary seed (the rosemary seed denotes hope, according to Ms. Huffman); Ed Madinger cited his past experience. Marty McDermott climbed up on a chair and let loose a roll of parchment paper thirty feet long, listing all of the taxes imposed by the state of Indiana. Marty became disenchanted with the Republican Party and in later years sought several nominations as a Democrat.

Bob Morris had a vast amount of business experience. John Mutz talked about his stint on *The Indianapolis News* and his time in Pittsburgh. Everett Newlon was my ward chairman but rarely attended or spoke. For F. Perry Ray, this was the first of many attempts for public office. Dick Retterer was an insurance executive and was the smoothest performer. George Rubin, a young attorney, also advocated broadening the base of the Republican Party. Otis Yarnell was a former president of a locomotive engineers union and stressed that the ticket should include a union member. Phyllis Zerfas, a medical doctor from Beech Grove, seemed to campaign for Barry Goldwater more than herself.

Martha Burnett was the only candidate for joint senator for Marion and Johnson County. By informal agreement, the joint senator member resided in Marion County and the joint house member came from Johnson County. Martha, being unopposed would pop into a candidate's meeting, bat her eyelashes and ask for "just a moment." As an unopposed incumbent she talked for thirty seconds and left. I made up my mind then that someday I wanted to be a senator.

Excluding the Victory Committee candidates, the camaraderie of all of the candidates was healthy. If one of the candidates could not show up for a meeting, several of the others having memorized the other candidate's presentation were able to pitch in and give the candidates' regrets and his two-minute speech. One lady brought her knitting to a meeting, and planted herself in a chair to be first in line at 4:30 for a 6:00 beginning. My business hours were such that I rarely could be anywhere until 8-8:30, and so, I would be the last on the sign-in sheet. I would start showing up at 9-9:30 and only have to stay around an hour or so.

My biggest campaign disappointment was when the Washington Township GOP Club met. Theirs was the largest GOP club in the county. A must attend situation. At that time Washington Township was noted for being able to deliver a huge percentage of the total Republican votes in Marion County. That year, I made it to the meeting about 9:00 as usual. The format that evening was different than most. The audience was allowed to question the candidates after their prepared remarks, thus dragging out the evening. My turn to speak was at 12:30 in the morning with an attendance of three: a disaster. The president of the club assured me that he was taking notes and was rating the speaking ability of each candidate and that he would inform the entire membership of the club regarding his impressions. I think that I talked for three minutes and answered a question posed by each person still awake. I must have not been too impressive because I made a poor showing in Washington Township in the primary election.

My usual "two minute" speech mainly emphasized the leadership positions that I had either been appointed or elected to in my pre-politics life. I would refer to the fact that I was a Southside veterinarian and lived in Perry Township. Easily half of the legislative candidates lived in north Indianapolis, mostly in Washington Township outside of the city limits, so the rest of us emphasized the importance of geographical balance for the final selections.

During the primary phase, basic governmental issues were not always important to many of the groups we addressed. To a large number of Republicans during this particular primary election in 1964, how conservative a candidate might be was more important than were state and local issues. Some of the candidates attempted to outdo others by being self-described as an "extreme conservative" in order to leave an imprint of conservatism on the minds of the voters. I had always thought that Republicans differed from Democrats because of their approach to limiting government and first attempting to solve a problem by not having to rely on government as the only participant in the final solution. This type of philosophy seemed to me to be enough of a litmus test for being a Republican.

That year, at all of these public meetings, the candidates for Congress were given five minutes to explain how they would run the country. The two main candidates, William Ruckelshaus and Don Tabbert, were accomplished speakers and their presentations were solid and interesting. However, Tabbert and the other candidates affiliated with the Victory Committee were not al-

ways welcome at a central committee party function. Brown had decreed that
any candidate who had not paid his or her fees and assessments to the central
committee would be prohibited from speaking at party and club functions.
Tabbert and a few of his fellow members of the Victory Committee would
stand at the meeting entrance and try to shake hands and pass out their literature.

As Perry GOP Club president I announced at the spring candidates
meeting, "All candidates who have shown their seriousness by paying their
assessment to the Marion County Central Committee will be allowed to
speak first. Those who haven't may remain and be introduced later." For this,
Dr. Charles Zerfas, the husband of Dr. Phyllis Zerfas, took me to task in letters on the editorial page of several newspapers. Candidates opposing the
regular organization thought my statement to be heavy handed; the regular
party politicians I associated with thought it was the right thing to do.

One issue much debated in the media in 1963 between Democrat
County Chairman Judson Haggerty and Dale Brown was whether or not the
new sales tax enactment should be repealed. Haggerty had challenged Brown
to repudiate any prospective candidate if he or she had voted to impose the
sales tax in 1963 or any candidate who did not seek to repeal the tax in 1965.
Dale replied, "The Republican candidates who I will support as chairman of
my party will have to specifically state they are for repeal of the state sales tax.
They must, as they have in the past, also endorse a ceiling on the property tax,
and any new legislation that will be proposed to help cities and towns must
be subject to a referendum." It was a dead issue. The public by now had ac-
customed themselves to the sales tax, were resigned to its imposition, and the
stance of a candidate on repealing the tax became a non-issue in the campaign of 1964. Dale Brown never did make any of the candidates pledge future action regarding the sales tax.

At midnight on primary night there was every indication that I would
not be one of the top fifteen vote getters. I figured it to be close, but with so
many candidates, the tallying and reading of the machines was not precise. As
I read *The Indianapolis Star* the next morning the unofficial results had David
Derry in 15th place with 19,626 votes to my 19,082. An also ran. So much for
my first political race. I hoped that I was gracious in defeat.

On the following Friday, *The Star* listed the official results. That morning, before I had even gotten out of bed, my wife and children ran into the

bedroom with the newspaper wide open, showing me the headline, with my picture in the printed text. It read, "Dr. Lawrence M. Borst, Southside veterinarian, was nominated Tuesday by Republicans for state representative from Marion County. Unofficial returns earlier had labeled him a loser. County Election Board officials attributed the revision to absentee ballots which were not counted until after machine votes were tabulated Tuesday night." I was now in 15th place with 20,534 votes and Derry 16th with 20,021 official votes. Edward Madinger at 14th gained from 19,576 to 20,545. Somehow I had 483 more absentee votes than did Madinger. To be honest about it all, and accepting the vote total change from unofficial to official, I imagine that there was some kind of influence from H. Dale Brown, coupled with the uncounted absentee ballots, which placed me on the ballot for the fall.

Surprisingly, only seven of the organizational candidates survived the challenge from the Victory Committee. Don Tabbert was easily nominated for Congress.

chapter 3

1964 Election

The Republic State Convention held at the State Fairgrounds Coliseum the month following the primary in 1964 has not been duplicated in suspense or in longevity in the many years since.

Before the day was done, the delegates ended up casting their votes on five ballots before the business of the convention was completed. The most hotly contested race had John Snyder defeating Richard Folz for the state treasurer nomination on that fifth ballot. The normal Republican State Convention takes about three hours from the opening prayer to the benediction; this convention lasted over eleven hours with the time for the actual voting taking eight and a half hours of the total time period. A total of 2,195 delegates cast their votes on the first ballot for the state treasurer, but only 990 delegates remained to vote for the treasurer's office on the fifth ballot; 1,817 delegates choosing not to stay for the fifth ballot. Milking the cows or watching their favorite television program became more important than staying to exercise their responsibility to the Republican Party.

D. Russell Bontrager won over Don Bruce and Ed Whitcomb in the contest for the nomination for United States Senate. Bruce, an Indianapolis broadcaster, was the incumbent 11th District congressman. Whitcomb at that time was not much of a factor—Bontrager won on the third ballot 1,142 to Bruce's 851.

The race for the gubernatorial nomination drew the most interest from the delegates. Richard Ristine had been elected four years before as lieutenant governor, while the governor who had been elected in Indiana during the same election was a Democrat, Matt Welsh. Ristine was opposed by Dale Brown, who supported Congressman Bill Bray for governor. Other candidates for governor at the convention were Richard Ellis, Bob Gates, Charles Hendricks, Robert Hughes (being championed by Senator Bill Jenner and the incumbent state treasurer), and Earl Landgrebe. Ristine received 839 of the 2,210 delegate votes on the initial ballot. Only Hughes and Ristine increased their vote totals on the second go-around. The down-to-earth politicking then began.

After the second ballot, Dale Brown called twenty or twenty-five of his convention floor managers together in the Fairgrounds Cow Barn. The building was relatively clean despite many years of housing cows, but still retained an identifiable particular odor. Some of the faithful stood in the gutters. The more knowledgeable occupied the front of the stanchions. The topic was whether to stick with Bray and possibly go down the political tubes or to make a move to another candidate.

Brown knew that I had supported Dick Ristine, and he asked for my opinion. This was heady stuff. I opined that Ristine was going to receive the nomination on the next ballot and that the Marion County organization should swing to him on the third ballot. The Brown lieutenants hooted at that and wanted to hang in there with Bray. Dale didn't offer an opinion until about ten minutes later. For a long time and for reasons unknown he had despised Jenner and so told his Marion County troops that he personally did not care who they voted for, so long as it was not Jenner's man Bob Hughes.

Going through Brown's mind was the disagreement he had with Dick Ristine over the tax increases that caused the 101-day special session. Brown had resigned his position as Republican state chairman because of the differences with Ristine. But more importantly, Brown blamed many of his internal political problems on Jenner's followers. These followers in Marion County were all supporting Bob Hughes for governor. Dale was not given to utter words of encouragement for Ristine on one hand. On the other hand, he figured that a follower of Bill Jenner had to be worse.

Bob Gates released his delegates to Ristine, who then won on the third ballot with 1,212 votes, 599 for Hughes and 266 for Bray.

Judge Jack Ryan had to be the most popular Republican in the state of Indiana. He drew no formal opposition and was selected as the nominee for lieutenant governor by acclamation.

Bob Bloem wrote in *The Indianapolis Times:*

> *Indiana's Republican convention nominated conservative candidates for its 1964 election campaign. But it refused to nominate extreme conservatives.*
>
> *For U. S. senator, delegates rejected the state's most right-wing congressman, Representative Donald Bruce of the 11th District. They stuck with long time legislative leader D. Russell Bontrager.*
>
> *For governor, delegates rejected Robert Hughes of Greenwood, protégé of the most right-wing senator Indiana ever had—William Jenner. Instead they stuck with hard-working Lieutenant Governor Richard Ristine. All signs indicated the convention still likes Barry Goldwater for the party's presidential nomination. Ristine made a point of saying so.*
>
> *Perhaps the victories of Bontrager and Ristine proved nothing more than that if you work long enough and hard enough for a nomination you'll win. Bontrager had been helping out with the GOP chores for some thirty years. Ristine has been titular head of the party since its 1960 governor nominee, Crawford Parker, fell by the wayside and lost out to Democrat Governor Welsh.*
>
> *Goldwater was virtually unopposed for the presidential preference in the primary. Republicans like Marion County's Chairman H. Dale Brown who believed Indiana isn't as far to the political right as Goldwater had no place to go. Brown's political opponents, in fact, latched onto the Goldwater gravy train and convinced Goldwater backers in this county that being anti-Brown and being pro-Goldwater were the same thing.*
>
> *Elsewhere in the state, too, the sweeping Goldwater victory in the primary was interpreted as the voice of the Indiana GOP. Actually it almost was, but not quite. The state convention apparently served notice that while Indiana goes to next month's national convention as a "Goldwater state," in state political matters Indiana Republicans aren't quite as far out to the right as Goldwater.*

Following the spring primary, the two separate groups of Marion County Republicans rarely met together. Both Brown and Tabbert made public assertions that there was a great cooperative spirit between the Victory

Committee members and the members of the regular GOP organization, but no one individual was ever in charge, and that the campaign had no single focus. Brown did form the United Front GOP Victory Committee to "bolster the presidency of Senator Barry M. Goldwater and local Republican office seekers." Named to the committee were: Don Tabbert, Charles Applegate, Judge John M. Ryan, William Sparrenberger, John Mutz and myself. So far as I can remember, this committee never met. Sparrenberger was the head of the Goldwater-Miller Committee in Marion County, and Mutz was coordinator of the Goldwater-Miller forces in Lawrence Township.

Enthusiasm for the Republican ticket, especially for Senator Goldwater, was most evident. The volunteer pool was huge. The conservative segment in the Republican Party now had a champion. Goldwater was energetic, experienced in government and offered ideas that seemed new. He spearheaded the troops that were tired of "big brother" government and residual New Deal philosophies. Twenty years before, a goodly portion of the active volunteers had been involved in World War II. They felt that the ideals that they had fought for in the war were being overlooked and ignored, and they knew that a change in governmental philosophy was needed.

Down in my territory, Rufus Dodril loaned an empty building to the Goldwater forces to be used as a public headquarters for the Perry Township GOP. Located on the southeast corner of Troy and Madison Avenues, the headquarters was manned and open ten hours daily including the weekends. Buttons were available as were bumper stickers and Goldwater literature.

I had never before been exposed to the fervor of the conservative portion of the Republican Party. This campaign was not a political campaign, it was a crusade. At times, and when talking to someone like Dr. Zerfas, this crusade took on a religious aspect. I had never heard of the John Birch Society. I had never heard of the Tri-Lateral Agreement. I had never heard of the green door, or red door, or some color door in Chicago, behind which, awful global things were plotted by the Rockefellers and other super liberal Republicans.

My running mates from the Victory Committee barely tolerated the infidels from the regular organization. They were all on a mission and the newly arrived or non-believers were asked to always sit in the back and keep quiet. I attended many residential meetings, usually having to negotiate a flight of stairs going down to the basement. The basement was fairly dark, as if illuminated by only a forty watt light bulb. A large American flag would be on display. The settings reminded me of the old black and white movies, where a meeting was being held with Peter Lorre guiding some secret conspiracy group. Testimony would be given about the glories of the John Birch Society and the heinous behavior of suspected members of the Communist Party employed by the federal government. Those attending these meetings truly believed that the election of Barry Goldwater would save the country from self-destruction. Or at least from federal government excess.

When called on, I would tell the assemblage that "I believe in the flag, I believe in the Constitution of the United States and the Constitution of the State of Indiana, and if elected, I will fight to preserve all three." I would sit down and receive polite applause.

The John Birch Society, which had been founded in Indianapolis some years before, became a mini-campaign issue. The Democrats demanded to know which of the Republican candidates were dues-paying members. Naturally, the media pounced on the issue and attempted to make it a big story. The society, whose secrecy did lend itself to second guessing by the general public, was made out to be a subversive organization plotting, behind closed doors, to take matters in its own hands to rid the nation of communism. Each candidate was sent questionnaires from the print media asking if he or she were a society member. The candidates were also asked if they supported the mission of the John Birch Society.

It was not until years later that I finally found out what the Tri-Lateral Agreement was. This agreement, which many of these arch-conservatives abhorred, was said to be set up by the bankers in New York, London, and Tokyo as an arrangement to control all of the currency and cash flow in the world. Or something like that. I did know that several of those from the Victory Committee also had no real idea of the agreement's mission or even if there really was a Tri-Lateral Agreement as they termed it.

A real defining moment for the Goldwater national campaign occurred when Nelson Rockefeller attempted to speak during the Republican National Convention in San Francisco. The floor and galleries were packed with Goldwater supporters. Rockefeller was booed unmercifully and his attempts to speak were drowned out by the delegates and spectators, though this was not the doing of Barry Goldwater or his staff. The reaction was spontaneous. It made a bad impression on television viewers. Older Jewish immigrants remembered howling Nazi crowds in Germany that had the same fervor. Many of the voters, not sympathizing with either faction of the Republican Party, felt that Rockefeller should have at least been given an opportunity to express his views. While Indiana and Marion County had voted overwhelmingly for Goldwater delegates for the Republican Nation Convention, Dale Brown and Russell McDermott cast their convention votes for Nelson Rockefeller.

During the fall of 1964, whenever a meeting request to the GOP Central Committee for a Republican candidate was made, Brown usually contacted me first. The speakers at these appearances were only from the regular organization and never from the Victory Committee. I did a lot of appearances.

Of all of the speaking assignments that I accepted, the one that still stands out in my mind was a meeting for the political candidates at the most orthodox of the Jewish synagogues. The dinner consisted of a huge ground beef burger, enclosed in a poppy seed bun and a giant bottle of Pepsi-Cola. I was the only Republican present. I think that the entire Democrat slate was there. I was treated cordially, even though I was never called on to speak. The moderator allowed that I was a nice young man and most likely a well qualified candidate, and maybe in another election, he might be able to recommend my candidacy to his membership but not this one. The tone of the evening's discussion had to do with the fear of the apparent extremism of the conservative movement in the United States and what effect such a philosophy might have on Israel.

Andy Jacobs, Jr. the Congressional candidate from the 11th District, did not have to plan a comprehensive campaign that year. The polls were in his and Lyndon Johnson's favor. Andy accused the Republicans of wanting to do away with the Social Security system. He promised to "strengthen, not abolish" the system. Jacobs won the election with 149,337 votes in Marion County as compared to Tabbert's 146,415 votes. County wide, the African-American vote was decisive. Totaling the congressional vote in the ten wards where African-Americans lived in large numbers, it came out 45,759 for Jacobs and 12,847 for Tabbert.

Johnson drew 152,413 votes to 143,309 for Goldwater in Marion County. Statewide, Johnson won in eighty of the ninety-two counties. Each of the Marion County Democrat House candidates prevailed by about seven to eight thousand votes. The Republican message, too extreme and non-focused, was not accepted by the voting public.

In the 1964 post-election analysis, Leslie Duvall wrote: *There are mem-*

bers of the liberal wing of the party that did do battle for the national ticket, although with varying degrees of enthusiasm. These persons certainly are entitled to future consideration but not the Romneys, Rockefellers or the Keatings. While the party should be big enough for varying points of view, the members should be big enough to abide by party decisions if they intend to exercise national leadership. Richard Nixon charged that Nelson Rockefeller "got his pound of flesh" out of Barry Goldwater's defeat. Rockefeller fired back that this was typical of Nixon, "being neither factual nor constructive." So much for post election unity.

Dale Brown complained that "the Republican national campaign, as well as the state campaign, was amateurishly handled." He continued, "In my opinion there is a world of difference between extremism and genuine common-sense conservatism. Because America so badly needs enlightened conservatism and because it is vital that the two-party system continue, our party is not dead. It has roots like the oak. It has enduring qualities which can outlive the curious combination of conflicting forces now propping up the Democratic majority." Dale also said, "Regardless of how you or I feel about certain issues—and I have always voted Republican and worked my heart out for the party—if those issues do not have sufficient appeal to the voters to convince a majority of them, then we must consider broadening the base and we must look for attractive candidates who believe in a positive Republican program that is truly realistic."

The election of 1964 completely changed the guiding philosophy of the Republican Party. It almost seems as if there are two Republican parties today: one attempting to stem the tide of government intervention, the other emphasizing moral issues. One portion of the party readily accepts compromise in order to make progress, while the other portion does not subscribe to the old adage of, "fifty percent of something is better than one hundred percent of nothing."

The actions or non-actions of Dale Brown in the fall election, combined with the defeat of most of the slated regular organization candidates, led to the formation of a small group of Republicans that eventually became the Republican Action Committee. The RAC deposed Dale Brown as Marion County Republican Chairman and installed L. Keith Bulen in his place.

chapter 4

The Age of Bulen

The sixties were the Age of Bulen as far as the Republican Party in Indiana was concerned.

Keith Bulen was a political genius. His political and organizational ability made him stand out as a giant among the little people. He was so far ahead of his time with his ability to motivate, to foretell the political future, to plan and to execute, that it took literally dozens of extra people in later organizations to produce the successful political campaigns that he did during the RAC heydays.

Lawrence Keith Bulen was born in Madison County, Indiana on New Year's Eve of 1926. He got his start in big-time politics at the age of sixteen handing out bubble gum to win votes as a candidate for Supreme Court judge at Boys State. He attended Pendleton High School and ran successfully for freshman class president. After winning a varsity letter in both basketball and baseball, Bulen graduated from high school in 1944 at the height of World War II and enlisted in the Army Air Corps. He briefly attended The Ohio State University while in the Air Corps and served overseas in the 5th Air Force. In 1949 he earned a B. S. degree in government at Indiana University, Bloomington, followed by a Doctor of Jurisprudence in 1952 from the Indiana University School of Law.

Bulen served as a county deputy prosecutor from 1952 to 1960. Elected

Young Republican chairman in 1954, Bulen challenged the party organization, led by county chairman H. Dale Brown. In 1960, he defeated the slated
candidates (one of which was current Indiana Court of Appeals Judge Patrick
Sullivan) and was elected to the Indiana House of Representatives. Following
the same script he was re-elected in 1962.

In September of 1962, I introduced myself to Keith Bulen. His reputation and accomplishments were familiar to me from reading about his exploits in the newspapers.

He was frequently mentioned in *The Indianapolis Times*, often in the
daily column written by Irving Leibowitz. For anyone who had even a slight
interest in politics, gossip and downtown events, the column was "must"
reading. I read it religiously. From the time I was appointed as precinct committeeman in Perry Township, I figured I should read about the events in the
world of politics.

Keith's name appeared often. I didn't know then that anyone could call
Irving up and schmooze with him and drop a few pieces of dark side information. In return, he might include something that would be favorable to the
caller and would mention his name in later columns. Keith would never admit that he was one of those who discussed inside-info with Irving, but events
seem to confirm a conspiracy between these two.

Keith was usually identified as the chairman of the Marion County delegation in the House of Representatives. That this delegation never had a formal vote as to who was chairman did not faze Bulen. You might say that
among that group, each one in the delegation assumed the mantle of chairman at one point or another. Richard Guthrie was the Speaker of the House,
but not the speaker for the Marion County delegation.

I decided that I wanted to meet the man and found out that Bulen's law
offices were downtown on the ninth floor of the Consolidated Building. A
group of young lawyers rented space on that floor from an older lawyer and
practiced in a spartan and reasonably priced cooperative environment. I
walked in off the street without an appointment and asked the lady if I could
see Mr. Bulen. Because Keith's legal specialty was criminal law, I suppose I
didn't appear as a typical client. There was hesitancy and then a disappearance
of the receptionist and then the appearance of Keith.

He was most cordial and unbelieving that someone from Perry Township would take the time to look him up and offer individual help for the up-

coming election. He had neither badges nor bumper stickers, and I suggested that he get some. These were delivered to me the next day. That day was the beginning of a great relationship with a man who was to become one of the closest friends in my life. That relationship was not always even-keeled; and there were times when neither of us would even speak with each other for days. Even though both of us competed unmercifully, I believe we always wanted the other to be there to share in the glory of any individual accomplishments.

Keith never denied that he was a "politician." To him, being a politician was being a member of an honorable profession. It was a calling for public service with a goal of using the political process to create a solution to get something done, not just for his political party, but for the benefit of the public too. Whenever a remedy or a solution was in doubt, if it came under the heading of good government, then it was good politics. Keith wanted to first and foremost win elections. Winning popularity contests was secondary. Positive results would take care of being popular. His bluntness was legendary. Being able to withstand a tirade was a trait that was totally necessary if you were going to be a member of the Bulen team for any extended time. Woe to the offender, especially if the offender seemed to be taking this one-sided discussion personally. With any sign of weakness, the tirade would become more intense and lasted longer. One could either completely ignore the man or else chuckle or laugh a little. His law partner, Charlie Castor, would simply turn around and walk out, slamming the door behind him. Charlie was very hard of hearing in one ear and would purposely turn his deaf side to Keith.

On the other hand, LKB was an absolute softy to the people he liked. Every committee person received a birthday and Christmas card. Valentines Day was a convenient excuse to send the ladies of the organization another card. If the date were known, an anniversary card was sent on the proper day. Florists in the area were kept busy with orders for hospitalized party members. Headquarters always sent flowers to the funerals of deceased party members or their immediate family. Ex-wives were remembered on their birthdays, anniversaries and holidays with flowers, gifts and cash. Keith instituted the central committee Christmas party where all who attended were fed and all left with a present.

He always treated the ladies well. I came to the conclusion that every woman around him fell in love with him at one time or another. The elderly women wanted to mother him, while the younger ones sought to please him. I never knew Keith to take advantage of this situation. When he was married, he was faithful. Between marriages when there was a dating situation, the bestowing of gifts and attention on the intended knew no bounds. He carried on the perfect courtship, one that most women only dream about. I can remember one or two of the brides-to-be were advised by my wife not to get married. "Continue the courtship," she said, because life would never get better.

President Reagan was going to appoint Keith to a United Nations committee. Protocol dictated a check of his background so that he might receive the proper security clearance. I was contacted by the FBI to answer questions regarding some of the features in his life. The opening questions from the agent were routine and easily answered. The agent then tried to shape a question, "It's a fact that Mr. Bulen has been married four times. Do you believe that he hates women?" I had to laugh and reply, "No, it's the opposite, he loves these women. The mistake is that he marries them." Case closed.

The elderly were special. Fiftieth wedding anniversaries were very special. My own parents did celebrate their seventy-fifth anniversary. Keith always thought it cool that Eldoris and I received a bouquet of flowers from my parents on our fiftieth wedding anniversary. He would always count the total number of years he had been married and then hope to make it to fifty.

Keith had written to my parents in 1997:

Dearest Mary and Lawrence,

Never met a Borst by blood or marriage that I didn't like a lot. What a tremendous tribute to the mare and sire of the line. I've had a world champion sire that repeated again in '96; however it pales beside your accomplishments and contributions to all who have known you and yours. You and yours have bettered my world for which I'm grateful and fortunate. So pleased that the Senator and Eldoris will share the 70th celebration with you and for what it's worth, I will rejoice as well.

As always,
Keith.

chapter 5

Republican Action Committee

On a cold November Sunday afternoon, Marion County Prosecutor Noble Pearcy and Sheriff Bob Fields rang the doorbell at our house following the November general election of 1964. The Republican Party was the big loser in the Goldwater campaign, not only nationally, but locally. The tone of the conversation from Pearcy and Fields was, "Something needs to be done, and changes in the local party leadership should be discussed." I was asked to join several of the present officeholders for a lunch at the Severin Hotel to discuss the state of the local Republican Party. I agreed to attend what may have been the identifiable beginning of a political movement that was to be known as the Republican Action Committee.

Pearcy, Fields, John Burkhart, John Sutton, Marsha Hawthorne, Louis Ping, Walter (Doc) Hemphill, Beurt SerVaas, John Niblack, Tom Hasbrook and I were the attendees at this first luncheon.

Burkhart and Pearcy were the main leaders in this small, unorganized effort. Nine out of the eleven involved were current Republican office holders. John Burkhart and I were the non-office holders. I had been appointed as Dale Brown's ward chairman for Perry Township and Burkhart had held a variety of GOP organizational offices having to do with finance and fund raising.

Discussions that began in November of 1964 intensified in early 1965.

The first decision that the group had to make was whether to affect a change under current party leadership or to take on the present party leaders and replace them with someone of our choosing. The consensus was that there needed to be total new leadership in the Marion County GOP organization. The group discussed the pros and cons of several individuals who might be interested and would be capable of leading and masterminding the overthrow of the incumbent duly elected Republican county regime.

These gatherings were not the most secret of meetings. With the many office holders involved, and with each office holder having one or two confidants, the word got out on the "street" that something was up. The regular Republican organization probably discounted these rumblings. Dale Brown had been challenged every year that there had been an election.

During Pearcy's tenure as prosecutor, ground zero for informal political discussions affecting anything in the county was at his home. Noble held an open house in his basement recreation room practically every week day beginning about 4:00 in the afternoon. Saturday and Sunday assemblages were also common. The bar was well stocked. The pool table was available. A pack of cards was in evidence at all times. Politics was always the main topic of conversation. While Leroy New, the chief deputy prosecutor, was minding the prosecutor's office downtown, various judges, officeholders, contributors, wannabes and nevergonnabes, would stop by and pay their homage. Those gathered were not all Republicans. Members of the Democrat Party also attended so the discussions were bi-partisan. Politically, it becomes dull to only talk about what is going on in your own party. Dissecting the other party's problems and validating street rumors is a normal course for any political gathering. I was a somewhat regular attendee since our home was a short block down the street.

Noble was a great guy but had difficulty in keeping a secret. He would start out, "Now, I shouldn't tell you, but, I know that you can keep a secret" and then proceed to spill everything. Since the formation of the group and subsequent meetings of the eleven people became known to one and to all, Keith Bulen began to call me and wonder whom this group might pick to lead their effort. I had no idea who was capable and asked the sixty-four dollar question of Keith. Of course, he would be interested. His relationship with Noble and Marcia Hawthorne, the county auditor, was not good. Keith and Noble had been in law school together. Marcia was Marcia, a very capable lady with very decided and forthright opinions which she was not afraid to express. Keith was too competitive for Noble and probably too brash for Marcia.

The group discussed Keith, but put his name on hold. He had successfully defeated the regular organization on two occasions but was thought to be too politically ambitious. Judge Charles Applegate was given much consideration. Pearcy and several of the members wanted me to take on the task. Something like that commitment was not feasible in my life. We would then bring the conversation back to Bulen. It was decided to put off the final consideration of a leader for this new organization for a few days and make a final selection the next week.

On the appointed day, by arrangement, Keith was strategically located on Monument Circle a short distance from the Columbia Club where our meeting was taking place. The committee finally made the decision and agreed that Keith Bulen would be the choice to lead the troops in an effort to depose the incumbent Republican county chairman. I was asked to convey the news. This I did, meeting Keith on the Circle. Marion County politics has never been the same since that day.

Keith, Buert SerVaas and Dick Pettigrew obtained headquarters space in a building on the corner of Market and Delaware Streets. Keith put together a "Mission and Method" for the new organization; a list of ideas for the members of the Republican Party in Marion County in an attempt to gain their approval and support. One of the pledges was to locate county headquarters at street level. County headquarters in 1966 was on the third floor of the Ober Building on Pennsylvania Street. Access to the third floor was by a creaky-jerky elevator that had seen its better days some twenty years earlier. It was not publicly accessible.

Bulen proposed that the new county chairman should be a full-time position, one who would receive a salary that would be equal to the highest salary of any elected public official in Marion County. This pronouncement was a giant departure from the norm, because previous county chairmen had not received a salary from the party. Some former chairmen had no visible means of income, but drove new cars and did well enough to pay the tuition for their kids to attend and to graduate from college. Living in high style with no signs of steady employment allowed for all types of rumors as to how the GOP party chairman could maintain such a standard of living. It was stated that the new organization would be more inclusive and would consider any person who wanted to declare for public office. These were the "aims" of the new RAC.

The stated Mission and Method was short, concise and to the point:

The mission of the Republican Action Committee is to put a new team in command of the Party in Marion County. A new team is needed to:
1. Find the best qualified candidates for public service;
2. Get them elected. There is only one Method under which a free and democratic society can operate—determine voter choices at the ballot box.

The statement continued.

3. In the May, 1966, Primary Election, Marion County voters will have a choice—a choice to reject present losing and unrepresentative leadership, a choice to elect a winning and representative leadership.

Bulen established a board of directors. Almost any bonifide Republican could be considered for membership on the board. Bulen worked hard to enlist Republicans to join the RAC. The first published membership list of the RAC board had well over 100 names. Joining up with this new political organization was not without its drawbacks. Everyone on that list knew that he or she was giving up any future opportunity for placement or advancement in the present Marion County political organization if the RAC was not victorious in its effort.

There were monthly meetings of the board, characterized by the absolute freedom of political discussion. The real decisions were made by the executive committee of the board, sixteen hand-selected individuals who met at least weekly with Keith: Charles Applegate, Larry Borst, Jim Buck, John Burkhart, Tom Hasbrook, Marcia Hawthorne, W. W. Hill, Ed Koch, John Niblack, Noble Pearcy, Louis Ping, W. T. Ray, Bill Ruckelshaus, Beurt SerVaas, John Sutton and Phyllis Waters.

Keith went out of his way to be inclusive. The participation of women and of African-Americans was a must to him. Nola Allen, a black lawyer, was his first assistant county chairman and also a GOP district officer. Phyllis

Waters was older than most of us and had spent her years as an educator. Bill Ray held many responsible positions in local government. Bulen would always slate some prominent person whom no one had ever considered as a Republican or even as a politically involved individual. Ray Crowe and Harriette Bailey Conn were selected to serve in the state legislature and Indiana Pacer Roger Brown on the City-County Council.

Geographical representation was also a necessity. The more the variety of involvement for these groups, the more voters might be touched and encouraged to vote Republican.

The RAC on different occasions placed advertisements in the Indianapolis newspapers outlining the aims of the new political organization. In one of the ads, the readers had the opportunity to cut out a ballot, fill in a blank as to who they thought should be the next chairman of the Marion County GOP and return the vote to a certain post office box number. The box number, of course, was the headquarters of the RAC. I was the one who counted the returns. Bulen, naturally, received the most votes on the returned ballots. Applegate was second and Dale Brown was third. Anyone could clip and vote. Not everyone got to count the ballots.

A second newspaper advertisement asked if any of the readers had the desire to become a candidate for any of the offices in the upcoming primary. Readers were asked to state which office they believed they would be best qualified for and a little about their background. When the form was returned, each applicant was sent a more detailed form requesting pertinent information. Education, employment, civic participation, arrest record, whether or not all federal, state and local taxes had been paid, all were pertinent. Each of those responding a second time was given the opportunity to appear before the RAC screening committee. At least two people who sent in resumes made it through the screening committee and eventually became members of the Indiana House of Representatives. These were Otis Yarnell and Wilma Fay.

Some candidates for offices to be voted on in the primary were recruited by the RAC, mostly to obtain a favorable geographic balance of candidates. All of the hopefuls were interviewed and recommended by the slating committee, which was chaired by John Burkhart. Dick Guthrie was a holdout. He had been a legislator and was the speaker of the House in 1963. He believed that Dale Brown had given him political life, and he was reluctant to oppose an old friend. Guthrie went on to serve with distinction on the Indianapolis Board of School Commissioners. Richard Retterer was the last legislative candidate selected before the primary filing deadline.

The strategy to win the race for county chairman was handled in a much different way than it had been in previous years by other rebellious groups. In those election years, the political groups had just filed a contesting slate of candidates, if not a full slate, only three or four individuals. The insurgents would then concentrate on the few. The strategy of the RAC was concentrated in securing the votes of those who could participate in the selection of the county chairman—the precinct committeemen who had the votes.

But now each ward and precinct was analyzed by the executive board, and the committeemen were evaluated. Was the committeeman a Dale Brown person? Could the committeeman be lobbied? Was he even going to seek re-election again? If a precinct did not have a filed candidate for committeeman, a person familiar with that neighborhood found someone to file and to run. If a committeeman was a Brown person and was going to seek re-election, in most cases the RAC left that race alone and did not challenge the incumbent committeeman.

I had cast my lot with the Republican Action Committee. I was the ward chairman for the RAC in Perry Township that primary. I had been the ward chairman for Perry Township under Dale Brown but had submitted my resignation and reasons for resigning shortly after the beginning of the year. About one-third of the committeemen were allied with Brown, and one-third were unaffiliated committeemen who were serving their party out of a sense of duty, and we felt we could convince them of our mission of good government. The other third of the committeeman positions were vacant. The significance of the vacancies was that the incumbent county chairman had the power to fill these vacancies before the general county GOP convention which convened every two years for the purpose of selecting a county party chairman. The county chairman normally filled these vacancies with his most loyal friends who then could vote in the county reorganization convention. The RAC easily found several hundred people to file, and to campaign for, precinct committeeman. In some cases, the Brown organization filed against the RAC candidates, but those cases were very few.

With this many neophytes involved, the opposition never had a chance. The RAC swept everything. Bulen had orchestrated a wipeout. The convention was posted for 10:00 on the Saturday morning following the Tuesday primary, and all the newly elected RAC people would be there to elect the county chairman. The meeting place was the basement of the Indiana Theatre on the north side of West Washington Street. The entrance to the basement was down a narrow stairway from Washington Street into the rather large room below. Keith and I got there about an hour before the announced convening hour. We took three or four of our largest committeemen with us to be lookouts or bodyguards or just to be around in case there was any trouble. Both of us had seen how Dale Brown in the past had clogged the aisleway from the street to screen out those who wanted to proceed down the steps. If needed, two or three really huge guys could stop any unfriendly or rowdy committeemen attempting to gain entrance.

There were no signs of trouble. However, we had a script on how the business would be conducted, with or without Dale Brown. Brown showed up briefly, gave no one any trouble, did not participate in the re-organization, and left a key to the Marion County GOP headquarters. He did not give any blessing to the new group.

I made the nominating speech for Bulen's election as county chairman. I have never been so frightened before, or since, when making any sort of presentation before any audience. Some of it may have been excitement. My knees shook. The paper in my hands rattled. My voice was about two octaves higher than normal. I did manage to get through the ordeal. Keith never allowed me to forget my moments of terror. Approximately every six months for the rest of his life he alluded to my fright. He loved to needle me because he knew that I was still uncomfortable with my nominating performance.

Keith had a handbill for all of the committeemen who attended the county convention. It outlined his pledges if he were to become the head of the Republican Party in Marion County. He stated, "I pledge, with your active support, to build a vigorous, effective organizational team that will ignite the imagination and enthusiasm of all people—locally, state-wide and even nationally."

The proceedings went well and everyone seemed to have a good time and went home charged up to accomplish the sweep in the fall. Keith was, of course, elected county chairman after this careful, brilliant campaign. The two of us, with Keith in possession of the key to the old headquarters, headed for the Ober Building. Cy Ober probably had given the rooms on the third floor to the party rent free. Cy was a generous individual who was sensitive to the party and some of its past financial difficulties.

We went up in the shaky old elevator and found Brown's suite of rooms. The key was not needed, because the door was unlocked and open. Inside was chaos, with papers everywhere, and files open and overturned. There were no records of the Republican Party, no lists of names, no receipts of past contributions. Nothing. The huge door to the room-size safe was wide open. In it on the floor was the only tangible object within the safe, a small cloth bag containing about a thousand political buttons. The fifty-cent-size lapel buttons simply read, "Brown" and they were white in coloring with brown lettering. Dale Brown never had the chance to pass them out in the convention. It was all over by then.

So, starting from scratch, Keith began the fall campaign immediately. He had fantasized about running such a political program for years. He was confident that someday he would have an opportunity to be a county political chairman. And he had considered thousands of scenarios and the means of putting such an effort together if such an opportunity ever presented itself. The political brochures he developed were the slickest and best ever produced: full color, with individual photos placed in a group setting, magazine quality paper. It was something to be proud of. Beurt SerVaas, Dick Pettigrew, John Burkhart and P. E. MacAllister raised the money to do all of this through a combination of fundraisers and solicitation of the Republican faithful.

Keith even knew a famous "voice" from southern California whom he wanted to hire to do the political commercials on radio. Keith had dreamed about employing the best. He convinced this Democrat "voice" of the good government efforts the RAC was attempting to provide for in Marion County and so the melodious tones of this super professional graced the airways of central Indiana.

Keith supervised a whirlwind of activity that summer and fall. Each and every candidate spoke to a small group of neighborhood Republicans at different locations several times weekly. The small neighborhood gatherings might have been in the morning or afternoon or even in the evening, but were always referred to as "teas" where the hostess showed off her finest china and silverware to her neighbors. Nominees would enthusiastically show up at the gatherings even when they were not scheduled to speak. Lee Eads, the fairly laid back nominee for sheriff, a professional lawman, at the first of these gatherings spoke in short clipped sentences such as Jack Webb might have in portraying Sergeant Friday on Dragnet. Before the election came around, Lee was taking his full five or six minutes at each gathering and making a whole lot of sense.

Research committees were formed, issues assigned. Each of the legislative candidates, for both the House and Senate, was assigned a position on more than one committee.

The issues were standard during this election. John Mutz found a giant chuckhole somewhere downtown and had a mini press conference in the middle of the street. He extolled the virtues of a countywide thoroughfare system, while the traffic was moving around on both sides of him and the television camera. Thousands of political door-hangers were delivered by the committeemen. Mailings of tailor-made literature were sent out.

Charlie Castor, Keith's law partner, was booking bets with the Democrat attorneys on the election results. The Democrats were giving odds and points (in the form of how many thousand votes their victory margin would be) and Charlie considered that a bet on the RAC winning in the fall to be a sure thing. Knowing Charlie, he was what is known in the betting world as a "chalk" bettor (betting only on a sure thing), I had to participate with Charlie in a small way. As a result, my family was able to purchase our first large TV set.

The November election results were more than positive for Bulen and the Republicans. Marion County was once again a force in the state Republican Party and Keith Bulen was now the acknowledged certified political genius in the state. Keith had provided a lavish spread of food in the ISTA building for the troops following the victory. Ever the worrier and negative person, he had made up his mind that if the Democrats did win on that November day, he would give the key to the party room and the food to Jim Beatty, the Democrat county chairman.

Warren Spangle, who ran the Indiana Restaurant Association, had arranged for a small private room at a restaurant on west 16th Street for several of us to sit around late in the evening and analyze the events of the day. I drove part of the group and had Keith and his wife, my wife, Spangle and probably the Castors in the car. We took the route on the west side of White River Parkway, going north to 16th Street from downtown. Somewhere along the river, very late in the evening and with no traffic to be seen in either direction, I stopped the car and loudly told Keith, "By God, if you are so great, and so effective, I want to see if you can walk on water." Keith struggled a little and acted like he intended to comply. Fortunately, others would not let him out of the car. There were many in the organization that evening who would have bet that he could have walked on the water across the White River.

Keith may have equaled himself in conducting subsequent campaigns, but never would he exceed that campaign of 1966, whether it was the primary or the general election. The following year's effort for Richard Lugar for mayor was significant, but did not have the newness or the vibrancy of the Republican Action Committee enthusiasm of 1966.

The Action Committee continued to provide Republicans victory after victory. Lugar was easily elected and re-elected. Edgar Whitcomb and Otis Bowen were elected governors of the state of Indiana. Bill Hudnut served one term in Congress. Then Keith began to sense it was all becoming a business and not as much fun as it should have been. Going full blast for seven plus years began to take its toll on his health. He cut his tenure as county chairman short and then resigned his positions as Republican national committeeman for Indiana, as well as 11th District Republican chairman, effective at the end of 1974. His successors were capable people who tried hard but seemed to be in the political arena for different reasons than was Keith. The party seemed to tread water until the morbid Democrat Party began to show life and start its own reascendancy.

The RAC of Marion County in the late sixties and early seventies has to be truly considered as one of the most efficient and productive local political organizations in American history. Boss Michael Curley of Boston, Tammany Hall in New York City, the powerhouses of Chicago and of Kansas City are probably more famous in the folklore of local political machines. There is one giant difference between those more famous political organizations and the RAC: no one from government in Marion County went to jail. The all-out effort was one that still can be categorized as "good politics makes good government."

The Borst family in 1966, (l-r) David, Lawrence, Eldoris, Philip, Elizabeth.

L. Keith Bulen: Insights

Keith Bulen was Marion County chairman for only a little over seven years. Another of his goals was to become a Republican national committeeman. He attained and served in that position most honorably. He was the United States delegate to the Economic and Social Council of the United Nations in 1970 and 1973, and was the United States observer to the United Nations Natural Resources Conference in Nairobi, Kenya in 1972. In 1980, Keith was Reagan's National Convention director and was the Eastern regional political director for the Reagan-Bush Committee with responsibility for the campaign in seventeen states in the East and Midwest.

He was called to serve at the national level. Appointed by President Reagan to the International Joint Commission (IJC) in 1981, Keith applied his organizational ability to resolving disputes and settling questions of policy involving the boundary waters between the United States and Canada. In 1984 Keith collaborated with Canadian E. Richmond Olson to perfect an agreement which resolved a forty-two year dispute between the city of Seattle and the province of British Columbia resulting in the "Bulen-Olson Treaty."

Keith was flamboyant. He liked being the center of attention whether in a small group or in a crowd. Keith was the voice that those around him could hear singing *The Star Spangled Banner* at the Indianapolis Colts games. He seemed to be able to control, modulate and project his voice. At Columbus, Ohio, with the score 45-0 (not in favor of the Indiana University football team) he yelled, "Wait till we get you in the swimming pool." Keith loved to sing. As a member of the Murat Shrine Chanters, he would send us tickets to the annual Triad production. One year he had a semi-solo, singing *Shenandoah*. This I never let him forget and I would break out singing the title of the song during his times of stress.

Keith was a traditionalist, wearing seersucker suits and white shoes in the summer. To really dress up he'd sport black and white shoes. He and I were born in the twenties and grew up in the thirties and forties when times were difficult and expectations not so great. Events that happened during the thirties were the touchstones of our lives. One of them was the Army-Navy football game always scheduled on the last week of the college football season. A kid in the thirties listened to the radio broadcast of the football game religiously. The mystique of the hundreds of midshipmen and plebes marching in with the goat and the mule was most vividly described by announcer Ted Husing.

As adults, Keith and I talked about going to an Army-Navy game, but I did not want to attend the game unless it was played in Veterans' Stadium in Philadelphia. The services had yielded to public pressure and to TV and had moved the game around on the East Coast to accommodate more fans. But for us it had to be Philadelphia. When finally the game was scheduled in Philly, Keith immediately contacted his friend, Congressman Bill Bray, to secure hard-to-come-by tickets. Bray was a long-time member of the House Armed Services Committee and would be the ideal contact for game tickets.

Bray reported back that he was having a difficult time obtaining the tickets. March turned into June and on into July and still no action from the congressman's Washington office. Finally in August came the word that tickets for the game were very scarce and Congressman Bray would not be able to accommodate Mr. Bulen; but the congressman would immediately begin to work on obtaining these tickets for the next year. This turn of events infuriated Keith but also challenged him. He knew somebody who knew somebody high up in the Pentagon. This contact resulted in four good tickets, but the tickets also came with four reservations on the Armed Service special train that would leave from the D.C. train station the morning of the game and take the VIPs and their guests to a rail siding next to the stadium in Philadelphia.

We were thrilled. Then, the two of us and our wives were invited to make use of the Army's chief of staff's private suite beneath the stadium. The day of the game was absolutely beautiful football weather, but the temperature was in the low twenties. Our wives spent the second half out of the cold and talking with half of the Army General Staff. The bar below the stadium was well stocked. What a way to attend and see a football game.

Keith had an apartment in the Watergate Apartments looking out on the Potomac. He and Charlie Castor decided that this was a necessity since they were in law practice together, and perhaps the practice might include business in Washington. D. C. We flew from Indianapolis on Friday before the Saturday game, got up early and boarded the train in downtown D.C. The train ride north was enjoyable. We were thrilled to be in the company of all the generals and staff people. Arriving at the stadium we worked our way from the train to the entrance of Veterans' Stadium.

Our seats turned out to be in a great location—top row seats on the fifty-yard line. In fact, they were in the same row as those of the Congressional members of the House Armed Services Committee. At first it was a shock to see Congressmen Bray sitting in the seat next to that assigned to Keith Bulen, and then it was my pleasure to watch Keith fumble around trying to be nice to Bill Bray. One thing about Keith, he was always adaptable. He commiserated with Bray about the congressman's difficulty in being able to provide four tickets for the incumbent Indiana Republican national committeeman, surely not an intentional oversight on Bray's part. He next mentioned that he had talked with the President regarding the game. As the master of the laid-back dig, Bulen asked why he had not seen the congressman on the official armed services train? Keith had to further lay on the sarcasm. If Congressman Bray wanted to get back to D.C. early, he, Keith, would spend some of his personal time and use some of his influence to have the congressman invited for the return trip. With that out of the way, Keith switched seats with me and had me talk with Bray all during the game.

Before the game, a Navy single-seated jet fighter buzzed the crowd. We were seated in the top row. The airplane came in one end of the football stadium and roared across our line of vision at a height from the football field below where we were sitting. I looked down on the pilot. That pilot is either, because of lack of common sense or extreme bravery, now dead or else a four-star admiral.

Army won the game. The occupants of the train were more than happy. Most had used the stadium suite more than once, and not to just keep warm. We also had a drawn out cocktail hour after the game while waiting for the train to be cleared to head south. Somehow on the way back, Keith and I were able to sit in the club car. The club car was a modern streamliner—stylized and shaped like the "Twentieth Century Limited," and it was the last car on the train. The table was contoured and rounded to fit the modern styling of the train, and everyone sitting around the table was packed in with no ability to extract himself or herself to make a trip to the bar or whatever. No problem. There were enough aides of the colonel variety to immediately answer your fondest wish. A drink or a sandwich or some shrimp magically appeared.

There may have been a two-star general in the car. If there was, he was not sitting around the table. Most were four-star generals, some of whom I'd read about. Keith announced that he had been a veteran of World War II and his friend, Borst, had served time in the Ordinance Corps and in the Alaskan theatre. The level of good fellowship was such that both of us were able to pull it off without getting thrown off the train. The discussion involved all sorts of military strategy and whether or not the President would be capable in a war situation. For all those generals knew, the two guys at the table must have some sort of political clout, or they would never have been asked to travel on the train. On arrival in Washington, D.C., business cards were exchanged and promises of getting together for lunch were made and each of us made our way home. That was about the only thing that Keith did not arrange. Each of the generals had his own staff car and aide pick him up at the train station.

It wasn't all politics with Keith Bulen. He had other interests, and owning, training and racing standardbred race horses was one of those major interests.

The first standardbred horse that Keith Bulen purchased was from Judge Nat U. Hill. She was a nondescript bred pacing filly out of the Frost line whom he had trained at the Indiana State Fairgrounds. This horse did not work out too well, mostly because of injuries.

In my travels on the horse circuit I had become aware that there was a promising two-year-old for sale at the fairgrounds. One evening, over a few drinks, Keith and Castor and Borst decided to purchase Sara J. Go, a bay pacing filly. The price was $15,000, which turned out to be three times the horse's worth. Keith and Castor assumed the majority of the purchase price and Keith provided the leadership in the handling of the horse's future. This was the first and last time that Charlie Castor put out a dime to support a racing horse. Charlie would never deign to bet two dollars on any of Keith's horses and didn't approve of paying money for something that could not converse with him in English. This was the same man who later would bet a fortune on silver futures in the world market.

Sara J. Go was not the answer. She did, however, provide a lot of exposure to finding out whether or not racing was a fun game. Keith and I decided that the yearling route was the way to proceed within the standardbred business. We went to Tattersall's auction one fall in Lexington, Kentucky, acted like we knew what we were doing and bid on a yearling stud colt by the name of Streakin Sam. I made the final bid of $4,500, much to Keith's amazement. He had agreed that the colt filled the bill on bloodlines, but neither of us had physically inspected the colt. He liked the breeding. I liked the price. I was convinced that Keith, left to his own devices, would get carried away and spend more money than I could afford. Following the sale, we went out back to the stalls to look over our new purchase. Looking in the stall, we couldn't see the colt at first. Streakin Sam was small enough, that when he stood next to the stall doors you would look over him. The colt was given to Jerry Landess in Portland, Indiana to train.

Streakin Sam turned out to be a fun horse. He won two-thirds of his heats during the Indiana Fair Racing Circuit: places like Anderson, Shelbyville, Converse, Goshen, Connersville and Frankfort. Sam won everywhere and became the two-year-old champion of the Indiana fair circuit. Following the Indiana Fair Circuit Jerry entered him in an overnight race in Celina, Ohio. The Ohio fair circuit was ten times larger than the one in Indiana and each of the fairs had a pari-mutuel system for the two- or three-day meet. Sam's pre-race odds were two to one, which was OK with us. My bet was a two dollar to win. Down the line at the next pari-mutuel window, the man behind the window taking bets and handing out the tickets yelled for everyone to hear, "I got a guy that wants to bet $100 to win on one horse." Probably that had never happened at Celina. I didn't even have to look to see who this big time spender was. I knew it was Keith and he was in his element. He was the center of attention and really ate it up. When the locals found out that these were big-time horse owners from Indianapolis, we were invited to several of the RVs parked on the grounds and offered all kinds of libations.

In 1976 Keith and I talked about returning to Lexington to bid on another yearling. I had somewhat different plans for my immediate legislative agenda. I was running for re-election and had been involved in attempting to legalize pari-mutuel horse racing. The general public had voted during the state-wide general election in 1968 on the advisory question of legalizing pari-mutuel horse racing. Otis Bowen had allowed this ballot question to pass while he was speaker of the House in 1967. The state-wide results were very favorable for its acceptance by the voting public in Indiana. Newspaper reporters had opined and several others had orated about the conflicts that I would have as a practicing veterinarian and as a one-half horse owner when speaking up for pari-mutuel. The Paul Oakes and Greg Dixons of the world got to my sensibilities. I told

Keith that instead of adding another half a horse, I wanted to get rid of the half that I did own with him. I wanted to remove any and all conflicts in order to push for legalization.

I turned down the opportunity to buy half of the yearling colt pacer named Abercrombie. Even after Abercrombie was brought back to Indianapolis following the sale in Lexington, Keith asked me to take a look at the horse. I did, and it looked like any other yearling that I had ever seen. The colt's breeding was not outstanding. The dam's side was fair. The sire's side was unproven. I again turned down the chance to become a partner in the ownership of Abercrombie, and lost the chance to become several times a millionaire. Keith called his longtime friend, Morris Mitchell, who put up the money and had the horse registered in his wife's name. Morris died way too early, not having been able to share in the colt's glory. His wife, Shirley, did the honors in admirable style.

Abercrombie was also sent to Portland, Indiana, to be trained by Jerry Landess. I can remember Keith calling me in early spring and telling me that he was bringing the colt back to the Indiana State Fairgrounds. Jerry had entered Abercrombie in a colt baby race and in his own laconic way, reported that Abercrombie had gone the mile in about 2:04, with fractions of 1:05 and 0:59 on a half mile track. In the 1970s, 2:00 was an acceptable time for an adult pacer on a mile track. For a two-year-old to go that fast so early in the year on a half mile track was unbelievable. Throughout that summer Abercrombie had a great deal of success, winning most of his races all around the Midwest. Keith received an offer of $70,000 for a horse that he had paid only $9,500 a few months earlier. Tempting? Castor would have sold in a minute and said so. Not the least bit tempting for Keith. He insured the horse with what purse money he had won during the previous summer and fall. Keith then decided to winter the colt in Indiana and go with his gut instinct that this was a once-in-a-lifetime racehorse. Abercrombie hit a "home run" on the Grand Circuit the next year.

For the start of Abercrombie's three-year-old season, Keith

borrowed a two-horse trailer and he and Ab drove the interstates east to the Meadowland Race Course in New Jersey. Keith did the stall work (so he said). He at least took care of Abercrombie for a few weeks. Since Ab was winning sizeable purses, money for Ab to really travel in style was then no problem. Keith in his usual way hired Glen Garnsey to train and drive Ab, because Garnsey had the reputation as the best driver-trainer in the United States. Abercrombie was adjudged to be the standardbred Horse of the Year in 1978. Most stud horses are syndicated following their three-year-old season. Keith, a traditionalist, wanted to race Ab during his four-year-old season, and to have total lifetime winnings of at least a million dollars. The horse's last season of racing was not his best. Fair, but not as good as the year before. Abercrombie fell a few thousand dollars short in purse winnings of attaining the seven-figure mark.

Syndication for breeding purposes was now in order. The law firm of Bulen and Castor tried to negotiate with one of the old line Lexington law firms. Keith and Charlie raised a lot of eyebrows with their Indiana demands but had to finally go along with the old Kentucky aristocracy. Castleton Farm, at that time the premier horse breeding farm in Lexington, became the lead partner and contracted to stand Abercrombie at their magnificent farm in eastern Kentucky. Even though Ab was not thought to be well bred, he was fast, had been a winner and his conformation was excellent. During the sixties and seventies most of the successful racing horses had Bret Hanover or Meadow Skipper bloodlines in their breeding. Abercrombie had none, so he made an outstanding outcross to all of the Bret and Skipper mares.

Abercrombie as a sire was an immediate success. For years now, his offspring have been good racehorses, especially at four, five or six years of age. His offspring seemed to have longevity and durability as racehorses.

chapter 6

Into the Sixties
Fall Election of 1966, RAC Style

The 1966 summer and fall political campaign in which I was again running for the House in the Indiana legislature was an extension of the Republican Action Committee's primary election effort to unseat H. Dale Brown as county chairman and to nominate its own slate of candidates. Keith Bulen, the new Marion County Republican Committee chairman, was able to use every effort and campaign technique that he had saved or had occurred to him during all of his years on the sidelines. The campaign was intense, enthusiastic, non-stop, focused, well funded and successful. The hand-out literature and mailing brochures that Bulen authorized and commissioned have not been equaled nor duplicated for any political effort since that campaign in 1966.

Surely we could do better in '66 than we had done in '64. All of the candidates for the fall election had been handpicked through the slating process by the Action Committee. Overall issues and strategies had been developed for the primary campaign, and these were simply extended to apply for the fall campaign against the Democrats. Most of the individual Republican candidates had researched and developed their own issues, and they had become the political authority regarding that subject during the campaign. Factoring in this amount of knowledge from the seventeen legislative candidates, the public had reason to feel overwhelmed by the information from the Republican slate.

Noble Pearcy was running for re-election as Marion County prosecutor; Lee Eads was the sheriff candidate. Those seeking judgeships in Marion County were Saul Rabb, Frank Symmes, Jr., Wilbur Grant, Ed Madinger, Rufus Kuykendall, Charles Daugherty, John Davis, Charles Applegate, Addison Dowling and Glen Funk. E. Allen Hunter, Marcia Hawthorne, John Sutton, Howard Bennett and Bill Mercuri were the nominees for the county administrative offices.

Beurt SerVaas was seeking re-election to the Marion County Council. Beurt had first been elected to the council in 1962 and also had served in that capacity from the beginning of Uni-Gov through October 2002. He may have been the longest serving Republican Marion County elected official in history. Bill Byrum, Dwight Cottingham, Ava James and Jim Redmond were also GOP candidates for council. On the Democrat side, Rozelle Boyd was a successful candidate for the County Council. Rozelle is still a member of the council and was a candidate for re-election in 2003.

Those candidates running with me for the Indiana General Assembly were truly a special assemblage of talent. Many had come to know each other well in the failed Goldwater campaign. At times, I found it rather intimidating to be around this group listening in on their vast amount of knowledge. They were not only smart and could put into words exactly what they wanted to express to the public, but each had a background in organizational politics. A few previously had been candidates for public office. Walter Barbour and Charles Bosma had experience as members of the Indiana House. Most were precinct committeemen and a few were ward chairmen. Each of us had his or her own assignment in our home areas while taking part in the county-wide campaign. The legislators were a team in every sense of the word. Of course, the spotlight was never wide enough for the light to shine on all of the legislative candidates at once. Some seemed to receive more media coverage than the others. No one minded; each would root for the other and not worry at all if others received the attention. All were focused on the ultimate goal, which was to be elected in the fall.

Ruckelshaus, a House candidate, later joined the Nixon administration as deputy United States attorney general. As second in command and temporarily in charge of the FBI, he was fired by the President, along with Attorney General Elliot Richardson, in the infamous "Saturday Night Masscre." Bill was the first director of the Environmental Protection Agency, and later served as CEO for two giant public corporations. Bill was one of the most humorous men that I have ever encountered. After his second beer his wit was unmatched.

Charles Bosma had served one term in the Indiana House and was seeking a second. Charles and his family managed a dairy operation in Beech Grove. Tall and commanding, with neither his integrity nor his morality ever having been challenged, he was almost completely involved in social legislation. Through his efforts during his legislative career, the handicapped now are treated in a much better fashion than before. The Bosma Industries serve as a reminder of his concern. His son, Brian, representing Lawrence Township, has been a member of the House for several years and is the leader of the Republican caucus.

Harriette Bailey Conn, an African-American attorney, was the conscience of our group. After serving in the Indiana House, Harriette became the first Indiana public defender. She served in this capacity for a number of years.

John M. Mutz served with distinction as a member of both the House and Senate but was seeking his first House term in 1966. John was appointed to the House Ways and Means Committee in 1967, an infrequent occurrence for a freshman legislator. In the Senate, he was chairman of the Senate Finance sub-committee for the budget. John later was elected lieutenant governor and was the Republican nominee for governor in 1988. He showed himself to be an expert in mental health legislation as well as in budget and financing. While in the Senate, he researched and wrote the legislation that became the state's Rainy Day Fund. John was also the first author on legislation that created the White River State Park Commission. He had been extremely successful in the private sector before entering politics and has enjoyed the same success following his stint as lieutenant governor. Mutz became president of the Lilly Endowment, president of an Indiana electric utility, and has served on the board of directors of several large corporations.

Richard E. Retterer, an owner in the Hermann Wolf insurance agency, was the sharpest dresser in the group. One of the few non-Catholics to have ever received the annual St. John Bosco Award for service to the youth of the community, he was involved in numerous civic activities. He later managed the Fourwinds Resort and Marina on Lake Monroe, and served as a gourmet chef in his own restaurant in the Broad Ripple section of Indianapolis.

Ray Crowe, another House candidate, the legendary basketball coach at Crispus Attucks High School, coached back-to-back state basketball champions in 1955 and 1956. By his own admission, Ray retired from coaching basketball and teaching much too soon. Keith Bulen had recruited Ray to become a candidate. Ray was a solid legislator, never missed a legislative day, and attended every meeting. He carried a little 3x5 card in his shirt pocket with numbers of selective bills written on the card. When a fellow legislator would ask if Ray was going to vote for his bill or for a certain bill, he would take the card out and look it over, much like a poker player looking at his hole card, close to his nose. Ray never exhibited a lot of emotion so you could not tell what he was going to say until the decisive words were uttered. He was a person that you could count on completely.

W. W. (Dub) Hill, Jr. has to rank in my "smartest people that I have ever known" group. Dub was a candidate for the Indiana Senate in that campaign of 1966. His expectations were never great, or so he said, and his sense of humor would always carry him through any adversity. In later years, I was the chairman of Senate finance and Dub was in charge of the budget. He had a desk in Room 430. In fact he shared the space; that room had a desk for me, Dub Hill, John Mutz, Tom Taylor and Carolyn Schott. Every day, Dub would spend a great number of minutes on the telephone in our office. I should have been listening to him. He was buying and selling securities and had to be advancing himself financially. Dub became a candidate for governor at one time, left the political arena, was a CEO of a telephone company and managed a rather large endowment.

Danny L. Burton was a partner in an insurance firm. He had been president of the Republican YRs when Keith Bulen talked him into joining the Republican Action Committee. Danny was the youngest and the most handsome of the legislative group. His seat on the House floor in the 1967 was between John Mutz and me. John and I would talk around him, and at times it would make him so mad that he would get up and stalk out of the chamber. Danny challenged the organization for a Senate seat later, was not successful, but was later selected by Keith Bulen to serve in the Senate. Danny's ultimate political ambition was to serve in Congress. I contributed a check towards that dream the day I overheard a telephone conservation in which he was mortgaging his personal automobiles in order to raise money for the primary election.

Indiana University and Danny did not see eye to eye during his first legislative term. IU was allowing Sunday afternoon visitations of boys in the girls' dorms for a few hours and under strict rules. Danny ranted about allowing males and females to visit one another. He led demonstrations against IU. He was like a bulldog on the issue. Thirty-five years later, Sunday afternoon visitation seems rather tame as an issue.

Danny was by far the best golfer in the group. Having now been a member of the United States House of Representatives for the past twenty years, Danny was also the best golfer in Congress for a period of time.

Walter H. Barbour had already served five terms in the Indiana House. He owned and operated an orchard in Lawrence Township and was our expert on agriculture and any kind of county or state fair or agricultural exhibition that existed. A real gentlemen.

Paul S. Partlow was a very successful realtor. A former director of the National Realtors Association, he lived in Washington Township. Paul was dapper. As an amateur photographer, he snapped innumerable photos of each and every legislative member of the House, placed the finished photos in an album, and allowed each legislator to purchase the finished product. Paul served only one term, primarily because of a gaffe he came to regret. Paul was at the microphone one day and was trying to explain the reluctance of a lobbying group to support a piece of legislation. He described the group as "being as nervous as a whore in church." Speaker Bowen slammed the gavel and admonished Representative Partlow that language such as that was not condoned on the floor of the House. Supposedly, Speaker Bowen instructed Marion County Chairman Keith Bulen that Partlow was not to be a member of the delegation in 1969. True or not, Partlow was never too active in Marion County GOP affairs after 1968.

Otis M. Yarnell was our union representative, a card-carrying member of a railroad engineer's union. Although the union was not a large one, he stood out as the only union member of the Republican ticket. Otis had been an unsuccessful independent candidate for the House in 1964. On his own, he responded to a RAC newspaper advertisement seeking candidates from the general public. Otis appeared before the RAC slating committee and was selected to run for the House. Otis was full of down-home wisdom, from a segment of society that most of us knew nothing about. He owned and ran a fishing bait shop in Wayne Township. When things became dull, Otis could always keep us interested with both fish and train stories. He smoked a pipe and had a great sense of humor.

Eugene H. (Ned) Lamkin, Jr. ranks along with a few others in a group of "smartest people that I have ever known." A medical doctor and an internist, Ned had his own medically allied businesses while also in private practice. Dr. Lamkin's knowledge is truly legendary. His mind is so retentive. He had the ability to express his thoughts in such a concise way so that even I could sometimes get a grasp on a detailed subject he was talking about. He served in the House for several terms, ran for the speakership one time, and has loyally supported the Republican Party in the intervening years. Dr. Lamkin made the original and early diagnosis of my prostate cancer, for which I am eternally grateful. I literally went into his medical office with a chronic cough and came out with a diagnosis of cancer.

Wilma Fay was the quietest of the legislative group. She was another House candidate from Wayne Township, and like Otis, one who had come "off the street" to be selected by the screening committee as a House candidate. Willy was a mainstay on the Appointments and Claims Committee. Always thoughtful, she could be counted on to make the right decisions for the good of the community and the State of Indiana.

Richard M. Givan was an attorney and House candidate from Decatur Township. Dick served on Judiciary and solved many of our legal questions. Always active in the legal community, he became an Indiana Supreme Court justice and for years was the chief justice.

Robert L. Jones, Jr., a tall handsome man with a shaved bald head, was at all times focused and earnest. He possessed several college degrees in education, and became the point man for educational matters. Field goal kickers, left-handed relief men and high hurdlers fall into a group of people that dance to a different tune. Bob was a high hurdler in college and was sometimes misunderstood. He did not survive the slating process in 1968 after his first term in the Indiana House. He then ran a very innovative campaign in the primary and won the nomination over the regular organization slated candidate. Following his service in the legislature, he was involved in a variety of educational ventures that serviced the private sector. He established his own church with its own congregation prior to his death.

Leslie Duvall, another candidate for the Indiana Senate, was an attorney with the Public Service Commission. Honest and forthright, Les was another legislator who was deeply involved with social issues and many aspects of the legal profession. He has remained active as a lobbyist and as a private citizen with the same interests.

Five attorneys, a medical doctor, a veterinarian, three in insurance, two educators, a dairy operator, a pomologist, a small business man, a housewife and a union member who sold crawdads and worms. Only two women and two African-Americans. A Lutheran, three Presbyterians, six Methodists, four members of the Christian Church, a member of the Friends Society and a Roman Catholic.

These nominees as a group were fairly representative of Marion County as a whole, although Washington Township was probably over-represented. But in 1966 Washington Township was the dominant area in the Republican Party in Marion County.

RAC was 100 percent successful in winning the contested races in Marion County in the fall election of 1966. Following the election, these newly elected Republican members of the House from Marion County, just described in detail, met to elect a chairman of the delegation. Keith Bulen had called the meeting. Entertaining some discussion, he announced his candidate for chairman to the fourteen of us in attendance—I was that candidate. This was the first that I had heard of the honor and it was the first time that any of the delegation was aware of Bulen's feelings. Two of the new House members blew up, shouting and saying that Bulen should "keep his nose out of our affairs." These were the same individuals who owed their election to Keith Bulen, loudly asking him to "shut up and get out of here."

Bulen persisted as he always did. He became as loud and as boisterous as any of the offended legislators. It got so that I was almost ashamed to vote for myself on the first ballot. Years later, Bulen would ask me if I had really voted for myself or had voted for someone else. Bulen had some method in his madness. He had cut a deal with others outside of our delegation to be sure that Bill Ruckelshaus would be the House majority floor leader for the upcoming legislative session and would be the GOP nominee for the United States Senate race in two years. He also had in mind to insure an appointment for John Mutz to the House Ways and Means Committee. Bulen pushed hard for me, because he also knew that the chairman of the Marion County delegation normally would be appointed to the chairmanship of the House Committee on the Affairs of Marion County.

John Mutz probably felt that he deserved the honor of being elected chairman of the delegation. Dick Retterer said he considered John to be more deserving of being selected. Two ballots were needed. The press reported that I had received eight votes, Mutz three, and Retterer three. That was not quite accurate since there were only two candidates. In later years, being chairman of either the House or of the Senate delegations was not the same honor, nor had it the allure that it had in the past. The process of electing the members of the House from individual districts, rather than electing fifteen members at-large from Marion County has been a huge factor in downgrading the importance of the chairmanship. In the Senate, the chairman of the delegation is the one who has the best and most efficient legislative secretary.

The general election in 1966 practically reversed the Democrat majorities of the 1965 session. Instead of Richard Bodine's being speaker, the Republicans would claim that honor, having elected sixty-six House members out of the one hundred seats. The Senate remained a Democrat stronghold with a twenty-nine to twenty-one majority and also having Lieutenant Governor Bob Rock as President of the Senate. Some of the newcomers elected to the House in 1966 from around the state were Phil Bainbridge later to become Democrat speaker of the House, Howard Barnhorst, Adam Benjamin, Quentin Blachly, Joel Deckard, Steve Ferguson, John Frick, Elwood (Bud) Hillis, Roger Jessup, Bill Latz, Thames Mauzy, Jack McIntyre, Howard Merz, Don Pratt, Ray Richardson, Dick Shank, King Telle, John Thomas and Charles Wise. Among the freshmen in the Indiana Senate were Jim Biddinger, Bob Fair, Joe Harrison, Alan Helms, Sidney Kramer, Dean V. Kruse, Al La Mere, Earl Landgrebe, Bob Mahowald, Emil Schmutzler, Gene Snowden and Jim Young.

Shortly after election day, our sixty-six Republican House members from all over the state met at state GOP headquarters to elect our leadership for the 1967 session. In some manner, Keith Bulen had entered into a deal with someone, or maybe several groups, not to support Otis Bowen in his bid to become speaker of the House. Keith informed the Marion County House delegation that they should support Charles (Billy) Howard for speaker. Howard was an insurance executive from Noblesville. He had served in 1963 with Keith. On the first ballot the vote was split thirty-three to thirty-three. A short recess was called and the elected House members sort of milled around in the party headquarters. Dr. Bowen had received only one vote from the Marion County delegation, and that was reported to be from Charles Bosma.

Published reports had the second ballot thirty-six to thirty, but I remember the announced results as thirty-four to thirty-two for Bowen. A single vote change.

Billy Howard was then elected chairman of the House caucus. Ruckelshaus was made majority floor leader. Walter Barbour was appointed chairman and Willy Fay was the ranking members of Appointments and Claims (the committee that hired all of the lay employees). Dick Givan became the RM of Judiciary. Ned Lamkin was made chairman of Public Safety. Retterer was named chairman of Financial Institutions. Bosma was rewarded with being the chairman of the Legislative Rules Committee. I was duly appointed to the chairmanship of the Affairs of Marion County Committee. Dr. Bowen seemingly held no animosity towards Bulen on this occasion, but later Bowen and Bulen were seldom politically compatible. Their goals may have been the same, but the manner in which each man tried to attain those goals was much different.

The Marion County House and Senate delegations had agreed on a five point program that was to be the basis of our legislative efforts. It was: (1) relief of property taxes through distribution to local units of some of the state surplus, (2) simplification of the purchase of auto license plates, (3) consolidation of county and city road construction and maintenance units into a Metropolitan Thoroughfare Authority, (4) mandatory yearly inspection of motor vehicles for traffic safety and (5) a crackdown on open pit dumping.

In 1967 the Legislative Service Agency (LSA) was in its infancy and had only been established in 1964, with a few employees. Today the agency is composed of sixteen legislators and a fulltime staff of sixty-five. It was established to professionalize the entire procedure of putting a bill through the legislative process. A legislator might have an idea for legislation that he or she wanted to introduce. The legislator would give that idea to someone in the LSA office to research the subject, who then would construct the new or amendatory language in proper form for introduction. During my first term in 1967 this typed-up legislation would then be given to Sam Lesh, who would assign the copy to his mimeograph machine people.

As the secretaries typed up the master copy, four or five carbon copies were also produced. Sometimes those copies of a bill that were carbon copies were smeared or wavy and hard to read. To have extra copies of a bill run off of the mimeograph machine was a chore. Sam might have made copies or he might not have made any copies. If he did not think that a bill had much merit on its own, he might have felt that it would have been a waste of his time to make duplicate copies and then would offer up excuses for not supplying the material. Sam was aware that during the sessions nearly 1,500 bills were introduced and less than twenty percent became law and he had favorite legislators to whom he gave special consideration. Freshmen were low on his list. Because of these factors, when a committee meeting was called for the purposes of hearing public testimony on a bill, the committee chairmen, and sometimes the author, were the only members of the committee who would have seen the proposed legislation prior to the hearing. If the chairman was so inclined, he would generously pass his copy of the bill around the table as testimony was being heard.

Public testimony would be taken on legislation in a committee setting and then everyone not on the committee would be excused from the room and the doors would be shut. If an author of a bill that had been presented at the public hearing was not a member of the committee, he or she would have to leave the room along with everyone else. The author could stay only if the chairman granted permission. The media also had to leave the room while the committee deliberated. By the time the testimony was over and the doors were shut, most of the members had now read the bill. The chairman would pose the question, "What do you want to do with that bill?" Someone might say that it could be a good bill if properly amended. An amendment would be offered but not necessarily written down for everyone to see. If the chairman was in an expansive mood, he would let the committee spend ten or fifteen minutes on a bill. Less than five minutes was the norm in which to resolve the fate of most proposals.

A vote would be taken by a show of hands or by a secret ballot. The chairman might then announce the results of the committee deliberations after the committee meetings or he might ignore the author and lobbyists and tell them to wait until the committee report, if any, was reported on the floor. Most lobbyists had the ability to receive inside information from the head of the secretarial pool or they would get the necessary facts from a committee member, so rarely was there a guessing game going on.

I can remember a public hearing conducted by the House Public Policy Committee in 1967 on the "Sunday sales" law. This issue had come before the General Assembly in previous years and was an issue that the newspapers featured and commented about on their editorial pages. Retail merchants, especially grocery stores, wanted the ability to open their stores on Sundays.

Such prohibitions against Sunday sales were termed "Blue" laws. There was no thought to allow sales of beer, wine and liquor. Against the wishes of the automobile dealerships, the proposed bill prevented auto sales on Sunday.

The committee was convened in one of the smallest meeting rooms that were available in the House. A huge crowd was waiting for the hearing. Retail merchants, automobile dealers were all in abundance as were entire church congregations. Once the legislators were seated, there was room enough for only a handful of people. Chairman Wayne Hughes announced that those for and against the bill would have fifteen minutes of testimony, each with no questioning from the committee. Dick Guthrie, who was Speaker in 1963, was the hired spokesman for one side. An equally expensive and effective person was the main speaker for the other side of the question. None of the committee members had copies of the bill.

Chairman Hughes cut off the testimony after the allotted time, shooed the crowd out of the room, closed the doors, and said to the committee, "This is a hot one." He also looked at me and said, "You seem to do OK, I am appointing you chairman in my place. Don't amend the bill and take a secret vote." With that, Chairman Hughes got up out of his chair and left the room. I think he knew that I would vote to amend the prevailing Indiana law and allow certain retail sales on a Sunday. He hoped that would happen. Representing Dekalb County, however, he feared the preachers and their congregations would take him to task if he voted for the bill. I tore a large piece of paper into small strips and gave one of the slips to each of the committee. They put a yes or a no on the paper. I then counted the votes, declared the committee to be in recess, and went out to report to Representative Hughes what his committee had decided. The result was fine with him. He had a Recommended Do Pass committee report prepared which he signed as chairman. There were never permanent records or even vote totals in the committees in 1967.

Guided by its authors, Mutz and Retterer, the Metropolitan Transportation Authority legislation for Marion County passed out of the Committee on the Affairs of Marion County and through the House on unanimous votes. The committee had public hearings outside of the Statehouse and drew opposition from the mayor of Indianapolis, John Barton. On the other hand, Democrat Mayor Elton Geshwiler of Beech Grove testified in support of the thoroughfare legislation.

As in all sessions of the General Assembly, there were several issues that unexpectedly came to the forefront and engendered a lot of maneuvering and debate during that session of 1967.

Keith Bulen and his chairman counterpart from DeKalb County, Senator Dean Kruse, a successful operator of an auctioneering business, attempted to play the part of kingpins in the House and guide a bill through that chamber that had to do with licensing auctioneers. In most cases, newly introduced legislation, which seeks to change licensing criteria, and is authored by a person who is licensed in the particular profession, will always contain new provisions that makes licensing more difficult. The legislation goes under the heading of "requiring more education so that the consumer is better protected." Sometimes these additional education requirements can only be obtained at schools operated by the ones asking that the requirements be changed. Dean and Bulen tried to work their magic, but it didn't work. The auctioneer's bill was not successful. It did not receive the necessary fifty-one votes on its initial presentation. On at least three occasions the issue was reconsidered and brought back for an additional vote under some rule or other. I believe that the session ran out of time before there was a majority for its passage.

A second contentious issue in the 1967 legislative session was the debate on the establishment and location of a second medical school for the state of Indiana. Each section of the state wanted the new school. The legislators from outside of Marion County were adamant in their opposition to legislation allowing the new school to be located in Indianapolis. Each of the areas in the state desiring the new school also vowed that there would not be a new medical school authorized unless it was located in their area. The House took votes to place it in Lake, St. Joseph, Allen, Vanderburgh and Tippecanoe counties. No one vote received a majority. My job, representing Marion County, was to split up the fifteen Marion County votes to make sure that no amendment received a majority. A Marion County legislator might vote for two locations and against three. We still had high hopes that the Indiana University School of Medicine would be able to expand and double its enrollment on the west Michigan Street campus. A year later, a compromise was suggested and adopted so that several regions in the state would begin educating the increased number of medical students at existing facilities for at least their freshmen and sophomore years.

Indiana Expo and Convention Center

The 1965 legislature had authorized bonding for a new convention center for Indianapolis. The language allowed for a three percent hotel-motel tax to be used to pay for the retirement of the bonds. Further, the Capital Improvement Board was required to secure two million dollars of "seed" money from some source prior to finalization of bonding and of construction. Thus, financial aid by the state became an issue and caused the whole topic to become a serious discussion item in the General Assembly in 1967.

The Capital Improvements Board then hired a facilitator, Thomas Smith, to give the board advice as to how to accomplish the project and where to locate and construct a convention center. Tom was an old time PR type, P. T. Barnum reincarnated. The more hullabaloo and hyperbole the better. He felt it was always safer to use extravagant clichés and diction. Tom, to his credit, did talk the city fathers out of their determination that the old City Market on east Market and Delaware Streets should be torn down and become the site for the new expo hall. The mayor's people envisioned a high-rise hotel with rooms in the upper stories, an exposition complex in some of the lower stories, and a city market in the basement and first floor. Tom envisioned the new building where it is today, facing the Statehouse. However, he wanted the two structures to be directly connected by an underground tunnel with a mechanical people mover.

Tom would bring a new schematic to the Statehouse every week. With his eyes lighting up and superlatives flowing from his lips smoothly, he'd spin his dreams. One drawing contained office space for each of the 150 legislators plus meeting rooms. For a measly $20 million of state general fund money the building would be titled The Indiana Exposition Center. He opined that conventions would flock to the new center because the underground tubes would keep all of the delegates out of bad weather. He boldly predicted that Indianapolis would receive most of the conventions that normally went to Chicago and Atlantic City.

Tom convinced Senator Ken Pedigo to pass a partial funding bill appropriating ten million dollars from state funds. I heard the bill in my committee but removed the appropriation at the request of Representative John Shawley, the chairman of House Ways and Means. Shawley always felt that anyone from Marion County was not to be trusted. He represented the Michigan City area which, other than for the state prison, never seemed to request or receive any state funds.

To John, Marion County was a giant sponge that sopped up most of the state monies. He would walk around with a yellow-lined legal pad clutched to his chest with his right arm. If asked a question regarding funding of some bill, John would lower the pad about six inches, take a peek, and then give an oblique answer. Shawley had been appointed chairman of Ways and Means because the Republican House fiscal expert, Representative John Coppes, of Nappanee, was out of sync with his northern neighbor, Speaker Bowen. Shawley decreed that no money would be given to Indianapolis by the State of Indiana to build anything as foolish as a convention/exposition center with tunnels and super-offices. Maybe a loan from the state, one within reason and only if the city reimbursed the state for any lost interest.

As a new member, I sat in the next to the last row of the House chambers. When the speaker called down the expo legislation, I slowly got to my feet and looked towards the podium. I swear that the microphone seemed to be a good mile away. I knew I could not make it down the aisle. In my hand, I had three different amendments, one for a loan of eight million, one for a loan of four million and one for two million.

Shawley got to his feet as I was passing and mumbled something about my being careful. I had no idea what I was doing at that particular moment in time. Much to the relief of Shawley and much to the disgust of Ken Pedigo, I pulled the amendment for two million out. Shawley would have killed any other amendment that I had presented. John would remind me from time to time every year after that about non-payment of the loan and accumulated interest payments. After the loan was repaid, his final comment on the whole situation was somewhat positive, but he said that he always knew that the interest would be forgiven. And it was.

There were other issues in the 1967 session.

During that first 1967 session I also made an unforgivable error. Two nice looking gentlemen, who said they were good North-side Republicans approached me to introduce legislation, which allowed drug stores to sell cold beer, whether in individual cans or by the case. I did not realize that this legislation would create all kinds of turf battles and animosities. I also was informed that the same legislation had failed many times in the past and that a really top-notch lobbyist would charge a minimum of $10,000 just to assure its introduction.

The two gentlemen inhabited the halls daily for the first half of the session. Each time I stepped out into the corridor, they would want to know the progress of their bill. They knew as I did which committee the bill was buried in. I would tell them I was working on the chairman for a hearing. I would tell them a lot of things. I became good at ducking them. They would write signs on cardboard and put the signs face inward to the chambers on the back dividing window. If ignored they would bang on the window with their key chains. I learned a lot of lessons from that episode. To this day, I have no idea who they were. I don't even know if they were drug store owners or beer salesmen or what. I learned to at least get a business card with names and addresses and telephone numbers. The bill was neither heard in committee nor did it pass into law.

I introduced legislation to create and to appropriate $500,000 for the establishment of a fifth state supported institution of higher learning in Indiana. Autonomous U. I am still introducing legislation attempting to establish a state-supported university in Marion County. I am no closer to that goal today than I was in 1967.

The first legislation that I, as a first-term legislator, had drafted and wanted to introduce, simply ordered the gasoline stations to include the total price of a gallon of gasoline on the pump price. The price of a gallon of gasoline was listed and then someone had to figure out, by hand, how much sales tax was owed and add that to the pump price. By law there were little charts stuck to the side of each pump. Some charts were too small to read, some were blurred, and for some strange reason most of the stickers were on the back of the pump. All payments were made inside in those days. Every once in a while the customer might find an operator too busy to accurately figure the additional tax on the gallonage charge, or spot an operator who added a few extra pennies to the tab. All of the new gasoline pumps were technically advanced and could have been calibrated to include the sales tax if the industry had so wanted. I thought this legislation a good idea that would relieve a great deal of irritation among my constituents.

A fellow legislator wondered what the retail gasoline people thought of the proposed legislation. I decided to find out. I sought out the chief lobbyist and director of the association. He thought that his association would not be very favorable to the idea but maybe my suggestions might have some merit. He asked for and took my copy of the bill and said he would contact me later. I assumed later meant the next day or two. Later meant two weeks later, coincidentally the day after the House deadline for the filing of a bill. Lesson: Don't be stupid. Always introduce the bill first and then seek advice from your most likely opposition.

I was the first author of HB 1188 in the same session. The city of Indianapolis had no master annexation plan. Indianapolis was annexing several miles from the normal city boundaries, and these disorderly annexations prevented long-range planning for several civil governments in the county and especially for the Indianapolis Public Schools. HB 1188 freed the Indianapolis Board of School Commissioners from a requirement that the schools join in civil annexations. The legislation amended the general school annexation statues and repealed a special act applying to Marion County, which mandated that the school district boundaries were required to expand and to follow all civil annexations. The location of John Marshall and Arlington high schools is a result of strip annexation. The legislation easily became law.

The enactment of this legislation was cited some years later by Federal Judge Hugh Dillin when he ordered a school desegregation plan for the Indianapolis Public Schools. In the order Judge Dillin referred to two bills that the legislature had enacted, HB 1188 and the Uni-Gov act. I was the original sponsor of each bill, but was never contacted during the deliberations on desegregation. The court and the attorneys in the case were not much interested in legislative intent.

The Democrats had campaigned on writing into law that beginning school teachers in Indiana be paid a minimum starting salary of $6,000. In the midst of a hot campaign, and acting alone without any consultation with any other Republican, the state GOP Chairman, Charles Hendricks, upped the ante and declared the Republicans would guarantee a minimum beginning wage for school teachers of $12,000. Further, he announced, the state would provide the money.

The Republicans were reminded of this pledge on several occasions during the session. Of course tax increases would have been in order if that promise was to be carried out. Almost at the very end of the session, Representative Ruckelshaus responded to the lack of positive action exhibited by his party during the legislative session in attempting to make good on the GOP chairman's promise. He assured all of the House members that the minimum salary had not been forgotten. Such a minimum should be the goal and the methods of financing that salary guarantee would be researched and the findings would be presented to the legislature in 1969.

One of the outstanding freshman Republican legislators in 1967 was Mike Rogers, representing New Castle and Henry County. Mike was a professional radio broadcaster and on the faculty of the School of Communications at Ball State University. His professional radio skills would soon be put to good use. The Democrat majority of 1965 had appropriated money to remodel the House Chambers. Jeanette Surina, the principal clerk, was in charge of the over-all project, and did an outstanding job, sparing no expense. Newly purchased furniture and equipment graced the chamber. It included massive members' chairs of leather with the seal of the state of Indiana embossed in gold on the back upright section; in fact, too massive to move around. A member wanting to move from the inside row seat to the aisle had a difficult time pushing chairs to the desks and struggling to get to the outside. The monster chairs were mercifully replaced with a smaller version for the next session.

Here's where Mike Rogers came into the picture. Mrs. Surina had the latest in sound equipment installed. The acoustics were excellent, the amplifiers more than adequate, the microphones sensitive, the latest in technology. The second week of the session, Representative Rogers took to the floor on a Point of Personal Privilege. In his best authoritative manner, Rogers lectured the members of the House on the fact that the microphones were working well and the House members should never tap them before speaking to see if the system was working. He went on and on about the wonders of modern science. He especially warned of damaging the fragile instruments. He did all of this in his best professorial tone. When Mike was finished and sat down in his seat, one after another, the House members marched up to the microphone, tapped it and sat back down. For the rest of the session most of the members would tap the mike and then look at Rogers. For his efforts of lecturing the House, Mike was awarded the nickname of "Mother." His brood never allowed him to forget that Point of Personal Privilege.

chapter   7

Direct Primary

As I had discovered after my entry into politics in the early 1960s, Indiana was one of the few states which did not nominate its candidates for the United State Senate and for statewide offices by utilizing the direct primary system. Instead, elected delegates from each of the counties gathered in a party convention every two years to nominate the candidates who were to be voted on statewide. It was a deeply flawed system.

I have been a delegate to the Indiana Republican State Convention every two years since my first Indiana convention in 1962. Dr. Don Scroggins, as Johnson County GOP chairman, offered me a proxy in 2002. Along with the appointment, he sent a note warning me that I would be responsible for paying the twenty-five dollar delegate fee.

In most cases through the years, I had been a candidate for the position of delegate. To be considered as a delegate during the May primary, a person must file a Declaration of Candidacy with the county clerk. Usually, a ward or township or county was allotted a certain number of delegates by the state committee, and the number allowed would be the number of individuals filing their candidacies for becoming a delegate. Many precinct committeemen felt that they deserved the honor of becoming an elected delegate. County chairmen would use the enticement of being a delegate to reward the party faithful. Sometimes a stray citizen would file and then the party apparatus would have to take over and conduct a "campaign." Slates would be printed. Committeemen would "push" the slates on the voters at their precincts. By having a great proportion of committeemen as candidates for delegate, the ward chairmen could make sure that a concerted effort to carry the slate would be made by those committeemen who were delegate candidates.

Once elected, many of these successful candidates would not have any interest in attending the state convention. Many did not want to pay the delegate fee that was collected by the state organization. In the 1960s the fee was five dollars. Forty years later, the fee is twenty-five dollars.

One of the years that I was Perry Township Ward Chairman, the township was allotted thirty-five delegates according to a formula used by the state GOP. Normally, this would attract two or three more filings than the allotted number of thirty-five. In 1968 several self-interest groups took issue with the Republican Party and some of its perceived stances. An organized conservative faction, a citizen party, and a few ordinary citizen voters decided that they all wanted a slate of delegates to the Republican state convention. When the dust had cleared and filing was concluded, eighty-five names were to be listed on the paper ballots.

The battle was on. Many voters were not even aware that they had the ability to vote for a delegate to the state convention. With the normal number of candidates for delegate in Marion County, their names would appear on the bottom row of the voting machine, sometimes to the far right side of the face of the levered machine, not very noticeable. The placement of those candidates for delegate was almost as far from the voter's normal inspection and eyesight as was the placement of those seeking to be elected committeeman. The voters in Perry Township became very aware of the contest that year: the polls were well manned, literature was printed and distributed and wagon books were kept up to date while the telephone calls were made.

All of our organizational candidates for delegate were elected. The Perry Township GOP even bested the GOP organization in Warren Township, a friendly rival. In those days John Sweezy was the Warren Township chairman, and John would invariably file only names that began with the letter A or B. One fellow I knew in Warren was elected more than ten times and never did attend a state convention. Warren Township always had quite a few open delegate slots that could be doled out as proxies.

The Republican State Convention, as far as I know, has been held in

Indianapolis in every even-numbered year. The convention is held in June following the May statewide primary. In the 1960s the headquarters and festivities were in downtown Indianapolis, but the convention and voting were at the State Fairgrounds, most often in the Coliseum.

Each person who had filed his or her candidacy for a statewide office to be selected by the convention delegates would reserve at least two reception rooms or suites in the old Claypool Hotel. The candidate and his wife or her husband would have an open house on the third floor and serve punch and cookies. An aide would wink at you and give you a card with a room number on it that was on another floor.

The second room would be on the fifth, sixth or seventh floor. Early in the evening, the room doors on this floor would be closed, and a knock would be answered by an underling who would inspect the proffered card. If all met the test, the delegate would be offered a drink of choice and something to eat. The office seeker's campaign manager and the candidate's county chairman were in charge. Small talk was in order in the beginning. When the hard drinks were delivered, the hard talk was not far behind. The visiting delegates may not have known it, but their names were listed on master files in each of the candidate hospitality rooms. His or her attendance to the hospitality room would be duly noted, and then the managers would attempt to surmise if this particular delegate before them was a "yes," a "no" vote, or "undecided."

The two-room system guaranteed that the candidates would satisfy the teetotalers who could never have voted for anyone serving alcoholic beverages and would also satisfy the "good ole boys" who wanted their candidate to have a tolerant attitude.

Even though the Claypool Hotel had elevators that worked to perfection the rest of the year, the night before the Republican convention, the elevators for reasons unknown failed to operate. The delegate and spouse had to navigate upwards from the third floor by using the exit stairs. The stairwell could accommodate, at most, three people on a step. Early in the evening going up was not too complicated. Later, as the party picked up, it seemed as if more were now coming down than going up. Most were carrying half-filled glasses. There was a lot of pushing and shoving. The closeness caused some delegates with conflicting opinions of the candidates for the contested races to be able to debate the virtues of their candidate practically nose to nose while trying to go up or down.

Each of the candidates would try to out-do his opponents. Bill Bray trucked in a live elephant one year. It was tethered on a lo-boy trailer on Illinois Street next to the Claypool. Trudy Etherington kissed all of the male delegates on their arrival at her third floor reception room. Kisses were more powerful than wine; Trudy was easily nominated the next day. Balloons were big giveaways, but they did not long survive in those days of indiscriminate cigar and cigarette smoking.

The Republican state headquarters and offices were on the mezzanine of the Claypool for a few of those years. To be invited to drop by for a drink in the headquarters was truly a badge of recognition. Only the top movers and shakers enjoyed the ultimate of the smoke filled rooms.

The convention of 1968 may have been typical of previous Republican conventions, but to me, all of the distasteful elements of what should have been a very important process in selecting our statewide governmental officers were exhibited. Forty-some Marion County delegates did not bother to show up at the Coliseum for one reason or the other. The back two rows of folding chairs were filled with delegates napping and sleeping away the party from the night before. A Nineteenth Ward adherent got into a fistfight with one in the First Ward. More was heard about Trudy's kisses than about qualifications of the other candidates. There was no question that the eventual nominees had been handpicked by a small group of county chairmen. The process may have been flawed, but at least the candidates who were finally selected met the test of representing the geographical reaches of Indiana.

The state convention of 1964 went five ballots. The number of delegates who waited to vote beyond the end of the fourth vote had dwindled to a ridiculous number. It must have been more important for the overwhelming percentage of delegates to get an early start for home than it was to stay around and vote for the candidates they favored.

I believed then, as I believe now, that the electorate must have a large role in selecting candidates for the fall general election. Political parties are a necessity, but this necessity does not give them the right to offer up a candidate or a group of candidates without the free input of the electorate. Any candidate must be required to face public and media scrutiny. Demonstration of the candidate's ability to think while operating in an unfamiliar or hostile setting is a must.

With this in mind, in 1968 I had the Legislative Council research the history of the direct primary in Indiana. Indiana laws had produced a variety of primary options, with a modified direct primary from 1915 to 1925 in the state. For many years the Indiana legislature had actually picked and selected the United States senator.

There was history here and there would be more. Unsuccessful legislation had been introduced in the 1940s to allow for a direct primary system. Again direct primary legislation was offered in several of the sessions of the General Assembly in the 1960s, but without any action taken. The same was true in 1969. I had legislation written and then introduced a bill that called for the direct primary for all of the statewide offices in Indiana. My co-sponsor was Senator Bob Mahowald.

Emboldened and with a modicum of encouragement, I decided to take my arguments to those in charge and addressed the Republican Platform Committee before the 1970 State Convention. I said:

> *The state nominating political conventions in Indiana must be eliminated. Indiana must join forty-eight other states in providing for a direct primary vote to nominate its major candidates for final consideration in the fall elections …*
>
> *The system that we now operate under is a disgrace to any thinking individual. We seem to be penalizing the voters in the effort to select those that will be candidates for the highest offices in the state …*
>
> *I have been a delegate to four of our state conventions and am an elected delegate to the 1970 convention of the Republican Party. I have seen perfectly logical and rational delegates, under instruction from back home, completely fall apart in their reasoning due to the influence of alcohol, blandishments, and promises and such. They can change their minds at the last moment, and wonder what the heck happened when their candidate got beat. The emotional impact and psychology of the night before the convention have as much, at times, to do with success or failure of a candidate, than all of his previous rhetoric …*
>
> *I have seen those that have worked for several months for a particular nomination to be completely shunted aside and this position filled by someone who had never had the foggiest idea of being a candidate for anything, ten days before the convention …*
>
> *The reasons are many. I would imagine that all of you have heard them before. I do say that it is time for a change in the present system. The public is not*

dumb. They know what is, and has, gone on. One of these days, they will want to vote for their choice directly ...

Needless to say I did not receive a standing ovation, nor was I instantly drafted to run for a statewide office. In an attempt to mollify some members of the platform committee, the chairman noted I held the appointive political office of assistant Marion County chairman. Actually, Keith Bulen, the county chairman, and I rarely spoke on this issue.

I tried again in the 1971 session. I reintroduced the legislation, but with a new co-sponsor, Senator Charles Bosma, who was also the chairman of the Senate Elections Committee. Finally, a public hearing for the Senate bill was held. Twelve people, including myself, offered testimony in support of the bill. This was to be one of the few times in my political career that the AFL-CIO and I were on the same page. Other proponents included the UAW, municipal workers union, Indiana Farm Bureau, and the Indiana Council of Churches.

John Price, secretary of the Republican State Committee, spoke in opposition, as did Ed Treacy, administrative assistant to State Democratic Chairman Gordon St. Angelo, and Gordon Durnil, campaign manager for Senate GOP nominee Richard L. Roudebush in 1970.

Price testified that the "pattern in states with direct primaries is that large, non-political interest groups, not responsible to the people, select the parties' nominees." Treacy read a statement saying that St. Angelo opposed the direct primary because he feared it would lead to less, not more, voter influence.

My own testimony added nothing new except that it enabled me to philosophize: "The more we involve people, the better the understanding of the problems, and the easier the solution."

Chairman Bosma said he thought that if his committee recommended passage of a direct primary bill, it would be the Borst-Bosma proposals with amendments limiting campaign expenditures. This additional proposal was a surprise, but one of the first lessons a new legislator learns is that the chairman is always right. The full Senate rejected the legislation by a twenty-two to twenty-seven vote.

Reintroduced in 1972, the legislation was similar to the previous year's bill and became SB 54. Once again the legislation cleared Senator Bosma's

Election Committee by a tally of five to two and was amended so that the bill might take effect January l, 1974. The Senate passed the legislation on to the House on a bi-partisan vote of thirty-six to eleven. This was quite a turn-around even with the makeup of the Senate being the same as the year before, excepting one member.

Most of the floor opposition to the measure was based on the idea that poorer candidates could not compete with wealthier ones if they sought the candidacy on their own. Senator Charles Wise from Muncie spoke against the bill, saying that it would favor the candidates with resources to buy more public exposure and added it is "no accident that the bill was sponsored by two Marion County senators." Senator Bob Sheaffer, from Shelbyville, agreed with Wise for many of the same reasons.

Senator Tom Teague, Anderson, supported the bill, saying it was "time we face the issue squarely. People should have an active part in the selection of candidates." Senator Robert D. Orr, a former Vanderburgh county chairman, surprised some observers by speaking and voting for the bill. Senator David Rogers, Bloomington, said he did not believe the "wealthy man advantage" exists anymore.

Meanwhile across the hall in the House, Representative Doris Dorbecker, the House elections committee chairman, was telling anyone who would listen, including the media, that Borst and Bosma were playing political games. She averred that all of the senators who voted for the bill knew she would never let it out of her House committee. She said that she had to follow the dictates that she received from Keith Bulen, her county chairman. Bulen and Orvas Beers and Joe Kotsos, GOP county chairmen from Allen and Lake Counties, pretty much steered the direction of the Republican Party in those years. They were not thrilled about having to give up their ability to select all of the GOP candidates for statewide office.

The direct primary system was installed in Indiana by legislative action in 1975. The vote came easily in the Senate. Up until the final minute of passage, the success of the bill in the House was short by two votes. As then representative, now senator, Lindel Hume of Princeton remembers, he and his brother Representative Donald Hume, were summoned into Speaker Phil Bainbridge's office. The brothers, Democrats, were against the direct primary system and were prepared to hold out at all cost. Those in favor were as determined. Lindel was handed a live phone, when he said "hello," the voice on the other end politely asked if he and his brother might change their voting stance as a personal favor. The voice on the other end was Democrat United States Senator Vance Hartke. Southern Indiana blood and background does make a difference. Direct primary passed by one vote in the House. In his next run for re-election, Senator Hartke had all kinds of difficulty in securing the senatorial nomination. Former state Senator Phil Hayes, from Evansville, running against him in the primary, conducted a smart aggressive campaign, and almost won.

Senator Bosma was the prime Senate sponsor of the successful legislation. In Bosma's legislation, only the political offices of United States senator, governor and lieutenant governor were to be placed on the ballot. The other statewide offices were still to be selected by a political convention.

The first significant use of direct primary was in the spring of 1980. Bob Orr was clearly the favorite to be the Republican nominee for governor. Senator John Mutz, Speaker Kermit Burrous, and former Shelbyville Mayor Ralph Van Atta all filed and ran for the lieutenant governor nomination in the direct primary. The race was close, practically a three-way tie. Maybe it was because someone got beat or maybe it was because Mutz was from Marion County, the legislature reversed its stance and put the lieutenant governor back into the convention system in a following session. No concerted attempt to reverse that decision or to bring the other state officials into the direct primary has been mounted since.

I believe that the primary system now in place does balance the traditions of the political parties by being able to select some of the statewide candidates but also allowing the electorate to cast his or her vote for the more important elective offices. Those candidates for United States senator and governor have usually worked hard to publicly project their image and programs. The voting public then does at least have an informed idea as to why and for whom they are casting their ballot for these offices.

chapter   8

Uni-Gov

Government consolidation in Marion County and establishing a state-supported university in Indianapolis were the two main issues of the 1968 political campaign in central Indiana. And they were, indeed, significant issues.

But with the Republicans on a roll in Marion County going into 1968, several House members took advantage of an earlier re-districting effort and decided to become candidates for the state Senate. I was one of them as were Walter Barbour, Dan Burton and Charles Bosma. Les Duvall, Joan Gubbins, George Rubin and Judge Jack Ryan won approval from the RAC screening committee and also became candidates for the Senate. Each of the slated candidates for senator was successful in the primary.

Republican House candidates in 1968 were David Allison, Harriette Conn, Ray Crowe, Doris Dorbecker, Choice Edwards, Wilma Fay, John Hart, Bob Jones, Dr. Ned Lamkin, Morris Mills, John Mutz, Don Nelson, Art Northrup, Ray Sanders and Otis Yarnell, all of whom survived the primary election.

The Marion County Republican fall campaign of 1968 went full steam. I rather doubt that any thought of not winning the fall general election was ever entertained by these Republican legislative candidates. Richard Nixon's candidacy began strong in Indiana and remained strong. His strength in central Indiana was such that Bulen ignored all of the state and local candidates from the latter days of September and concentrated totally on the presidential race.

Uni-Gov was a bill creating new administrative authority, more citizen representation, greater governmental efficiency, and basically extending the boundaries of Indianapolis to the Marion County lines. Once the 1969 legislative session began, we determined that the prospects of passing the legislation were much better than the delegation had originally thought. There was more legislative support from around the state than we had imagined. I think the prevailing opinion was, "If those guys in Marion County are that crazy, then it will serve them right when we pass this Uni-Gov and then they will fall flat on their faces." Before the session, some of us had thought that the 1969-1970 years might have to be a time needed to "educate" the rest of the state on consolidated government and then the proponents would be better organized in 1971 for an all-out effort. Upon assessment of the general support within the assembly, the Marion County leadership in the legislature made the decision to concentrate on government reorganization and to defer the establishment of a new university as a secondary legislative issue to be concentrated on in the future.

Before totally abandoning the quest for an autonomous university in Indianapolis, I called for an evening meeting at the Columbia Club with the president of Indiana University, Joe Sutton, the president of Purdue University, Fred Hovde, and John Hicks. John was the right hand man for President Hovde in all facets of Purdue involvement. I knew Hicks. At one time during a Senate finance hearing on the budget, I had complained that Purdue had not given me enough information about the university for me to make a rational decision. From that day forward, I received dozens of packages, letters, charts, reports from every conceivable school at Purdue. I labeled it the "Dump Truck Theory" of John Hicks. An imaginary dump truck would back up to my front porch every day and deposit its cargo of mail in front of my house. My mailman complained. He was forced to carry the mail that would not fit in the street side mail box to my front door almost every day.

At this moment, I told those gentlemen at the Columbia Club that the Marion County delegation was not going to pursue autonomous university legislation in 1969 but we would do so in 1971. The two universities already had held preliminary discussions on combining some of their similar missions in Indianapolis in the name of efficiency. They agreed to keep working on integrating and uniting with the idea of establishing an autonomous state university in Indianapolis at a later date. A like cooperative effort was also in store for higher education facilities in Ft. Wayne.

But first Unigov had to be dealt with. The bill was complicated in its eventual structure and took much planning.

It was Buert SerVaas who coined the acronym Uni-Gov. One afternoon, a dozen or so of the loosely structured research and investigative group who were looking for ways to make government within Marion County more efficient were sitting around Mayor Lugar's conference table, when Buert came up with the name. Before, the project was addressed as some form of consolidated government. Buert, ever thinking ahead, had rejected in his own mind "consolidated," "unified," "multiple," "countywide" and other words that might fit.

The quest for delivering governmental services in a more efficient manner had been ongoing for several years, of course. Efforts of the 1967 legislative session spurred the discussion to extend, countywide, as many services as possible, with the simple aim to eliminate overlapping jurisdictions between city and county governments.

House Republicans in 1967 had been extremely aggressive in moving towards consolidating some government functions in Marion County. With complete cooperation from the Senate Democrat majority, several of the goals that would pave the way for Uni-Gov were achieved. Funding for the new Expo Center originated in the Senate with Senator Pedigo as its author. Services in the areas of drainage, air pollution and transportation were extended county-wide.

Immediately following the legislative session of 1967, a small group of Marion County Republicans began meeting weekly at John Burkhart's home to discuss bettering government services and improving the quality of life in Marion County. Ardeth Burkhart would serve a meat loaf or a fruit salad or sandwiches while we sat around the dinner table discussing possible future legislation. Buert, Dick Lugar and Tom Hasbrook attended regularly. Carl

Dortch, then the executive director of the Indianapolis Chamber of Commerce, John Mutz and Ned Lamkin were also involved on a regular basis. Keith Bulen, as Republican county chairman rarely attended but did support the discussions.

After several weeks of give-and-take, two main issues were identified as projects for the 1969 session of the Indiana General Assembly. Number one on the agenda would be the creation and establishment of an autonomous educational institution of higher learning in Indianapolis. Secondly, research would begin on drafting amendatory legislation that would combine most of the governmental services throughout Marion County.

John Rabb Emison was retained to research procedures on creating public universities in Indiana. The report was completed and submitted to the ad hoc group in the fall of 1968. As has been written, the pursuit of an autonomous university in Indianapolis was to be deferred until 1971.

Attorneys Lou Bose and Charles Whistler volunteered to begin the arduous task of writing a workable plan for Marion County government reorganization, the plan that would eventually become Uni-Gov. Most every young Republican attorney in town was enlisted to work on the proposed legislation. Each section of the code that was to be amended had an assigned team that worked independently from the rest.

Most of the work began in 1968 following Dick Lugar's installation as mayor of the city of Indianapolis. None of the framers of the legislation gave any thought to not having a Republican majority in the legislature in 1969. Every one of the House and Senate aspirants assumed that he or she was going to win again in the fall of 1968. Gross conceit or political stupidity dominated Republican thoughts.

As time went on, political practicalities began to surface. The writers were not quite sure how to eliminate the law enforcement duties of the Marion County Sheriff's Department. Because the sheriff is a constitutional office in Indiana, the department could not be simply eliminated by an act of the legislature. The procedure for amending the Indiana Constitution is time consuming and so was not considered. Thought was then given to expanding the Indianapolis Police Department countywide and retaining the Sheriff's Department as a civil division only, with the sheriff serving subpoenas, warrants and such. An outline was developed making the Indianapolis Police Department the surviving entity but it was ultimately rejected. Recognition of other problems associated with the two departments eventually cancelled out the whole idea of law enforcement consolidation.

One problem was the magnitude for the fiscal liability of future pension expenditures for the Indianapolis Police Department. The pension benefits had been negotiated and legislated by Indianapolis city government. If consolidation throughout the county were to occur, the boundaries of the police service district would then be extended countywide, requiring that all of the taxpayers in this extended district to be liable for future pension payments. County residents would then have had to pay for a service that they had not received.

In 1968 all of the township fire departments were volunteer, each having only one or two full time employees, mainly dispatchers. Wayne Township was unique with seven or eight individually-created volunteer fire units. The decision-makers of Uni-Gov concluded that extending Indianapolis city fire services countywide, and eliminating the volunteer departments, would be an enormous undertaking, with respect to manpower, costs and resentment to be incurred.

Future fire pension liabilities were also a consideration, as they had been for the city police. Consolidation of Marion County fire services was not seriously considered because of the foregoing and other valid reasons.

Since the awarding of beer, wine and liquor licenses was based on the population figures of the police service district in Indianapolis, it was felt that the rest of the state might have serious objection if the number of licenses available was adjusted to the total population of Marion County. The authors of the legislation carefully froze the number of licenses already awarded. A later lawsuit and court decision overturned the legislation and increased the number of permits because of the increase in total population.

The creation of the Metropolitan Planning Commission caused some very serious philosophical debates. The fact that the new commission would be comprised of appointed members, with no elected members, was cause for concern for some. The new entity would plan for future growth and oversee all zoning ordinances. Previously, all zoning ordinances had come before the city council. The new legislation reduced the number of these ordinances but still provided for council review on demand. These accepted checks and balances were not resolved until the original legislation had passed over to the House.

One primary reason for revamping government in Marion County was to eliminate the posts of Marion County commissioners. These were elective positions in all of the counties in the state, and the three commissioners seemed to squabble frequently over hiring practices, personal use of gasoline credit cards, not attending meetings and the awarding of contracts. Most of these problems made the media. Fortunately, two of the commissioners supported their own elimination. The legal duties of the commissioners were divided up among the other countywide office holders by the Uni-Gov policy-makers.

For legal reasons and to preserve historic heritage, all of the recognized cities and towns in Marion County were preserved with boundaries remaining intact. Each of the excluded cities—Beech Grove, Speedway, Lawrence and Southport—were given the ability, under certain restrictions to expand their boundaries through annexation. City and town government under Uni-Gov was much the same as it was before the changes were made.

Sanitation was expanded countywide. Development and the creation of new parks became a hybrid. Each of the excluded cities which had a public park system did maintain that system, but also had to contribute to the newly formed Uni-Gov Park Department.

There never was any serious thought given to unifying the school systems in Marion County.

Some of the decisions that were required to make up the structure of this new government were debated at length. The decision to provide for a strong mayoral type of government was made. One fundamental issue to be resolved was the percentage of council votes needed to over-ride a veto by the mayor. Making that only a majority vote, rather than two-thirds, brought back into play a balance of authority between the council and mayor.

The number of councilmen to be elected in the county had to be determined. The Indianapolis City Council was composed of nine members. Six of the councilors resided in their districts and were elected from the individual districts, but were voted on by all of the voters in the city. The additional three council members were the three highest "losing" candidates, assuring that the minority had representation on the council.

The Marion County Council, on the other hand, consisted of five councilmen, each from an individual district. The thought at first was to provide for fourteen council members. Through continued discussions, members were added. The first draft of the legislation made in Mayor Lugar's office was for twenty districts plus five to be elected at-large. The more districts, the more support for the legislation. The selling point was that with more, smaller districts, there would be more grass roots.

The final decision was to create twenty-five districts and to add four at-large councilmen. It was felt that whichever party a mayor might represent, by adding the at-large positions, the mayor would, and should, have a working majority within the council. The perception was that the four at-large would always tip the balance of numbers within the council. The county election of 1999 disproved that theory when the new mayor and the four at-large councilors were Democrats but the Republicans prevailed as the majority in the council.

About the last question the writers of the legislation had to deal with was what to do with the dog pound. The mission of the pound and of stray dog control did not conveniently fit into any particular niche. Originally, I had wanted to include the dog control under the new Public Health Department. For reasons that may not have been particularly valid, this proposition was rejected. At the last minute before finalizing the drafting process, as an addendum, stray dog control and the pound were placed at the end of the chapter on Public Safety. The police did not want the responsibility in 1969 and the police do not want this same responsibility now. The problems with dog control continue to this day.

Two public hearings on Uni-Gov were scheduled and conducted in the City-County building. The committees of the Affairs of Marion County, both from the Senate and the House, were present to offer statements and to answer questions from the public. Less than 100 citizens attended the meetings. The main question then and later: "Why not a public referendum after passage of the bill?" The answer was that there had been ample public hearings and input with open discussions in every part of the county.

The last of many drafts of the proposed legislation was finalized and put into proper fill form near the end of 1968. The decision-makers agreed that the legislation would be introduced first in the Indiana Senate. I had served one term in the House and had switched to running for election in the Senate in 1968. Even as a freshman legislator I was given the responsibility of being the bill's author and chief spokesman in the Senate. The legislation was introduced early in the session.

Advance copies were distributed to those reporters and interested observers shortly after the first of the year. Somehow the copy for Ed Ziegner, of *The Indianapolis News,* was either mislaid or else placed on the desk of some other reporter. That I was not responsible for the delivery of the advance copy made no difference to Ziegner. I was royally berated and challenged in a way that I had never experienced before. The additional fact that his wayward copy was found twelve hours later, on another city-room desk, made no difference. I remained persona non grata with Ed for many years. He never did acknowledge that we had tried to deliver an advanced copy of Uni-Gov to him.

The framers of the legislation did an absolutely outstanding job. Very little of substance needed change. After the bill's introduction, on January 21, 1969, I went over the introduced version checking for mistakes or omissions. There were many typos and misspelled words. Instead of a comprehensive amendment correcting these minor problems on a line-by-line basis, I chose to have a complete redraft with all of those secretarial problems changed. I wanted a clean bill that could be presented as un-amended and reintroduced the legislation on February 4. I have a difficult time remembering the bill numbers assigned to my legislation. So, this second time around for the Uni-Gov legislation, I waited in the Senate secretary's office for a while and watched the numbers being assigned. I waited until it was time for an easy bill number for me to remember came up, and then gave the new version to the secretary. Uni-Gov then became Senate Bill 543. Later the opposition reminded everyone of the second introduction as proof that the bill was far from perfect and only a work in progress piece of legislation. It would be pointed out that I had made over one hundred amendments to the first filing, reason enough to vote against passage.

Most of the opposition to the bill was from those people who might be losing some of their legal responsibilities. The volunteer fire departments knew that the legislation did not allow for a countywide fire system, but in their own minds they figured a mandated system was inevitable. The County Commissioners Association did not like the elimination of the three commissioners in Marion County. Taxpayer associations felt that there would be no significant efficiencies in consolidated government and there would be no property tax saving. The associations would estimate that costs could not be contained and individual property taxes would soar. The conservative faction of the Republican Party remained unconvinced that this new form of government met their philosophical standards. The mayors of the excluded cities did not want to give up any authority and did not particularly care for their constituents voting for the mayor of Indianapolis, as well as voting for the mayor of the excluded city. African-American leaders were afraid that their community in the central city would not be heard and would not have representation under Uni-Gov. Being against change was a basic tenet for much of the opposition.

The legislation was voted out of the Senate Committee of Affairs of Marion County and was sent to the floor with the recommendation of Do Pass as Amended. The amendment within the committee was one that I proposed. In an unofficial survey of legislators representing those counties adjoining Marion County, I found that there was no support of the legislation; in fact they were vocally opposed. They and their constituents conjured up the specter of Marion County annexing everything in its path in all directions. Hancock, Morgan, Hendricks, Johnson and Hamilton counties were all fearful of the possible consequences of the legislation. My amendment would prohibit annexation outside of Marion County, but would permit the city to rent or to purchase property in surrounding counties as was then permitted. The amendment was meant to garner at least a few votes in the House and Senate. No legislator from an adjoining county ever did vote for Uni-Gov.

The discussion during the second reading debate and amendatory action was fierce. Senator Joan Gubbins, a Republican senator from Indianapolis, led the charge by the opponents. Still the crippling amendments that were offered by the opponents were all defeated. A good portion of the Senate body sat and enjoyed the spectacle of a split Marion County delegation. Senator Bob Nash from Tipton was so turned off by the tone of one of the opponents that on leaving the chamber he promised me that he would vote for the legislation. What the proponents had to sell was that this legislation would provide good government. We all felt that politically such progressive action would also be good. Senators Rubin, Ryan and Burton were rock solid in their support of the legislation.

I had not quite made up my mind when I would call the legislation down for the third reading. I waited a few days for tempers to settle and to see if we could get a little more support from within the Marion County delegation. Supposedly, others from outside the Statehouse were working other areas of the state for positive votes. Keith Bulen made several contacts with other county chairmen. Buert SerVass talked with Chamber of Commerce types. My personal vote count was good, so I waited for a time when all those committed to the bill were sure to be on the floor of the Senate.

In those days, the legislature only met in session every other year, it was not uncommon to have Saturday morning sessions. Usually they were abbreviated so that the members could get an early start on their way home. I decided to call the Uni-Gov legislation down for third reading on the Saturday morning of February 15th.

Senator Jack Ryan had decided to help out the cause of Uni-Gov by entertaining three members of the Millard Fillmore Society (a fraternity within the membership of the Senate), all of whom were opposed to the bill's passage. A private room within the Athletic Club was reserved for any of their members who desired an intimate discussion, with private lockers and favorite labeled bottles. The Athletic Club had the reputation for quality service and its discreteness towards its members was at a very high level. It was a perfect hideaway. Jack's later explanation was that he wanted to get the three anti-votes so "Jacked" that they would not be able to attend the Senate to vote against the bill. The three identified Senators answered roll call. Ryan did not.

I was not about to debate the bill without Ryan. I called his house once, then twice. He finally answered, listened to my plea to "get the heck downtown to the Senate floor," but could not comprehend how his three guests of the night before were in attendance in the Senate.

I called a third time and found out that he was out of the shower. There was no answer to the fourth call, so I surmised that Ryan was on his way. I then contacted the state trooper who was on a Senate security detail and asked him if he would somehow monitor the progress of Senator Ryan from his north side home to the north door of the statehouse. I can't say that the judge was tailed by a variety of law enforcement officers, I can only imagine. I received a message from the trooper that the judge's car had pulled into the parking lot. The Senate was still on the third reading calendar. I had previously passed, but I asked another senator if he would yield to me on his call. He did and I asked that Uni-Gov be placed before the Senate to be considered for the third time.

As I made my call, Senator Bosma jumped out of his back row Senate seat and immediately left the chambers and headed home. Some secretary had to collect all of his papers and bills left in disarray upon his leaving. As the saying goes, Senator Bosma had friends on both sides of the issue and did not want to disappoint his friends.

Most third reading debates are restrained following the fierce and free-wheeling discussions of the second reading phase. There were no new facts to be given out from either side and so it went with Uni-Gov. The recorded vote in the Senate was no surprise to me. The vote was twenty-eight senators voting for the legislation and sixteen in opposition. I know of at least four of the senators who voted against passage who had told me they would vote for the bill if they were needed. Buert contended that he knew a few more yes votes that might have been available.

Representative E. Henry Lamkin was to be the prime author and main spokesman for the legislation in the House. We had felt that acceptance by the one-hundred-member body would be more difficult than in the Senate. By this time the bill needed little amendatory attention. The legislation was on a fast track and survived second reading amendments and became eligible for third reading on February 27th. Coming to the final days of the legislative session, House Speaker Bowen was asked by the media when he would schedule debate and consideration on Uni-Gov. He had not made out his bill schedule, he said. Some of the media interpreted this to mean that the speaker had not made up his mind about the bill and might not even allow the legislation to be considered on the floor of the House. Speaker Bowen said that he needed more time and personal assurance that the majority of Marion County citizens favored the proposal. I figured that such a statement was from a man that wanted to become the governor of the state of Indiana and he desired to show the prospective voters in Marion County that the legislation would not be rushed through without thoughtful consideration. The mayor of Indianapolis, Dick Lugar, interpreted Bowen's reasoning for non-scheduling as being the obituary for Uni-Gov.

The mayor immediately called a press conference and denounced Bowen for delaying the hearing on the bill. Lugar then gave out the unlisted telephone number of the speaker and urged Marion County's citizens to call in and express their sentiments. In retrospect, all of Lugar's actions were a comedy of errors. His subordinates had given the mayor the wrong telephone number. He had wanted the callers to go through the general switchboard of the House rather than calling the speaker's private secretary to register their opinions. The opponents of the legislation called and called and called completely tying up Speaker Bowen's private line, a really organized effort. It was reported later that 1,086 calls were logged against the legislation and 102 in favor. I am not quite sure of the accuracy of that tally.

I was in my car when the news was flashed over the radio that Lugar was upset and was denouncing the speaker. I got to a pay telephone and called Keith Bulen and told him that I had heard the mayor's statement on the radio. I felt that the mayor's actions toward Bowen could not help with the passage of the legislation in the House. I suggested that he call the mayor and have the mayor personally hand deliver a note of apology to the speaker in the statehouse. The mayor did not deem it necessary to hand deliver an apology, but he readily contacted the speaker with his profuse apologies. The mayor also sent a written note later in the day. Otis Bowen accepted the apology and, while he was at it, may have extracted some political favors for later years for his conciliatory attitude towards the mayor.

On the final day of the session, Uni-Gov was handed down for third reading. Dr. Bowen also noted, "If the representatives do not accurately reflect the sentiments of their county, the remedy is at the next election."

In his closing arguments, Representative Lamkin spoke with confidence and persuasion. He said, "Many who oppose this proposition possess a fear of change, a fear of disintegration of our cities, a fear of representative government. It's a kind of fear that spreads decay through a city.

"Indianapolis is a great city, but like so many of our cities, it is in danger of becoming a doughnut—a suburban circle around a dead core. Indeed, no man is an island anymore. We must live together with our neighbor and accept his burden—or move somewhere else.

"This is a bill of faith in representative government. As President Richard M. Nixon has suggested, let us pull together. That is what we must do in Indianapolis and this bill is the start in this direction."

The Uni-Gov legislation passed the House by a vote of sixty-six to twenty-nine. Governor Edgar Whitcomb signed the act into law on March 13, 1969.

It should be noted that Mayor Lugar had organized his own lobbying effort with the out-of-county legislators. He visited with all of them either at a breakfast or a lunch, usually in groups of four or five.

Carl Dortch, executive vice-president of the Indianapolis Chamber of Commerce, filed a friendly lawsuit against the Uni-Gov bill to ensure it would survive an anticipated string of legal challenges. The Indiana Supreme Court unanimously upheld the act. The lawsuit was filed within ten minutes of the bill signing by Whitcomb. A lawyer was waiting in the Supreme Court Clerk's office with a prepared suit and filed it immediately in order to make sure that a competing lawsuit would not take precedence over the friendly suit.

Post passage proved to be hectic. The legislation did not take effect immediately upon signature by the governor. The effective date of the new legislation would be January 1970, more than nine months in the future. Now that there was an actual Uni-Gov stature on the books, those who had paid little attention to the legislature and those that were opposed to the enactment scurried around in an attempt to negate some of the provisions of the new law.

Any of the excluded cities could look at their geographical boundaries and round them off by annexation procedures. In the most extreme instance, the City of Southport's mayor, Gene Wilson, had visions of creating a second class city with a population of over 25,000 overnight. He and the Southport City Council filed annexation ordinances that added many square miles to the territory of the city. Thousands of acres. Many ordinances. I spent many nights making appearances at the public hearings in opposition to the ordinances. In one way or the other, each of the ordinances were defeated and Southport remained a fifth class city.

The city of Indianapolis also attempted to annex acreage in order to "square" off the police district. One of the few city annexations that did succeed was the one that annexed my animal clinic into the city proper. This allowed me to pay for all of those services that I had never received. I could hardly object.

Many months after the implementation of Uni-Gov, Keith Bulen was quoted by John Apple of *The New York Times,* that "Uni-Gov was [his] greatest political coup." During the many months of discussion, I cannot remember a time when the political implications of Uni-Gov were ever internally discussed. The media, in an obtuse manner, may have raised questions.

The moon, stars and planets were all aligned for passage of the legislation. Republicans governed all of Marion County in 1969. The situation of having a Republican governor, legislature, mayor and Marion County councils in the majority, probably had never occurred before and may never occur again. Keith Bulen in his rare appearances with the writing of the bill did give his tacit approval to the new form of government.

It was within this scope and framework that changes were made to provide for a cohesive and coherent government in Marion County.

Another problem that needed to be addressed in that 1969 session was one of state highway improvements. Southern Indiana legislators had always complained that you cannot drive from here to there in southern Indiana. Any city can be substituted for "here to there." It might have been from Indianapolis to Evansville or Indianapolis to Lawrenceburg or Indianapolis to New Albany. The advent of the federal interstate system provided relief for most of the travel problems and, other than the isolation of Evansville, there is not much of a highway connector problem in Indiana these days. For the 1969 session the Southern Indiana highway problem to be addressed was the auto travel from Indianapolis to Bloomington and on to Bedford on Indiana 37. It was a two-lane highway, with dangerous curves, a maze of stops and starts in Martinsville, cars pulling boats on their way to and from Monroe Reservoir—all an absolute nightmare.

Since I boated on Lake Monroe and had traveled Indiana 37 many times I personally was full of sympathy. Representative Steve Ferguson and I set out to "doctor" a bill so that the legislation would be acceptable to the full Senate. Steve and I met in the office of Senator Alan Bloom, the Senate Pro Tem to work out a solution. Any solution had to include enough monies to provide for the construction of four lanes of highway on Indiana 37 to Bedford. The precise costs of reconstruction of Indiana 37 had been determined. That amount was subtracted from the net amount of new taxes imposed and collected and the remainder of the money was to be distributed to local government entities under a new formula, the Local Road and Street Fund (LRS) built into the Motor Vehicle Highway (MVH) funds.

I had decried the misuse of state collected gasoline tax monies by some counties, so I was challenged to develop a new formula for distributing the remainder of the new gasoline tax increase. The new LRS distribution formula required long-range road and transportation plans to be developed by county government. A highway improvement plan would require detailed engineering, and the newly collected money was to be spent on worthwhile projects and not to just oil the gravel road in front of the county commissioners' homes. The distribution of the money from the two additional cents of gas tax favored the more populous counties at first because of their numbers of staff, but then LRS brought about a more professional approach that was instituted by all of the counties for local road improvement.

Representative Ferguson was almost a one-person show in successfully shepherding the money-raising legislation through the General Assembly. The new gasoline tax money financed the re-building of Indiana 37, which is now named for Ruel Steele, a former state senator and a former head of the state highway system.

Lugar's comments about Uni-Gov

Bob Bloem, a journalist, moderated a television panel and asked Mayor Dick Lugar, "to tell a little about the genesis of Uni-Gov, what its purposes are and what we expect of it?" Lugar's reply was:

Uni-Gov is based on two general ideas: first of all, that most taxpayers want more for their money and they resent duplication of governmental services. Hardly a political campaign goes by in Marion County without duplication in drainage or snow removal being an issue. And the second thing very important is that tax payers have the feeling that they can not get action and that they can not put their finger on someone who is responsible. Take the snowfall problem. There are five jurisdictions in Marion County to remove your snow, people are very unhappy over the inability to organize this function cohesively. In order to do this, we suggested that we need an executive branch of government that brings the fifty-eight units together in eight departments. A mayor, elected by all people of Marion County, would name the department heads. They would be responsible to him and to an elected council of at least twenty-five individuals, the bulk of these, maybe all of them, if the bill finally evolves that way, would be elected by districts. This way council members with committees can ride herd on the executives to assure a checks and balance system and the participation of more people in elected government. And finally, the taxpayer can look to the mayor and to the council, all of whom are elected, to bring about responsible results and efficiencies. Presently, the taxpayer is rather frustrated in this respect, one unit of our government, Health and Hospital Corporation, spending eleven to fifteen millions of dollars, is not responsible to anyone who is elected and is appointed at such a glacial pace that the turnover hardly takes place during even the term of the mayor. So what I think we are driving at is efficiency and pointing a finger at someone where the buck might stop.

chapter 9

Code of Ethics

A bill to establish a code of ethics for the legislator and one that would require financial disclosure and financial conflicts began in a sordid way in 1969. I was offered a bribe for my "yes" vote.

A bill due for a public hearing and a vote before a committee of which I was a member was favored by a well-known public lobbying organization. I had not paid much attention to the bill or to any discussion of its merits. When I finally read the legislation, it seemed straight-forward with no particular problems. I figured that there would be no serious debate and that the legislation would easily pass out of committee.

The chief lobbyist for the proponents asked for a few minutes of my time, stuttered around, and told me how important it was to his organization that the legislation reach the floor of the Senate for a final vote. Without asking me what my thoughts were on the legislation, he flat out said that if I voted yes in committee he would deliver a large color television set to my home. To say that I was taken aback would be putting it mildly. I asked him to repeat what he had just said. I thought that surely I was not hearing correctly. The offer was repeated. No hesitation. No qualifications.

An offer like this was a stunner. Did these guys actually think that I would be open to outright bribery? What made them so sure of themselves? If they thought that bribery might be possible, did everyone else around the leg-

islature have the same thought regarding my morality? Later on, I wondered
how they arrived at a TV, and not a dozen golf balls or something like that.

The committee hearing was not to be until the next day. I stewed and
fretted for most of the day. Finally, I went to see a senior member of our caucus. I sat across from his desk and poured out the story. I probably was a little
emotional. He was calm, dragging thoughtfully on his cigarette. When I finished, I expected him to rise up in righteous indignation. I expected him to
call out the guards, the state police, or at least call a caucus to discuss the bill.
I expected him to console me and to soothe my hurt ego. Instead, he asked
me, "Do you suppose that you could get a TV for me?"

Color TVs were the "in" thing. Our family did not possess one. For several years I refused to buy one. Our children did not understand why we were
the only family that they knew of in Perry Township without a color TV set.
The kids would invent excuses to visit a friend down the street, just to watch
"Lassie" or some popular program in color. I finally bought one. The "marked paid" bill of sale was firmly scotch taped on the back of the set. The children rationalized that their dad was too cheap to buy this new fangled device
and wanted to wait until the prices dropped.

If I was truly stunned the first time I was bribed, it was doubly so the
second time. I said "no," thanked him for his time, and left. A few waste baskets and cardboard boxes were dented on the way out.

The hearing the next day produced a recommendation of Do Pass by a
vote of six in favor to my no in opposition with practically no debate. Suspicious as I was by this time, I could not help wondering how many color TV
sets were scheduled to be delivered that afternoon. Third reading passage in
the Senate produced only one or two no votes. The bill became law during
the session. The sad thing is that it was fair legislation and did not need a fix.

That evening, I really needed to talk with someone about the two different injustices. Senators Phil Gutman and Jack Ryan and I went out to dinner at the Columbia Club. Ryan probably paid the bill, as he always did. We
not only had dinner, but we closed the place down. Ryan was either on the
board or was president or something in the club, and Jimmy and the staff
would not have dared to have asked the judge to go home. The discussion
became animated, ridiculous, hilarious and stupid as the hours marched on
until well past the witching hour. Nothing was exactly settled, but a multitude of options and scenarios were explored.

My take on this episode was that legislators could be badly exposed to all sorts of charges and innuendo with the merest hint of impropriety. What if the knowledge of the offer had made the rounds of the rumor mills of the "halls?" How could a legislator defend himself from false charges? From my experience, it was apparent that there was no forum where any elected legislator could address and rebut false charges. Nothing was in place in the House nor the Senate to allow for any defense.

In 1972 I wrote and introduced what I called the "legislative ethics" legislation, written to protect the legislator. Most present legislators and lobbyists think of the legislation as a consumer protection device to insure that the public has a forum to question the ethics and conflicts of a particular legislator. This is only partly true. That's a secondary result. I intended to provide a forum I could use in any situation where I might need to clear my reputation.

I was surprised at the reactions I received from fellow legislators when I finally did introduce and file the legislative ethics bill. The attitude was that I was concerned with the morality of one and all, attempting to solve a problem that did not exist. The prevailing opinion was that this was not needed and if any problem arose, it could be handled "internally." Larry Conrad, then secretary of state, fully agreed with the ethics legislation and encouraged me to pursue it. He was the first state public official to publicly declare his personal and campaign financial activities. Larry even sent a folder of research material he had collected and also wrote to me on September 14, 1973: "I recommend, as I have in the past, that the General Assembly investigate the wisdom of enacting certain ethics legislation as it relates to the executive branch of state government."

I had sent a copy of the proposed ethics legislation to Representative Bill Latz for his comments. The first comment was: "preposterous." Another comment: "My own conscience serves me pretty well right now. Yours does too, sly fox. If your bill would be printed as our Code of Ethics in our Legislator's Handbook, I think it would serve all of us very well." Bill made other comments but by and large, what he wrote was typical of the thoughts of many legislators. The prevailing opinion was that legislation would not be needed. We should just print a code up and put it someplace that was inconspicuous to the public and quit stirring up trouble.

Many of the elected officials could not foresee the future. Accountability, openness and "transparency" were just a matter of time. The old order was being challenged. A new political rule book was soon to be written: one that said the public had a right to know much more about the system and much more about those in charge of it.

Before passage of my legislation in 1974, there were several adjustments and compromises. Instead of a "legislative ethics" bill, it was now a "legislative financial disclosure" piece of legislation. Congress had enacted this, so the idea was not too hard to swallow. Ethics committees were mandated to be appointed in each of the chambers. These committees were charged to write a code of ethics for their body and present the code to that body in the form of a committee report. The proposed legislation was ultimately amended to include the executive branch and certain of the higher salaried Indiana government employees.

Later in the proceedings when I realized that the Pro Tem was not going to allow the ethics bill to be considered for a vote by the full Senate, I developed a little strategy. I used leverage on the President pro tem by refusing to call down the supplemental budget bill for a vote. I even elicited a promise from the co-sponsor of the bill, Senator Jim Plaskett, not to call the bill down if I was not in the chamber. After I had disappeared from view for a couple of hours, took a long walk, kicked a few cans along the way, and returned, there was seemingly a change in attitude of the leadership. The legislation was debated, passed by the Senate and became law.

It has been my privilege to have been either the chairman or a member of the Senate Ethics Committee since its inception. Fortunately, it is not a busy committee. The chairman has great leeway and so is able to informally answer most questions without a formal complaint or hearing. Legislators' questions usually involve questions over a pecuniary conflict between an aspect of their personal life and a vote that is to be taken on the floor. The Senate rule that requires that all of those on the floor to cast their vote supercedes abstaining. Normally, the legislator will ask for a "point of personal privilege" and inform the body of his or her possible conflict.

There is a Code of Ethics for the Senate. The code has changed little since 1974. I know of no outright bribery, nor have I heard any legislator saying that he or she was offered something of value for a vote. The professional lobbyists have too much to lose if they are ever accused of such an act. Helping a legislator to understand the reasons that he or she should vote a certain way is much more sophisticated today than it was in the days of the color TV incident.

Here I am (1969) with "It's Purple Martin time" badge on my lapel in front of Lieutenant Governor Dick Folz, presiding.

Courtesy B&L Photographers

Speaker Otis Bowen in 1967 with pages David Borst and Noble Pearcy, Jr.

Representative Frances Gaylord, Speaker Otis Bowen, Representative Vicki Caesar in House Chambers in 1967.

Representative Ned Lamkin and I flew to Atlanta to see the new stadium in 1970.

L. Keith Bulen, William Ruckleshaus, and I engrossed in State Convention strategy in 1968.

chapter 10

Taking Back the Senate

Sometime during the summer of 1970, Senator Phil Gutman called me
to ask if I thought it was time for the Senate to be in charge of its own affairs.
Up until this time, the lieutenant governor had named the senators who
would sit on the committees along with designating the chairman and ranking members who would conduct the committee business. He even decided
the names and the compositions of the committees. The listing of assignments to committees by the lieutenant governor even allowed him to name
the session-ending conference committees. In the previous session, Lieutenant Governor Dick Folz, a Republican, had by-passed the chairman of Senate
finance, Senator Joe Harrison, to appoint Senators Les Duvall and Bob Orr
as conferees on the budget. He not only excluded the committee chair but
had ignored any Democrat input. Chances are good that the previous presidents of the Senate had consulted with the pro tems regarding recommendations and had more or less followed those suggestions. That situation changed in 1969, and that was the beginning of the members of the Senate wanting
to assume full responsibility for their own appointments and their actions.
Allowing the lieutenant governor so much authority was not a part of the
Indiana Constitution, but by a rule of the Senate, became a tradition from
one session to the next.

Because he demonstrated a great deal of ability as a legislator and as a
writer of legislation, Senator Gutman was popular within the Republican

caucus. His campaign theme of "taking back the Senate" gained enough acceptance for him to make a formal declaration of candidacy to become president pro tem of the Indiana Senate in 1971. Senator Duvall also announced his own candidacy for the position. Gutman and Duvall were not the only candidates. Senator Jim Gardner from Fowler and Senator Martin (Chip) Edwards from New Castle also were trying to develop support.

My personal philosophy told me that what Gutman was attempting to accomplish was proper for the Senate. The lieutenant governor was not an elected member of the Senate, and I also believed he should not have the administrative authority over the Senate proceedings. Senator Duvall was a political teammate of mine from Marion County and one of the most honest and dedicated individuals that I have ever worked with. Senator Duvall may have thought that the senators should be in charge of conducting their own business affairs, but he was unwilling, out of consideration for a fellow Republican, to dilute the authority of the lieutenant governor in 1971. My decision was made much more significant because both Senators John Ryan and George Rubin told me that whichever candidate I chose to support, would also receive their support.

The first or second most difficult telephone call that I have ever had to make was the one that I made to Les Duvall. I explained my position regarding the Senate, and he sympathized in a way, but reiterated that he would feel uncomfortable stripping Dick Folz of his authority. If Les had agreed to allow the Senate to conduct its own business, I would have supported him for president pro tem. In the very last days of the contest, Keith Bulen, ever wanting to be involved, would call me daily for an update of where the votes for Gutman were coming from and how many total votes Gutman had been promised. He just knew that he could sway a couple of Senate votes for Gutman. One of the votes from Marion County that had been counted on to be in favor of Gutman, and one that Keith had promised to deliver, did not happen.

There were twenty-nine Republican senators following the election of 1970. The vote was fifteen for Gutman and fourteen for Duvall. Gardner and Edwards dropped out of the race. Chip Edwards was elected as majority caucus chairman and Gardner was appointed majority floor leader. Duvall was selected as chairman of public policy, Rubin as chairman of judiciary, and Ryan as chairman of financial institutions.

In my own case, about a week after the election, Gutman called and wondered who I would recommend as chairman of the Senate Finance Committee. I assumed that since Senator Harrison had been chairman the previous two years, and had supported Gutman, that he would once again be selected as chairman. Gutman said that the choice was made easier because Senator Harrison said that he had no desire to continue on finance. I was stunned.

The session before, while a member of the finance committee, I was far too busy with Uni-Gov legislation to pay a whole lot of attention to what the committee was proposing. I only knew that members met in the glass-walled room in the rear of the senate chambers. They would gather there while the Senate was in session and would peruse the assigned bills and the budget. The room was constructed in such a way that the senators and those in the outside hallway could see what the committee was doing. Also, the senators in the room could see out and observe the Senate floor action and hear the legislative debate over the intercom. We would no sooner talk about one of the bills assigned to the finance committee than one of the committee members would stand up and say, "I have to vote on that bill," meaning the bill on the floor of the Senate. Hearing that, all of the committee members got up and filed in to the chamber to cast their votes. Rarely did the members quickly return to business. The committee proceedings started and then stopped a good many times.

I cannot recall attending any public finance committee meetings. I doubt if there were many. Mostly, in closed-door meetings, the committee passed the assigned bills around the table and decided then and there which ones to recommend to the full Senate.

Gutman had made his decision. He wanted no publicity on any of his committee assignments until the middle of December 1970. We both attended the Indiana Society in Chicago in early December. The talk of the politicos there was who would be chairman of Senate finance. My name had been rejected early on by those in on the know. I was a non-factor. Gutman's eventual announcement caught a few people completely off guard. I have since chaired the finance committee thirty-one out of the last thirty-three years.

I firmly believe that the lieutenant governor should now be relieved of his constitutional duties in acting as the president of the Senate. In the years before Bob Orr became the lieutenant governor, the person's duties were few, so he had time to devote to chairing the Senate. The legislature was only in session sixty-one days every two years. Being president was not time consuming nor an imposition on other official duties. Now, with the onset of yearly sessions and the proliferations of special sessions, an inordinate amount of time must be allocated by the lieutenant governor for the business of the Senate. Bob Orr, as lieutenant governor from 1973 through 1981, was the first in that position to be entrusted with significant administrative duties by the governor. The legislature itself is designating the lieutenant governor as the head of more and more newly enacted programs. The elected lieutenant governor surely does have more important responsibilities than to babysit the Senate.

During the eighties under the Senate presidency of Lieutenant Governor John Mutz, some in the Republican majority thought that this was the most opportune moment to begin the constitutional amendatory process of relieving the lieutenant governor of his duties in presiding over the Senate. The resolution was introduced and debated. John expressed his extreme concern. Even though he had been a senator at one time, and even though the demands on his time were excessive, he felt that his personal integrity was being challenged, and he would much rather that we table the idea until another time and until a different lieutenant governor was president of the Senate.

The 1971 session could be characterized as a "dueling banjos" scenario. Whatever legislation Speaker Bowen sent to the Senate, it would be massaged and changed by Gutman. I became involved in the property tax relief portion but was not a 100 percent willing participant. The House passed a tax relief package. The Senate changed it around and the Democrats in the Senate were successful in changing the local option income tax from a flat rate to a progressive rate. Gutman lured seven Democrats to vote for the bill's passage. It did pass with twenty-six votes. I voted against my own bill. Senator Gutman, in a show of trust, then made me a conferee on the legislation.

In the normal legislative course of session-ending action, playing "one upmanship" with the House was the thing to do. Gutman and I would simply concoct several conference committee reports just for the heck of it. There were stacks of reports lying around his office, all variations of the property tax relief theme. One was even typed up and reproduced minutes before the deadline. No constructive legislation resulted. To this day, both houses of the legislature are guilty of promoting last-minute legislation, knowing full well that the legislation has no chance of passage, but trying to convince the public that their body is the only one that has the interests of the populace at heart.

Both the Senate and House wanted to institute a local option tax on income, increase the sales and state income taxes, increase the corporate tax three percent and raise the cigarette tax by four cents and increase taxes on alcoholic beverages ten percent. All of this legislative action was planned without knowing whether or not Governor Whitcomb would sign or veto the proposals.

Edgar Whitcomb as governor was an easy target for both Bowen and Gutman. Whitcomb had made a "no new tax" pledge, but Bowen allowed the House to pass legislation that would increase state taxes. Gutman, then chimed in and was quoted, "We are not proud of what has happened in the last few years. You only have to walk out in the halls of the Statehouse to see what state of disrepair our state is in after two years of the present administration." One would have thought that Whitcomb was a Democrat instead of a sitting Republican governor.

During a late-night debate on taxes and property tax relief, the back-and-forth discussions at the microphone boiled down to a "he said" exchange. The topic was whether Governor Whitcomb was really against all forms of new taxation or whether local option and other techniques were acceptable to him. The leadership decided to ask the governor to restate his thoughts before the two Republican caucuses. Whitcomb agreed to once again explain his philosophy.

The Supreme Court chamber was the only room in the Statehouse large enough that could accommodate those planning to attend. The legislators left their respective chambers and milled about the entry door of the court chamber. Whitcomb was late arriving. When he did appear, he strode through the waiting legislators. The legislators all surged around and in back of him as he approached the door of the court chamber. Whitcomb was the first to approach the door; he grasped the doorknob and attempted to open the massive oak door. Nothing opened, nothing gave. The doors were locked. The surge of legislators pinning the governor and the first wave of leaders fell flat against the door. Cries of "back off" were heard. A dignified proceeding ended up as a comical happening. Whitcomb still didn't want any new taxes, local option or whatever.

At the end of each session, committees from the House and Senate are appointed to call on the governor and ask him if there is any more state business that should be accomplished before adjourning *sine die*. The members of the committee from the Senate reported that the governor's door was locked and that the lights in his office had been turned off. The Senate surmised that Governor Whitcomb had no other undone business for the legislature.

chapter 11

Visible, Substantial, Lasting

Otis Bowen campaigned for governor in 1972 on the promise of reducing the property tax for each homeowner. Asked how it could be done without raising other taxes, his reply was, "It cannot be done without a tax increase." His Democrat opponent agreed and that was the last of the discussion about a tax increase. Ordinarily, if a candidate admitted that he was thinking of raising any tax he would be hounded, at least, by the media, if not by members of his own party. That was not the case with Otis Bowen. Escalating property taxes had been discussed yearly as long as Dr. Bowen had been a legislator. With his November victory he now had a mandate to reduce property taxes.

Following the election, J. B. King, Bowen's campaign manager, called me and asked if I could meet with him and Representative John Hart and go to work on property tax relief. Not having been an insider in the recent campaign, I was surprised by the call, assuming that such a detail as how to provide for the property tax relief had already been thought out.

Governor Bowen's criteria for the package were simple: visible, substantial and lasting. This is where our discussions began. The substantial part of Bowen's request proved to be the most difficult. Five percent property tax relief was wimpy. Fifty percent out of reach. Twenty-five percent tax relief became the goal.

The next worry was how to prevent a tax "creep" from taking place once there had been a reduction. A frozen levy was agreed on to insure that the property tax would not continue to go higher and higher in each budgetary cycle. An announcement of the freeze on the levies was delayed until Hart had an opportunity to present the program to the House.

John Hart knew government financing. He was as knowledgeable as any legislator that I have ever worked with. John seemed to have an idea a minute. If I didn't like one idea he would think a second and come back with another.

The House was deemed to be the easier of the two chambers in which to pass the tax relief package, and since there would have to be both sales tax and corporate tax increases involved, constitutionally the legislation needed to begin in the House.

In the Senate, acceptance of the tax increases and the imposition of local option taxes was not a foregone conclusion. Of the fifty senators, thirty were Republicans. Theoretically, the package should have had smooth sailing in the Senate, but the personality and the makeup of the majority was such that we knew there would be difficulty in securing the twenty-six votes needed for bill passage.

To pay for the new Property Tax Relief Credits (PTRC) a two-cent sales tax increase was necessary, but because of the amount of new money available the across-the-board cut in property taxes had to be reduced to twenty percent. A County Adjusted Gross Income Tax (CAGIT) on individuals was written as a local option tax to allow substantially more tax relief. More relief was available only if a county so wanted and acted. I asked that a referendum for increased levies for education be included as an option in the proposals. I also wanted the corporate gross tax to be phased out at the rate of one-tenth of a percent each year. Governor Bowen, leery that the opposition may have accused him of favoring business, demanded that corporations pay more in taxes and required an increase in the Corporate Adjusted Gross Tax.

The package ended up in a fairly simple form. King, Hart and I kicked around ideas and J. B. would then go off somewhere, write them down, show the work product to the governor, come back for another meeting, and we would take on a new phase of the overall package. Fitting the work product into the Indiana Code became the difficult part of putting the tax relief idea into legislative form. Because of the late start in formulating a program the

final resolution of the reform was not finished until conference committee
time.

Governor Bowen, of course, deserves the bulk of any credit for the enactment of the 1973 Property Tax Relief Program. He had campaigned for
governor on the proposition. He set in motion the writing and the structur-
ing of the legislation. His personal leadership in the end helped to carry the
day.

Lieutenant Governor Bob Orr deserves special recognition, for it was
his vote that broke the twenty-five to twenty-five Senate tie vote allowing the
bill to increase the sales tax to pass third reading. Bob Orr is a great student of
political history and knew only too well that Lieutenant Governor Richard
Ristine had cast an affirmative vote in 1963 to break a twenty-five to twenty-
five vote in the Indiana Senate that authorized the implementation of the
sales tax in Indiana. That vote by Ristine, captured in dramatic fashion by a
newspaper photographer, greatly affected his future political career. As the
Republican nominee for governor in 1964 the voters were constantly reminded that Ristine was the cause of the sales tax.

The president pro tem of the Senate, Phil Gutman, never has received
proper recognition for his part in the successful passage of the tax relief program. Thirty Republican senators should have been enough to supply the
twenty-six votes needed to support their governor. A few of the senators had
campaigned on the promise of "no new taxes." Several had never voted for a
tax increase and never would no matter what the situation. After counting
noses (votes for tax relief), Gutman realized that he was four votes short of
obtaining twenty-six votes in the Senate. All fifty senators would have to be
present and voting in order to create a tie vote enabling the lieutenant governor to become the twenty-sixth vote. That meant that Gutman had to sway
three in the Democrat minority.

Gutman talked to and identified the three members of the minority
who, under certain conditions, would cast their votes for property tax relief.
The governor also talked to several of the prospective votes. Three Democrat
Senate heroes, Senators Plaskett, Mahowald and Frick ended up supporting
the governor. Their own political fallout was severe; none were ever re-elected
to the Senate.

Bowen also had to do some horse trading of his own within the Republican ranks. He went out of his way to mollify and to make future promises to

Senator John Augsburger. Phil Gutman had a long talk with Senator Earl Wilson and requested his attendance in the Senate to vote and to provide for a twenty-five to twenty-five tie. Earl was not about to vote in favor of any type of tax increase. After promising Gutman, Earl had second thoughts about being singled out, and literally, on hands and knees, crawled out of the back of the Senate, went through the swinging doors and tried to disappear. Gutman sent a State Police Trooper after him. Earl was apprehended with his wife west of the capitol on west Washington Street. He had to be coerced to return to the Senate. Earl Wilson had previously served over twenty years in the United States House of Representatives. This made us wonder if all of this was normal in the halls of Congress.

The first of the package of bills to be voted on was the increase in the sales tax. When the votes were counted, the board showed that the measure had not received the necessary twenty-five "yes' votes. Gutman called for a recess, and Orr left the machine on with the "yea" and "nay" lights glowing. The senators scattered for lunch and Gutman again went to work. Senator John Mutz did not support the legislation. I had hope that he might change his mind. He and I had our lunch in the most conspicuous place that I could think of—the Statehouse cafeteria. None of the media would think of John's being there.

The Senate was reconvened later in the afternoon with the board all lit up still displaying the votes. During the recess the lieutenant governor had locked in the votes on the board and posted a State Police Trooper to watch over things. During the morning and afternoon floor debates, Orr kept the voting machine unlocked, allowing the individual senators to switch their votes back and forth, red to green to red. As the first author of the legislative package, I had no clue what was happening.

The necessary tie vote was achieved. Bob Orr cast the tie-breaking twenty-sixth vote with enthusiasm. And finally, by combining the efforts of Senator Gutman and the governor the needed votes were secured and each of the bills in the property tax relief package passed the Senate and was sent on to a conference committee.

At the end of the entire legislative session, on the evening that the Senate would vote to approve changes made to the tax package by the conference committee, Senator Wilson made one last charge at defeating a sales tax increase. He attempted a filibuster. This idea must have come to his mind through his experiences in Congress. Earl had made up his mind that he would talk past the midnight adjournment time. Earl talked about hunting. He was a great railroad buff and he regaled the Senate about his past experiences as a railroader. At first we all saw a smidgen of humor in what Wilson was attempting. Those senators who still had bill concurrences to be acted on became somewhat edgy since their own legislation would die along with the tax package. Finally, Senator Gutman walked to the lectern that Wilson was using, placed his mouth near Earl's ear to make sure he could hear but that no one else in the chamber could, and whispered a message. Earl heard and understood the message. He looked a little flustered, shuffled his papers, and then sat down in his seat without a further word.

The Fourwinds Resort and Marina was being built at Lake Monroe, which was in Senator Wilson's senate district. The new hotel needed a liquor license. The hotel was being built on state-owned property and needed an act of the legislature to obtain the permit. Senator Gutman had whispered in Earl's ear, "no tax relief package, no liquor license." The way to a man's heart is not always through his stomach.

The conference committee report was accepted by the Senate and the total tax relief package was enacted into law. The legislation was effective in lowering and controlling property tax rates. Amendatory legislation by succeeding legislatures removed many of the restrictive control measures allowing for a new hew and cry about high property tax rates thirty years later.

Sassafras

Without anything else constructive on my mind at the beginning of the 1973 session, I got a novel idea. As it turned out, I should have ignored the idea and gone on to other more productive things. But my ego also kicked in, and so I was about to put together a production that would be completely foreign to anything I had ever done.

I noticed other legislators distributing food items and knick-knacks produced in their districts, or they would hand out an item that was made or manufactured in their locality. It might be a bag of mushrooms, or a smoked turkey, or a jar of Amish jam, or a whatnot handmade from an elm tree. The recipient would be expected to remember not only the donor but also the area that the donor represented.

Representing part of the southside of Indianapolis, a portion of Perry Township and a segment of Greenwood and Johnson County, I could not think of any significant product grown or produced or manufactured in District 36. If I had thought long enough, I probably could have decided on an item. Oh, the greenhouses on Bluff Road produced tomatoes in the summer and mums in the fall. And purple cabbage plants were grown and harvested in October. Turnips on south Meridian Street were also plentiful in the late fall. These couldn't be given to fellow legislators with any certainty of freshness. Alpine Corporation in Greenwood produced high quality stereos. Too expensive.

Somehow I decided that in each session I would give the legislators a bundle of sassafras root. Whenever sassafras appeared in stores, my mother would brew up the tea and we would all drink it, and supposedly feel better for it. A spring tonic was the way she explained it. Better than sulfur. Brewing sassafras does have a great, penetrating smell. Hot sassafras tea is warming and has a distinctive taste.

No question about it: I would yearly give each legislator a bundle of sassafras root. They would be forever grateful and would retain a long and favorable memory of the person who gave them the sassafras. Their families, too, would be appreciative and would revere the thoughtful and generous senator from south Indianapolis.

My friend, Mike DeFabis, was president of Allied Grocers. I called and asked if the sassafras was on the grocery shelves. He wondered why I would ask; his stores had not stocked such an item for years. "Why not?" I asked. "When I was a kid it was a necessity in every home at springtime!" "Most people go to the new health food stores for tonics," Mike informed me. Made sense. But would he be able to buy some sassafras from a vendor so that I could hand it out to the legislators?

DeFabis did secure and deliver to the statehouse several sacks of sassafras. He wouldn't take payment. He considered it to be a political gift for a senator with a stupid idea. I had expected the roots to be sorted and string-tied into little neat bundles as I had remembered it from years before. The uncut roots were delivered loose and after a few were sorted out and tied together, hands became red and rusty looking with an odor that seemed to linger forever. I left the bulk of the task to interns and such.

With each bundle of sassafras to be delivered, I had a 4x5 card made up with a salutation:

HEAR YE, HEAR YE, Now let it be known —
SASSAFRAS
A potent medicinal, is said to thin the blood, rid it
of the various bilious bile-like spirits and any other
terrible pizzens and demons. Properly brewed, it will
rejuvenate the mind, cleanse the body and purge the soul
of all evil thoughts. By so doing, compassion abounds,
all rancor is gone, sweetness and light descends.

Use this root in good faith so that your thought will be
pure, and your decisions will be fair.

To make sassafras tea, just place plenty of the roots in
water and boil until the water turns nice and red. Add
sweetening, sugar or honey, to taste and drink hot or cold.
Some people will like to add a bit of Indiana cream as well.

The Southport Sage

I thought the message and the sassafras would make the members conduct the rest of the legislative business without "rancor."

All of this happened in February and I was not too attentive to the task. The roots were not bundled and the distribution was sporadic. I think that only a dozen or so of the senators received any sassafras at all. None of the House members or the staff were given the opportunity to partake of this wonderful elixir. I modestly gave up on this idea for fame and sought recognition elsewhere.

Late in the summer, we noticed a pungent odor on the fourth floor. In 1973 the half floor up the stairs from the fourth floor of the statehouse was not as developed as it is today. I used some of the space for storage of personal items connected with the legislature and files from Senate finance. The left-over sassafras had been loosely bagged in a paper sack and stored in one of the rooms on the fifth level on top of a stack of boxes. The summer sun beating on the statehouse roof, the lack of air circulation in the closed room, the one small window catching the sun from the west and probably a high humidity index, all had combined to begin cooking the sassafras roots.

I quickly figured out what we were smelling; by golly, the smell was just like our kitchen at home when my mother was brewing a pot of sassafras.

chapter   12

Inches Prevail

In the early 1970s a move to switch to a metric system from the accepted English system was all the rage in the United States.

I had introduced a bill requiring Indiana to convert to the metric system—from inches, feet, miles, ounces, in a certain time frame and with the legislation also calling for an emphasis on teaching the metric system throughout the public and private schools in Indiana. My interest and the stimulus came from my admiration of Bill Greathouse. Bill was an outstanding elementary teacher at Edgewood School in the Perry Township school system, the type of teacher you hoped would teach your own children. An activist, constantly writing letters to the editor and organizing statewide seminars on the metric system, Bill knew the metric system was eventually going to be the worldwide standard. All of his pupils learned the metric system. Bill organized statewide seminars. He offered me reams and reams of background material so that I could be conversant in the matter.

The legislation was not accepted by the legislature. I then used a common legislative technique: transferring the basics and philosophy contained in the introduced legislation, combining the gist of the proposal and creating a common Senate resolution. The resolution, having no legal status, was considered and voted on by the Senate, and thus allowed the proponents to brag a little and rethink their strategy for the next session.

Congress enacted the Metric Conversion Act in 1975. It was meant to ease the country into the metric system. As time went by, all sorts of opposition sprang up. Senator Richard Lugar issued a statement in opposition to mandatory conversion. Senator Birch Bayh hoped that federal agencies would be sensitive to public opinion before converting. Representative Bill Bray was a board member of the "Metric Rebellion," which was leading the opposition in the state of Indiana.

Representative Dave Evans nominated lawyer Bob Wagner to president Jimmy Carter's metric council. Wagner was to bring Hoosier opinions to the council. The president, if he ever did read the reports or took notice from the "advice" from Indiana, would have received a one-sided opinion. Wagner was the originator of the anti-conversion "Metric Rebellion" in Indianapolis.

Wagner reported that he had been besieged with more than 1,500 letters in support of his efforts to thwart conversion. In his usual flair for the dramatic, Wagner said that conversion would be a disaster, would be costly ($100 to $200 billion), and would create chaos. "We Won't Give an Inch" was the motto of Wagner's organization. He said he had 5,000 names on petitions of support for his new group, but no incoming dollars. He found that the verbal supporters gave no money to the cause. He also said that he had spent $2,000 of his own money and "hundreds of hours" on Metric Rebellion.

Wagner had his supporters write to their congressmen. He himself personally visited special interest groups in Washington, D. C. trying to drum up support. One office he visited, he said, was the National Metric Council, which he described as being "financed by big business and has very sumptuous offices." An apt description from an attorney who specializes in labor issues.

Even Governor Bowen chimed in, saying that converting road signs in Indiana would cost over a million dollars. Bowen also made known that conversion would not be high on his agenda for action.

The National Weather Service must not have gotten the drift of public opinion. It announced that the service would go "all metric" by the middle of 1980. Temperature reading in both Celsius and Fahrenheit would be given for three months beginning in June, 1979. Then it would drop the Fahrenheit readings and report only the Celsius degrees. Rainfall would be reported in centimeters by December 1979. The original plan was to have this all accomplished by July 1978. Storms of public protest arose, and governmental delay ensued, allowing the politicians to take the temperature of their constituents on this issue, probably in Fahrenheit, rather than Celsius.

I wrote to all of the members of the Indiana Senate Republican caucus, asking them to include a question about the metric system in their constituent polls. Most did. Senator Marlin McDaniel wrote to me with the observation that the public did not want highway mileage and temperature reporting to change. He suggested that Indiana ease into the program by converting liquid and weight measures. Then the state should wait five to ten years to accomplish total conversion.

Having assimilated all of these weighty utterances, it was not too difficult to come to the conclusion that mandatory, or even voluntary, conversion would not occur in Indiana in the foreseeable future. My graceful retreat was to propose legislation that would call for a statewide referendum and allow the voters in Indiana to decide the issue.

Nothing positive happened. The referendum proposal was not even assigned to a committee for consideration. The most common reaction from my constituents has been "let the rest of the world convert to inches." The average guy on the street did not want to hear about the home run going so many meters, rather than so many feet, and they would write that they were used to the 100-yard dash. Bill Greathouse still thinks that metric conversion is a good idea. Bob Wagner continues to be dramatic, politically powerful, and chairman of the board of the White River Park Commission and can be measured as an all-around good guy—in inches, of course.

chapter 13

Pilot Project for Reassessment

Innovative proposals scare legislators, so when the Indiana legislature responded in an uncharacteristic manner in 1975 in approving an untested proposal that I made to them, it was somewhat surprising. And it was also unusual for them to appropriate $400,000 for an attempt to improve on the property assessment methods that had been in place for a hundred years in Indiana. A special interim study committee was authorized to determine how best to use computers in assessment procedures. Eventually, the research task was assigned to the Commission on Taxation and Finance Policy, of which I was a member. The commission, through its director, Scott Lloyd, developed a set of criteria for in-depth study.

The commission contacted each county assessor to see if there was interest in participating in the pilot project. Ten counties indicated an interest. Johnson County was deemed to have characteristics that were average in the entire state. Bill Combest, Johnson County assessor, was very enthusiastic and became deeply involved in the project. The commission envisioned that if successful in Johnson County, the project could then be implemented in each of the other ninety-one counties.

The goal of the pilot project was to demonstrate how local government can apply existing modern technology (at that time—computers) in ways to improve efficiency and reduce costs.

A contract was let in July of 1979 to Computer Systems and Services of Springfield, Ohio, to develop a computerized property tax assessment system. As part of the agreement with CSS, the state would obtain the right, in Indiana, to use the developed program, including its software.

Nearing completion of the project in February, 1981, the project manager noted that "an objective review of the pilot project will show the specific objectives and primary goal of the project have been achieved. By comparison with the attempt of other states to develop computer assisted assessment systems, Indiana's approach has been a resounding success." Everyone felt that providing the software to the other counties would result in substantial savings for the counties.

Bill Combest wrote on December 1981, "Being on site in the pilot county and seeing the results of the project on a daily basis, I can assure you that the computer project has accomplished all that we expected and more. The many accomplishments made in the pilot project can and should prevent the need to re-invent certain computerization methods. The pilot project can serve to save money for other Indiana counties." Mr. Combust described the final results as a long-term investment for the state and wanted everyone to know that the appropriated money was spent wisely. No one got rich during the lifetime of the project.

Everyone who had a hand in contributing to what we thought were practical recommendations was elated and certain that the rest of the state would accept the recommendations. It soon became apparent the members of the State Board of Tax Commissioners were less than enthused. They felt that their advice had not been sought. The board did not appreciate a legislative study— with results and recommendations—invading their turf. It was their way, or no way. Even with the intervention of Governor Orr, the report continued to collect dust. Counties were even encouraged to purchase hardware that would not be compatible with the new software. Vendors were encouraged to sell software that was not current and that would have to be replaced in a year or so. It was the art of bureaucratic foot-dragging at its best and succeeded in costing the taxpayers of Indiana several hundred extra millions of dollars.

Now, it is generally recognized that computers and assessment of property do go together, but Indiana still does not have only one software model. The tax board has not generally selected a program as being official. Re-assessment costs are exorbitant. Each assessment costs more than the last. Standardization and professionalization are the keys to cost containment and for achieving statewide equity in assessing procedures. Future legislatures will likely consider removing assessing from local township and county political control and involvement. Indiana may want to investigate professionally trained individuals who would be immune to political pressure. Indiana will also want to progress to yearly assessments based on market value. Computerization and standardization are the main ingredients that will lead to fair assessment values throughout the state.

"How ja doin"

It wasn't politics that brought Ed Lewis into my life. It was horses. Sometime in the early summer or 1977 I received a call from Lewis, who was known as perhaps the most influential non-elected Democrat in the state. Ed said that a mutual friend, Noble Pearcy, had given him my name and telephone number and wondered if I would answer a couple of questions about owning a standardbred racehorse. That call was the beginning of a close friendship that lasted until Ed's death in 1996.

Ed called me because I was described as being "honest." Honesty to Ed Lewis was an inspiring trait. He had known too many con men and had become a little disillusioned with the human race. Most people wanted something from Ed—a job, or a position, or a favor or money. He considered those who cut a corner here or there and ran a little scam to be perfectly normal. Those who did not operate that way and the few who wanted nothing were always a source of amazement to him.

If you heard "how ja doin" when the telephone was answered, you knew Ed Lewis was on the line. Ed's conversations were usually snappy, direct and to the point when he was the caller. When he returned a call his tone of voice told you that he was busy and you should appreciate his taking the time to return your call. Very few people could call Ed Lewis and get through directly. The list of those whom he would immediately talk with over the telephone was short and always changing. His unmatched influence in the Democrat Party was such that a whole body of informers routinely called and wanted to pass on the latest rumor. When you might actually have a conversation with Ed in his office, you were immediately impressed by the stack of pink "IMPORTANT MESSAGE" slips piled up near the phone.

Ed Lewis was a very sophisticated individual who maintained a certain persona by outwardly acting entirely unsophisticated. His "aw shucks" southern Indiana style suited him fine when he wanted to use it. A very intelligent man, he was a graduate of Butler University School of Journalism in 1949 and the Indiana University Law School in 1956. His reputation included the title "godfather of judges."

Many who had known Ed for years never realized that he actually owned a necktie. His clothes were expensive but never in fashion, nor did they ever seem to fit. I told him he should have become a Hawaiian. No shoes, loud shirt open at the neck and hanging out over his pants. The contrast between his sartorial style and that of his law partner, Bob Wagner, was rather startling. Nevertheless, those who met Ed and noted the lack of fancy clothes soon dropped any negative feelings because the man was so forthright and interesting.

The respect and admiration Ed Lewis and Evan Bayh had for each other was very special. I think they thought that each was the most important person in his own life. When Evan was governor, he would announce to one and all that there was not a drop of alcoholic spirits, other than a bottle or two of Oliver's Indiana fermented wine, in the mansion. Aside from the case of Becks Light beer for Ed Lewis, the governor's boast was correct. The Bayhs were always able to scrounge up an ashtray for one of the multitude of times that Ed had failed in his daily effort "to quit smoking." Lewis had the honor of being the godfather of Evan and Susan's children.

My being a particularly close friend of rabid Republican Keith Bulen and of rabid Democrat Ed Lewis was puzzling for many in the world of politics. The answer to have having a close personal relationship with Ed was complicated yet very simple. Partisan political disagreement stops where friendship begins; conversely, friendship takes a hit—sometimes fatal—when political divergence becomes personal. Life would really be boring if the only people we liked to spend time with agreed with us about everything.

Ed Lewis could tolerate Keith, but not Keith's law partner, Charlie Castor. Lewis maintained that it was Castor who had arranged for someone to place a "bug" in his office trying to gain information about one of Vance Hartke's senatorial campaigns. Lewis had to laugh at the clumsy attempt, because the "bug" was installed in an unused room of a defunct corporation. There was also the delicate situation when it was discovered that someone outside of his office building was inside a parked van with the latest in electronic equipment "eavesdropping" on Ed's office conversations. All of this had occurred before I met Lewis, so

I just listened to the ranting and never had to rebut or to defend. Legal action gained Lewis some satisfaction from the instigators.

Ed and Noble Pearcy were good racehorse handicappers and often made pilgrimages to Churchill and Louisville Downs. Noble made handicapping race horses his hobby. He subscribed to thoroughbred journals and knew and studied sires, breeding, "nicks," speed rating and track conditions. But he didn't exhibit the courage of his convictions at the two-dollar window and so usually came home a loser. Ed, on the other hand, was a good hunch bettor after studying the *Racing Form*. I personally could study the *Form* and pick the winners as consistently as Lewis, but I never did learn how to bet properly. Ed knew how to spread his bets around rationally. Noble would sit in the backseat of the car on the drive south to Louisville and mark up his *Daily Racing Form*. By the time we arrived, Noble knew exactly which horses he would bet on and for how much. Then, standing in line at the betting window, he began to have doubts. If the person in front of him bet more than two dollars to win on a horse, all of the research he had done and all of his confidence in his handicapping would disappear. Pearcy would bet on any horse that the stranger in front of him had bet on, Lewis would rag Pearcy about how many horses he had wagered in the same race, and Pearcy would claim that the reason that he had so many tickets in his hand was that the teller had made a mistake and punched out the wrong combo.

Ed and I owned several racehorses in partnership. One year we had a horse racing at Hoosier Park and doing well. Ed was determined that he was going to talk Governor Bayh into attending a horse race for his first time at Anderson. It was a hard sell. Evan's greatest fear as governor was that he would be remembered for only having one accomplishment in his eight-year tenure, and that was of forever being referred to as the "Gambling Governor." I arranged to have our good horse entered into a claiming race, in which an owner may enter his horse, but if another owner puts in a "claim" for the horse, the horse is then owned by the new owner for an announced pre-determined dollar amount. I made it known to the Indiana drivers and trainers that if anyone claimed the horse, I would personally want to kill them, since Ed and I thought of this as an exhibition and did not want to lose the horse.

Ed in the meantime had talked the governor into attending the racing session to present a trophy to the winning horse in the "Governor's Handicap." Ed had invited scores of his friends to the Penthouse Suite at Hoosier Park for dinner, good fellowship and the chance to see Governor Bayh award the Cup to Lewis when Ed's horse won the race. But the horse came in fifth. Making the whole evening more embarrassing, the horse was claimed at a price less than his true value by some itinerant trainer out of Ohio.

I made the on-the-spot executive decision that the race we had just witnessed really was not the one where the governor would hand out the hardware. It would be in the next race on the program. Bayh came down from the suite after the following race, gave the trophy to someone in the winner's circle and never broke stride as he took off for Indianapolis. The track management and the new winner both were surprised to have the governor of the state of Indiana in the winner's circle presenting a trophy for a featured race that no one had ever heard about. Ed and I fully understood what a "downer" was after going through that evening.

The Lewises and Borsts did a fair amount of traveling together. On one of our trips, we reserved the empty space at Mount Rushmore for Evan Bayh. The judicial chambers at Nuremberg were visited. Beer was evaluated in the Alps and in London's Ritz Club. On another occasion the four of us drove to Harrisburg, Pennsylvania to attend a mixed standardbred horse auction. The next day driving north through the Amish country, Ed took his usual little snooze sitting in the front seat. He was pretty zonked and slept quite a few miles. In fact he slept so many miles that when he awoke, Eldoris informed him that he had just slept through Intercourse. Intercourse, Pennsylvania of course. Quite the country—the previous night he had his raincoat stolen from the car while we were eating dinner in the Hoar House.

Boarding an airplane was a trying time for Ed. Two pre-boarding martinis were the norm and it took another two while in-flight to sustain him for the landing. He was one of those individuals who could handle takeoffs, but coming down to earth was an ordeal. How he could have survived three years in the Pacific in World War II while serving on a submarine remains one of those mysteries of life.

DMSO

Sometime during Governor Otis Bowen's second term, his wonderful wife, Beth, was diagnosed as having multiple myloma, a type of cancer that, in her case, primarily affected the bones. The bones such as the ribs or the long bones of the arms or legs, became deficient in calcium and lose their tensile strength. The bones would become very fragile and could fracture with a minimal amount of pressure. Radiology of these cases shows that some of the bones might have "holes" in them.

Beth struggled with the effects of the disease for some time. Dr. Bowen later told me that she had fallen and suffered several fractures. Beth was in terrible pain. The usual pain relievers did little to ease her pain. Heavy and continuous doses of narcotics might have made her life tolerable. But at what price? There would have been no real quality of life for either of the Bowens.

The governor literally spent all of his free time, night and day, with his wife trying as best he could, to make her life easier.

I received a call one evening at my home from the governor. He sounded desperate. He was willing to try any kind of medication to give his wife some relief. Up to this point, as a medical doctor, he played by the rules and did what the specialists suggested. Nothing really helped Beth. Maybe there was some kind of patent medicine that might be of benefit.

He had heard of dimethyul sulfoxide solvent (DMSO). He had been informed that among the drug's various properties, topical use of the drug might somehow relieve his wife's pain. He asked if I could recommend its usage and did I have any of the drug on hand at the veterinary clinic. My first reaction was, Wow. I'm an animal doctor. I am not licensed to give advice for human usage for any drug.

I had seen the drug being used around the horse tracks with varying success. I told him that DMSO had only been released by the FDA to be used on equine animals, and very definitely not released by the government for humans. The more we talked, the more sense it made that they at least try DMSO. We did not have any of the various forms of the drug in the veterinary clinic. The thought did go through my mind that by ordering the drug from a supplier, then giving it to a human being for the human's own use, I would be breaking a couple of laws regarding the licensing of veterinarians.

Bowen assured me that no one would revoke my license to practice veterinary medicine as long as he was governor.

I was still a little uneasy and made the governor promise that he would never tell a soul about getting the DMSO from a veterinarian. He sounded sincere when he made the promise. I also made sure that Dr. Bowen was aware that one of the side effects of the drug was its vile odor and resultant taste. For some reason the drug would penetrate the skin and fascia and deeper tissues almost immediately with an application on the skin. I also warned him to wear rubber gloves when he swabbed the skin, because after the applications, both the patient and the one applying the drug would have a horrendous garlic taste in the mouth and on the breath, no matter how little or how much of the DMSO was applied. Nothing could be done about the patient experiencing the sensation, but the person doing the applying could protect himself.

DMSO did work. Beth Bowen received a lot of relief from her extreme pain. It was an actual godsend. Using the drug may have been a shot in the dark, but it was well worth the ethical and legal chances taken. I had provided the Bowens with several tubes of the DMSO gel. We ordered more, and then I believe the governor found his own supplier. The drug sources being local made everything easier, because they made home deliveries.

Dr. Bowen had not been out of office very long when I received a copy of one of the nationally distributed women's magazines with an article in it written by Dr. Bowen. The article chronicled the sickness of his wife. It talked about their never-ending faith. And, yes, his thanks to that veterinarian in the Indiana Senate who had supplied the DMSO for his wife. So much for a promise of secrecy. Even with the national publicity, I have yet to receive a notification from the Indiana Board of Veterinary Examiners regarding any investigation.

The Insect Issue

Jack Colwell, political writer for *The South Bend Tribune*, had some fun at the expense of the Senate with this story about some school children's suggestion that the legislature name the ladybug as an official state insect.

The state insect bill has been swatted down after a State Senate debate in which it was suggested that the squirrel be named the Senate mascot.

A squirrel sure would have felt at home. There were a lot of nuts in the Senate chamber for an hour-long debate Tuesday afternoon during which amendments were passed to designate an official state worm and an official state animal.

All the hilarity broke out during consideration of a bill sponsored by Senator Clarence Kelley, R-Mishawaka, to name the ladybug as the official state insect.

While Senator Kelley was serious about his proposal, which originated with school children at Jefferson School in Plymouth, fellow senators could not resist attempts at humor and frivolous amendments that finally "did in the measure."

An exasperated Senate president pro tem Philip Gutman, R-Ft. Wayne, realizing the Senate was holding itself up to justified public ridicule and scorn, moved that the bill including the amendments on worms and animals, be laid on the table. That's parliamentary jargon for killing it.

Gutman's motion was unanimously adopted.

Kelley, obviously disappointed at the results of what had seemed to be a harmless civics lesson for the Plymouth students, told the Senate he had requested the tabling even though it would leave "some disappointed young people in my area."

The fun started when Sen. Lawrence Borst, R-Indianapolis, the usually serious-minded chairman of the Senate Finance Committee, sought to amend the insect bill to add designation of the fox squirrel as the official state animal.

On lengthy prepared remarks, Borst said the squirrel is "a typical Hoosier" and like a politician "is a tireless stump speaker." Some of the lines were better than that. Some worse.

Sen. James Gardner, R-Fowler, who had reluctantly let the insect bill out of his Public Policy Committee, then made the suggestion, with a bit of sarcasm directed at his joking colleagues, that the squirrel be made the Senate mascot.

The squirrel amendment was passed in a voice vote.

chapter 14

Legalization of Pari-Mutuel and Establishment of the Lottery

Pari-mutuel betting on horses became a major issue in the 1970s and it was an issue in which I was particularly interested. My interest dated back to my first session in the General Assembly in 1967, when I served in the House of Representatives. Dr. Otis Bowen was the speaker. One House member conceived the idea of approaching the legalization of pari-mutuel by passing legislation that would allow for a statewide, non-binding referendum on the question. I was the co-author of the resolution. Bowen was personally opposed to any form of gaming, and the resolution languished until the final hours of the session when he allowed it to be considered. The resolution passed.

The referendum was on the ballot statewide in November of 1968. The public voted favorably in eighty-eight of the ninety-two counties. Statewide public opinion polls showed a favorable acceptance for pari-mutuel by about a fifty-five to fifty-eight percent margin. Later polls would show that a lottery had an acceptance factor of over seventy percent. Table betting or casino never exceeded a favorable margin of thirty-five percent.

My love of horse racing was deeply ingrained. Indiana has been referred to as the "kindergarten" of standardbred horse racing. In the Benton County village of Oxford, population 700, barns, signs, and water towers bear the legend, "Dan Patch—1: 55," a tribute to the onetime world's record pacer.

Dan Patch had made his record setting dash in 1906 and his achievement was not surpassed until thirty-two years later.

Dan Patch and I were reared in different generations. We both relished horse racing competitions at county fairs, racing against and winning against all comers. My fascination with standardbred racing began by watching Sep Palin and Doc Parshall race at the Champaign County fair in Urbana, Ohio. Hugh Parshall is a Hall of Fame driver/trainer of standardbreds. He was also a veterinarian and owned horse farms and maintained standardbred training facilities in Champaign County. County fair time meant that it was time to watch the races. The buggy or automobile would be backed up to the outside track fence and become the central headquarters, around which the family would come and go throughout the day. High noon at the fair meant fried chicken and bean salad with the first race heat one hour later.

In the early days of harness racing there was neither starting gate nor tote board. The horses would be walked up to the starting line and then the starter would clang a rather large bell and off they would go. If for some reason, a driver tried to cheat a little to get a head start on the rest of the field, the starter would clang the bell several times more and call for a re-start. Some tracks would stretch a rope across the track, drop the rope and yell, "GO!" Not at Urbana. It would not be unusual for there to be up to five or six re-starts. The race horses then were tougher than they are today. They were bred for endurance, while today one-mile speed and quickness are stressed. The old-time horse normally raced two or three heats (a heat was a distance of a mile whether the track was one mile or one-half mile around) each and every week.

Tote boards and pari-mutuel did not appear in Ohio until the sixties and seventies. I rather doubt that pari-mutuel betting will ever appear at the Indiana county fairs. But it doesn't mean that a knowledgeable person cannot put a bet down on a race. The county fair boards in Indiana have a tendency to discourage one of their locals from becoming a "tout," as is a common practice in England. Connersville is always more open than other fairs. There, the far tree on the right side of the track close to one of the stalls is the place to go.

Currier and Ives depicted the early beginnings of standardbred racing as being a sport of gentlemen. Long Island was the site of most of the races. Interest in the long-legged trotters pulling the high-wheeled sulkies was kept alive by such diverse groups as farmers with grazing land to spare for an extra mare to breed, or the Amish who revered strong trotters which could pull a buggy for miles and miles, or the small town professional who kept a team of matched driving horses. Another gaited horse that has increased in popularity over the years is the pacer, which is not quite as flashy in style but is faster, easier to train and has a more even temperament.

During the early 1900s the Midwest became the center of racing, breeding and interest of the standardbred industry. Indianapolis at one time was headquarters of the United States Trotting and Pacing Association, but that office has been in Columbus, Ohio for many years. The state of Ohio has led the nation in numbers of standardbred foal registrations fairly consistently. Indiana even without pari-mutuel had usually been in the top ten in registrations. The state had maintained its standardbred industry for all of those years without governmental subsidy or legal pari-mutuel.

I became interested in trotters and pacers as a kid looking forward all summer to the county fair. I said that someday I would own a racehorse. Eventually I did purchase, sight unseen, a three-year-old pacing mare, Becky W; my first horse but not the last. She raced for two years with indifferent success. Moving to the next level I became involved in horse racing with Keith Bulen, Ed Lewis and Dr. George McClarnon. These gentlemen weren't in it for the thrill of being an owner. They wanted an operation successful with only winning horses in the stable, horses who could garner enough purse money to pay the bills. Before pari-mutuel, anyone positioned in the industry in Indiana had a most difficult time in even breaking even on the overhead. Those involved were doing so because of tradition and the horsemen's ever present attitude of extreme hope for "next year."

Near the end of the 1973 session the legislature passed legislation creating the Standardbred Board of Regulations. I had written this legislation as a stop-gap measure. I really wanted pari-mutuel for horse racing legalized. But in the meantime, I thought that the industry should be encouraged with a little help and possibly those already involved would be able to survive for a few more years. An appropriation from the state general fund was made to the board. A portion of the appropriated monies would be given outright to subsidize county fairs that conducted a standardbred racing meet. Half of the state money would be used as a match to the purse money provided by each county fair. Other money would be used by the new board to publicize the fairs and horse racing meets at the county and state fair levels.

But who would manage the new appropriation? Since there had never been any state involvement or state regulation of horse racing in the Indiana, assigning responsibility was not easy. As was the wont of the legislature at that time, when in doubt, give the new program to the lieutenant governor. Since he was the commissioner of agriculture, making this delegation of supervision to him seemed to be a perfect fit. Lieutenant Governor Orr happily accepted the new board's mission and immediately appointed John Hammond as the member of his staff to give guidance to the newly formed board. John was not in the least familiar with the equine industry or racing in general. In spite of that, John was a quick learner and did a most thorough job in seeing that the program was successfully implemented.

The manner in which the Standardbred Board carried out the philosophy behind the legislation was outstanding. The county fairs are funded from the money they can generate at fair time, income from events throughout the rest of the year and by a property tax levy. The money and the administrative help from the state were much appreciated by the fair boards. The state's subsidy prompted more counties to resurrect dormant racetracks and began racing again during their fairs. The yearly general fund appropriation reached $120,000. Even during the lean fiscal years for the state, Janet Bozelli, a staff member of the State Budget Agency, made sure that the appropriation level would increase at the rate of inflation even at times when other program levels were being reduced.

County fair horse racing in Indiana is one of the most pleasant experiences that a person can have. Every week you are able to visit with old friends and talk about horses. Those who race, or just plain watch, are a part of a special fraternity. Most of those who bring their racing stock to the fairs get up at 4:30 each morning and feed and clean stalls and maybe train two trips (the workout—one trip on the track under harness—maybe four to six miles of jogging and speed training). Then the owner pulls his eight-hour shift in some factory and comes back home to train a second horse.

During the summer the fairs at Converse, Shelbyville, Frankfort, LaPorte, Corydon, Muncie, Connersville, Goshen and Portland are spread out to allow the owners as much race time as possible. Points are awarded for finishing positions in each race with the top eight or nine eligible to race at the Indiana State Fair. In my case, if I won, fine. If I didn't, at least I could tell you which fair had the best foot long hotdogs or largest elephant ears. No pari-mutuel. No fancy hype. Be sure to take the kids. Great American people and a great midwestern custom.

My fondest wish was to be able to repeal the legislation that had established the Board of Regulations. Two horse racing boards can be confusing. I hoped too, that someday pari-mutuel racing would be legalized. When that happened then the need for the Board of Standardbred Regulations could be eliminated.

Following the advent of pari-mutuel, the Standardbred Board's actions fell from view and called meetings were few. The leadership of the board was hit and miss. At one time in the nineties, the board had gone for two years straight without a formal meeting. One of the directors was a college student at Purdue, but upon graduation moved to another state and took all of the pertinent records with him without leaving a forwarding address.

My first attempt to repeal the board met with resistance from the bureaucracy. Though oversight of the board and its activities was a pain to the lieutenant governor, his staff finally realized that I was attempting to repeal a portion of their fiefdom. A repeal was unacceptable I was told. Should not happen. And it didn't.

During the next year, though, I think that some of the lieutenant governor's staff had second thoughts. For their benefit, I agreed to compromise legislation that would allow the administration to save face by phasing out the Standardbred Board. To this day, I would doubt if the board members were ever asked for any advice. At least the appointees received no salary, only a per diem for meetings attended.

The serious push for the legalization of pari-mutuel horse racing began in the 1975 session. Representatives Craig Campbell, Don Nelson and Paul Mannweiler were co-authors of the bills introduced in the House. I co-authored the bill with Senator Louis Mahern when it came to the Senate. The introduced legislation passed both houses. Governor Bowen vetoed it. The legislature missed by only one vote in the Senate of overriding the governor's veto. Prior to the veto, Attorney General Ted Sendak had written an official opinion that the legislation was unconstitutional because the bill imposed several penalties that were too severe. Governor Bowen ignored this reasoning but thought that the legislation was unconstitutional anyway.

The next year, the short session of 1976, I introduced much the same bill in the Senate. It passed in both the Senate and the House. Again, Governor Bowen vetoed it and issued much the same veto message as he did the year before. I knew the bill was unconstitutional from the first day of its introduction because the bill had originated in the Senate. Legislation that raises new revenue must originate in the House of Representatives. At times, I have a difficult time in fathoming the lack of understanding of the media and of some of our governmental leadership. Here was a clear case of an unconstitutional procedure clearing both houses without some sort of outcry from the media or from the opponents. There was no attempt to override the veto in 1976.

Prior to the convening of the 1977 session, Sendak declared the newest version of pari-mutuel as unconstitutional, well before it was even introduced. Once again the legislature approved pari-mutuel for horse racing and once again Governor Bowen vetoed the legislation. This time, both chambers overrode his veto.

Pari-mutuel was then only temporarily legalized in Indiana. Joe Nixon, the publisher of the *Wabash Plain Dealer* and part owner of the Nixon Newspapers, Inc., had always been opposed to any form of gaming. He filed a lawsuit challenging the constitutionality of the new act. The lawsuit ended up before the Johnson County Circuit Court and Judge Robert W. Young declared pari-mutuel betting to be a lottery. The Indiana Constitution forbids a lottery, he declared.

Lottery was a fighting word in Indiana.

There were historical reasons for Indiana's strong objections to a lottery. In the early to mid-1800s a lottery was a popular way to raise funds for governmental services all across our young country. The lottery method of raising funds to build the National Road was in vogue in Indiana. In some cases the only winner was the person who organized the lottery. These promoters would sell the tickets, and then high tail it back East without holding a drawing or awarding money and prizes.

Indiana basically became bankrupt in the late 1840s, largely because of the unsuccessful canal mania which had gripped the state. The eastern bankers who bailed Indiana out of its own mess demanded that a new constitution be written and adopted in 1851 and absolutely prevented the state from going into debt and from legalizing the lottery.

On appeal, in 1979, the Indiana Supreme Court upheld the lower court.

The Supreme Court decision prompted the late Bob Collins to comment in his column in *The Indianapolis Star*:

> *Notice to horseplayers: don't place any hunch bets on "Supreme Court" this year. Odds are only three to two.*
>
> *People who made New Year's resolutions not to wager an illegal dollar in Indiana this season are good for 365 days. However, more than a few judges, policemen, prosecutors, politicians, and journalists will once again step outside the law to back up their opinions.*
>
> *But the worst blow to the old ego is the fact the Indiana Supreme Court considers wagering on horses more luck than skill. The mere thought is insulting to a horseplayer.*
>
> *This finds him in the same category as a driver who tries to find a parking spot in downtown Indianapolis after 9 AM: a man who tries to purchase a special advertised car by a used car dealer; or a lawyer who tries to get elected judge with a name that begins with one of the last six letters of the alphabet. The court says that a man who puts in hours of study and research can't select winners any better than someone who pitches darts at a tout sheet. How degrading.*
>
> *It took me twenty years to decipher the racing form. Now I am told that placing money on a horse's nose requires no more skill than putting a kernel of corn on a bingo card.*
>
> *Perhaps it has something to do with the separation of church and state. Money from legal pari-mutuel bets goes to the state. The Lord gets all bingo losses.*
>
> *But no skill involved? If it were not illegal, I would wager that the Indiana Supreme Court reached its decision immediately after the august justices returned from a race track—and that there were three losers and two winners.*

The vote of the Court on pari-mutual was 3-2 backing Judge Young's decision. One of the Justices who had just been appointed by Governor Bowen to the court cast the deciding vote. I personally lost a lot of respect for the judiciary from that time on for substituting their personal morals and opinions for legal facts and definitions. There had been thirty-five courts and judges in the United States that had rendered an opinion on the issue of whether or not pari-mutuel is the same as a lottery. Not one court had ever even delivered a split decision in voting for affirming that pari-mutuel and the lottery were two completely different systems.

The legal team that fought Nixon's lawsuit were overconfident from the start. I think that a sharper and more intense presentation might have carried the day. A prominent horseman recruited and paid the bills for the legal team. He was so confident of the outcome that he had purchased a large tract of land in Hamilton County for a racetrack that he wanted to build.

The opposition forces to pari-mutuel were euphoric. They could not conceive that the constitution might be amended to allow pari-mutuel. In an odd turn of fate and with the will of the electorate, what ultimately did happen was the outright legalization of pari-mutuel and lottery and bingo and casinos. I have often wondered if Joe Nixon, Paul Oakes, Reverend Grover Hartman and the three Supreme Court judges ever looked back in retrospect, and quietly chastised themselves for opening the doors to all forms of gaming when they might have objectively thought through the different scenarios and allowed pari-mutuel to stand as passed. At that time, I personally knew nothing about bingo, had never purchased a lottery ticket in another state, and was completely opposed to table games, casinos and slot machines being legalized in Indiana. Without the lawsuit and the Supreme Court's decision on the constitutionality of the pari-mutuel legislation, there never would have been an attempt to amend the constitution and consequently no river boats, arguments about pull tabs, or a casino in Orange County.

Attempts were then made to pass a constitutional resolution in 1982, 1983, 1984 and 1985. Each year the Senate passed the resolution rather easily. Each year the Speaker of the Indiana House assigned the resolution to an unfavorable committee. One year there was a five to five vote in the House Commerce Committee, which meant that the bill died because of a lack of a majority vote. In the Senate, the resolution was not scheduled for a hearing in two of those years.

After having breakfast with Speaker J. Roberts Dailey, Representative Sam Turpin cast the deciding vote against passage of the resolution in 1985. I was crushed. Representative Mannweiler was both the sponsor of the resolution and the chairman of the Commerce Committee. We knew that Turpin would be the swing vote, and I had relied on telephone calls from horsemen that were his constituents to sway his vote. Sam was quoted as "not listening to the speaker and being able to stand on his own two feet."

I had never met former Indiana Governor George N. Craig. I still did not have the opportunity to meet the man even after he came to the statehouse and testified against the passage of the resolution. Governor Craig concentrated his opposition on the lottery, saying, "I am one who firmly believes that becoming a huckster of a lottery just is not a function of state government. Putting an official stamp on gambling. That's what I don't like about it. Hell, if you want to play poker in the basement with your friends, that's all right."

Actually Speaker Dailey maintained that he was not opposed to pari-mutuel but was violently opposed to a lottery and other forms of gaming. Following the 1985 committee vote, I thought that I had heard him tell me, "next year." For me, my wait till the next year was like anticipating the arrival of Santa Claus. The feeling was real, but the nagging thought stayed with me wondering if he really meant what I thought he said?

The bulk of the floor debate in the Senate on the amendatory legislation to the Constitution centered on the wording of the contemplated resolution. One resolution would have dedicated any profits for the benefit of public education. Another wanted one-half of the income to be deposited into the state general fund and the other half to be divided between the cities, towns and counties. Senator John Bushemi made the most telling remarks in attempting to limit the constitutional amendment to allowing for the legalization of pari-mutuel only. Other suggestions would state in the constitution that only a lottery and pari-mutuel could be established. I settled on the wording to simply erase the old language written in the constitution that banned the establishment of a lottery and the sale of lottery tickets. This would allow me to pursue pari-mutuel and others to develop legislation to create a lottery at some time in the future. Not even in my wildest dreams did I ever think that there would be a General Assembly in Indiana that would allow casinos in Indiana. How wrong I was. Riverboats had never been a part of my reasoning. If I had acceded to John Bushemi's wishes there would have been a lot less stress in most of the legislative sessions since the constitution was amended.

The passage of the pari-mutuel legislation contained a local option feature. The county council of any county would have to pass a resolution permitting the establishment of a race track facility to conduct pari-mutuel racing within that county. Two counties—Madison and Shelby—took that action immediately. These two counties were able to secure interest from track developers who wanted to locate a track in those counties. The Marion County Council also approved pari-mutuel racing subject to zoning ordinances. Someone in an interested group of developers jumped the gun by securing options on acreage in the Southeast part of the county for a race track. A neighborhood uprising caused by the premature announcement of the plans eliminated Franklin Township from consideration. A group of lawyers and developers had designed a facility and reserved land on south Emerson Avenue in Perry Township and had entertained serious thoughts of building a track. Zoning requirements stymied their plans. The City of Lawrence opened its arms in an effort to entice a track. Purportedly, zoning and finance was no problem. The closeness to Hoosier Park in Anderson was reason enough for the Racing Commission to frown on that application.

The Resolution passed two separate legislatures and was scheduled for public referendum in the fall of 1988. Being as confident as I was of the public acceptance of the amendatory language, I began in the 1988 session to plan for legislation to establish a lottery and to legalize pari-mutuel. A Concurrent Resolution "requesting the commission on state tax and financing policy to consider the advisability of preparing legislation establishing a lottery and pari-mutuel betting in Indiana" was adopted in each of the chambers on a voice vote. This resolution gave me the latitude to begin compiling data and doing research on both subjects.

Later, I was asked if a bill would be introduced in 1989 if the public did adopt the changes to the constitution. My normal terse reply was, "I don't have a bill as yet, but there will be one. We'd look pretty stupid if people decided to change the constitution and there wasn't prepared legislation."

Horseman friend Ralph Wilfong hired one or two people to write the legislation. Ralph had signed one fellow from Ohio to a $25,000 contract to research a pari-mutuel bill. Ralph had hired a second gentleman from Illinois who was nationally renowned at something or the other in the equine industry. Wilfong was a do-it-yourself type. He had no real trust in government's being able to accomplish any task in the proper manner. He was taking no chances. I never did meet or consult with Ralph's hired help. Whether or not they were paid for doing nothing remains a mystery.

Those opposed to the passage of the Resolution in 1988 were extremely busy. Citizens Against Legalized Gambling raised over $300,000 for a fund to lobby the public to vote "NO" during the referendum. I had asked the Secretary of State to reserve the number one ballot designation for the referendum so the public would not be confused with the other referendum questions.

The Citizens group was funded by such outstanding Hoosiers as Columbus industrialist and philanthropist J. Irwin Miller, Indianapolis attorney and civic leader Henry Ryder and Harry Pierson of the Indiana Farm Bureau. The opponents formed a speakers bureau and nearly every Protestant church and community service club in Indiana heard from those opposing Proposition 1. I attended at least fifty of these meetings debating with Paul Oakes/ Grover Hartman. Grover was the president of the Indiana Council of Churches. The Catholic Church representative on the council was careful to abstain from any of the anti-lottery opinions of Dr. Hartman.

Phone banks were used by the opposition in the more rural areas of the state. They placed advertising in seventy-three newspapers and radio ads were placed on sixty-five radio stations in Indiana. The opponents felt that they were reaching over half of the population of the state. A million pieces of literature were sent to known opponents of Proposition 1.

Where were the proponents of Proposition 1? I thought that the vendors for the lottery would organize some sort of pro movement. Over the years a vendor of lottery games from Maryland was designated by his peers in the industry to call me at home at six-month intervals and invariably asked, "how the association could be of help to me or to the lottery effort in Indiana?" I was not exactly sure what the telephone caller had in mind but my recommendation always was, "just stay the heck out of Indiana until lottery is legalized." And they did. The horse associations had a miniscule campaign in one or two rural areas of Indiana. In short, the proponents made no concerted effort to sway the voters of Indiana to their way of thinking. I also felt confident enough of voter attitude and in the final determination that I did not advise the proponents to conduct a media campaign.

Statewide the public voted for the constitutional change in an expected manner. Sixty-one percent supported Proposition 1. Marion County voted in favor 149,529 to 74,931, about two to one. Eighteen counties voted over sixty-five percent in favor. An additional fifty-eight counties voted favorably in excess of sixty percent. Six counties voted fifty-one percent or more against the proposition.

It was time for the legislation.

The final proposed legislation dealing with pari-mutuel was based on the Ohio statutes. I had sent away for all of the pari-mutuel laws in the United States. No two were the same. Probably, most had originally passed in a basic form but in the intervening years had been amended completely out of shape. After reviewing the Ohio legislation I made several trips to the state capitol in Columbus. The fact that I had raced horses at Scioto Downs made me more familiar with the Ohio rules and conduct of a race meet. Representative Corwin Nixon, the Minority Leader of the Ohio House of Representatives, owned and managed a standardbred racing facility in Lebanon, Ohio and had written all of the equine legislation during the preceding thirty-five years in Ohio. When I asked for a copy of the Ohio racing laws it took two weeks for them to peruse all of the Code sections and get it all together. I think that Corwin was given free rein to put anything in the Code that he wanted, and he simply stuck in a new amendment wherever he wanted.

The Indiana law is much more favorable to the horse owner and the track owner than any racing law in the country. Most states would siphon off some of the profits for projects that had nothing to do with horses or with racing. I did write a section in the bill that appropriates $150,000 of the profits from pari-mutuel to the Purdue School of Veterinary Medicine for equine research. Several years later the tax from the betting that was returned to the state of Indiana was reduced to further encourage the track at Anderson.

Paul Estridge, Sr. had convinced me that the key to financial success for a horse track was the off-track betting parlors. He campaigned for the inclusion of two parlors for each established track. After reviewing the track projections that he had contracted for, I knew he was correct and that if two were minimum, we should make it four. One of the two main features of the racing bill is the absolute requirement that for a track to be licensed in Indiana, the track must have 120 days of live, on-track racing. Without that provision there would not be any live racing in Indiana. Only the off-track betting parlors would be in business, receiving a racing signal from somewhere else in the country. Hoosier Park should draw an average of 900 patrons for a day with the standardbreds and about 1,000-plus for thoroughbreds. It may be their location or a lack of promotion, but I would think that the management would, financially, be further ahead if they just closed their doors and raced the horses without the spectators and the hired help they have to keep on the payroll.

The second requirement that makes horse racing an economic development tool is the mandated requirement that all of the races at the licensed race tracks be televised to the off-track betting parlors in Indiana. Hoosier Park at Anderson is now able to televise the Indiana races to other off-track betting parlors in the country, which does help them financially.

Paul Estridge, Sr. was there at the first when legalizing efforts began. Paul, on his own, made significant contributions for the final version of the enabling legislation. His dream of building and operating a horse race track finally came true in the latter part of 2002 with standardbred racing. His track, Indiana Downs, just north of Shelbyville, welcomed the running horses in April of 2003.

The sixty-five cent subsidy for horse racing that is collected from each admission fee to the riverboats was inserted in a bill that passed the House. I truly have no idea what the thinking or computation was to arrive at that figure. The theory was that the casinos would take patrons away from the racing tracks. On another front, Indiana was the first state to establish a lottery and then authorize pari-mutuel. The subsidy has grown in 2002 to a figure in excess of twenty-eight million dollars per year. No other state in the union takes such good care of the track owners and the horsemen as does Indiana. Originally the subsidy was figured to be about one-third of the present figure. The track owners are guaranteed thirty percent of the admissions income and receive another ten percent that accrues to the Racing Commission. The rest of the subsidy is applied to the purse money of the competing horses and to an Indiana sires and Indiana owners only race programs.

The pari-mutuel program in Indiana has not worked as well as I had hoped. There has not been the investment in farms and facilities that there should be with the state subsidy, nor a great increase in the numbers of new owners and trainers. The new standardbred breed association has done little to promote the industry outside of their own membership. The only concerted lobbying effort the Indiana Standardbred Association made was during the 2002 session when the promoters of pull tabs promised the association almost $250,000 each year for "operational expenses."

I feel that the multiple owners of Hoosier Park and Indiana Downs at Shelbyville should have more of an interest in expanding the equine industry in Indiana. The possible implementation of pull tabs and slot machines at their tracks seems to hold their attention more than interesting more spectators at the races. I observed a dozen paid lobbyists attempting to kill important legislation in 2002 that was critical for the well being of the state, simply because the legalization of pull tabs was not included. Sometimes good government has extreme difficulty competing with outright greed.

The pari-mutuel legislation was well written and has not been significantly altered since its passage. Mike Schaefer, the Indiana Horse Racing Commission's first chairman, got the commission off to an excellent start. Since then, though, the commission has been in turmoil and has not received adequate direction and legal advice for several years. I would hope that the industry would step in and make their presence known and help correct deficiencies. Too often, a politically-appointed board or commission over awes a lay association. Politics can give; it can also take away. No governor wants any part of his administration to really fail. Any lay association should work within the system forcefully and directly and not just sit back, do nothing, and feel helpless.

Two racing tracks for Indiana are a plus. The commission and its director someday may want to use some of the riverboat money to develop a strategy that would enhance the equine industry in Indiana. Racing can be a boon to the agricultural industry and can be most beneficial to a great number of Indiana citizens.

And so, to the forbidden word—the lottery. Suddenly we were ripe for it. As the pari-mutuel legislation was based on the Ohio structure, the legislation creating the lottery was mostly taken from the Florida law. Legalization of the lottery was not a recent happening in the country. We were able to build the Indiana legislation on the success of other state's experiences.

If anyone really had studied the legislation creating the Indiana lottery, they would have been struck by its similarity with the legislation bringing about the Indiana automobile license branch reform. The best advice that I had received from others was to make the lottery administration as autonomous as possible. Being a semi-governmental agency, hopefully, would remove the lottery from a taint of political control. The lottery commission members were free to promulgate their own rules and regulations. They'd even be able to have their own personnel regulations, salary and fringe benefit schedules. The rules of public disclosure are not as wide-ranging as is the case for the rest of the rest of state government because of the need of operational secrecy and the desire of absolute honesty. The legislation producing the lottery also has had little need for amendments since its passage.

The session of 1989 was rather strange. There were fifty Republican House members and fifty Democrat House members, with each selecting a co-speaker who presided at alternate intervals. The lottery legislation encountered no difficulty, but the pari-mutuel legislation was assigned to a dark corner in Representative Pat Bauer's domain. Finally, on April 26, I was asked to make a concession (compromise) that I had known would be demanded of me for the release of the pari-mutuel bill. The terms for agreement with the House Democrats were far less than I had anticipated—total acceptance of the legislation that I had authored for a promise to allow the first fifty million of lottery profits to be use to balance the biennial budget. Easy choice.

There had been one change in the verbiage of the lottery bill. I had named the fund that was to receive the profits of the lottery as the Indiana Pension and Infra-Structure Fund. Governor Evan Bayh made that one change, a change that has made a lasting impression, by renaming the fund as the Build Indiana Fund. I was not invited to the governor's office for the ceremonial signing of either the 1989 passage of the legislation or for the 1992 revision of the pari-mutuel legislation. In both cases Bayh was quoted in the newspapers as knowing that I was out of the state, but he would save a symbolic pen that was used for the signing to give to me. I am certain that there was an oversight on someone's part about where he could have reached me. I am still waiting for the pen.

The Conference Committee on HB 1409 was signed and passed by the Senate forty-one to nine and by the House seventy-six to twenty-four in a special session of the General Assembly the first week of May.

With tongue in cheek, Senator Joe O'Day took the floor of the Senate and said, "Senator Borst, you have pulled one of the greatest coups that I've ever seen in my fifteen years in the Senate. You got pari-mutuel betting without the people of Indiana voting for it." At the last minute, the countywide referendum had been removed from the legislation and was replaced with the county council having to authorize the system in each county.

chapter   15

White River State Park

One of Indianapolis' principal attractions today is the White River State Park in the downtown area. It took a lot of effort by a lot of legislators, politicians, business leaders and civic-minded citizens over several years to see it realized.

The General Assembly in 1979 began the effort when it passed HB 1752, which authorized formation of the White River State Park Commission. It also appropriated ten million dollars to begin developing the park. The Lilly Endowment came up with five million dollars in additional funds. A zoo, a sports medicine complex, amateur athletic facilities and green space was envisioned for the park.

Earlier that year the Greater Indianapolis Progress Committee had appointed attorney Charles Whistler to survey the public for suggestions for the park. Carl Dortch was named chairman of the new commission. I was quick to remind him of earlier efforts to establish a series of urban parks next to the White River south of Southport Road.

The first report of a park design team was submitted in April, 1980. The overall theme would be a world-class park with an international appeal based on Food and Fitness—to be called the Celebration of Life. The Indianapolis Water Company's Canal was to be enhanced. The plan suggested an adaptive reuse of the historic Water Pumping Station on Washington Street, also a reuse of the Acme-Evans Milling Company and its silos. It was also suggested that the new Indianapolis Zoo be located in the park, along with a large plaza capable of handling festivals, concerts and celebrations. The construction of a public exposition hall was included in the plan, along with a dramatic focal point or observation structure that would physically draw immediate attention to the park.

This last suggestion made in November 1981 resulted in a concept for a central dominating tower conceived by Cesar Pelli, an Argentine architect. The tower was to rise 750 feet above Indianapolis, making it the tallest structure in Indiana, 273 feet taller than the AUL building. There would be a central elevator, but a person so inclined could walk continuously up and around the tower to the observation deck, a matter of over a mile and a half. The tower would have been a series of open arches stacked on top of each other, from bottom to the top, and around the circumference from side to side, creating a cone-shaped effect with the circumference becoming smaller and smaller nearing the observation deck.

Indiana Appeals Court Judge Patrick Sullivan thought the tower a bad idea. Quoted in *The Indianapolis News*, he said, "I saw the tower when I was walking past the model of the park on display on the second floor of the Statehouse. I walked by it several times. And each time I thought, 'By God that's ugly.'" Sullivan admitted, "I don't know architecture from nothing but I do know that tower looks like an oil derrick or something made out of chicken wire." Judge Sullivan then wrote the director, saying, "I have yet to hear anything complimentary about the ... proposed Indiana Tower, and I have heard at least fifteen persons express violent distaste for it. I could say it offends my aesthetic taste but it is worse than that."

Chances are that this might have been the best brief and decision that Judge Sullivan ever rendered in his illustrious career. The judiciary spoke. There is not a central centerpiece in the White River State Park.

There was not much development activity for the next few years. The commission was living off of interest earned from the state appropriation. In December 1984, Governor Orr put forth the plan to expand the statehouse office complex. Authorization for bonding by the State Office Building Commission was OK'd by the 1985 Indiana general assembly. The legislation was written to be most flexible, with the purposes for bonding not being mentioned specifically. Not being specific came back to haunt us later on.

Specific bonding for a new relocated state museum was taken out of the legislation at the last minute by the administration. The secondary purpose of this new bonding authority was to float bonds for improvements to the park and for a new Indiana State Museum.

Ken Cochran, executive assistant to Governor Orr, in July 1985, announced plans for the statehouse government complex. In addition to a main new building, and renovation of the government center, the plans also called for the renovation of the statehouse. Also proposed was a judicial building, two parking garages, a building for the Indiana Environmental Protection Agency, and an Indiana State Museum. This new museum was to be built in proximity to the Harrison Eiteljorg Museum of Indian Heritage.

Old Indianapolis Public School 5, on North California Street had been given to the state of Indiana. The school had a sentimental value having in the past educated many of the city's finest. Many immigrant children had attended this downtown school. The school may have had historical significance, but the building was not in the master plan for the White River State Park. The commission voted one day to tear down the school and began to do so within hours. A wrecking ball wrecked for a few days. Then an injunction was obtained to stop the destruction until the historic preservationists had a chance to explain the significance of the school. A judge eventually agreed with the preservationists that there had been hasty action and ruled that certain parts of the building were to be retained. The façade of School 5 was saved, stored in a warehouse, and reinstalled in the finally completed Indiana State Museum.

Representative Ray Richardson took the first shot at plans to bond for the new museum. He complained that the House of Representatives had no knowledge of bonding for the new state facilities. Ray was a busy legislator and may well have missed that testimony. He was later joined by Representative Pat Bauer and Representative Paul Hric in wanting further hearings on plans for the complex, and especially on the means for funding of the new museum construction. Bauer, Hric and Richardson professed support for the museum, but merely wanted the veil of secrecy lifted. Ken Cochran was sent to allay their concerns.

Cochran explained that a paragraph added in a Senate committee and the reference to extra space for executive department made inclusion of the museum in any bonding effort legal. Representative Richardson characterized this as a "sneaky" procedure and vowed that he would file a lawsuit against any plan for more state office space if the project included a new state museum. I then wrote to Richardson:

> *October 7, 1985*
> *The Honorable Ray Richardson*
> *Dear Ray:*
> *The situation regarding the two museums is perplexing. I sometimes wonder if the House pays any attention to what is going on in the Senate, and vice versa.*
>
> *As I read your comments, and I may be wrong, you are concerned about state bonding monies being used for the actual construction for one or both of the museums. The strategy that was outlined before the Senate earlier this year was to include bonding monies for purchasing land to expand the state office building complex. This land would be at the northwest corner of West and Washington Streets.*
>
> *Once purchased, Lilly and Eiteljorg would pay for the construction of the Indian Museum. Architects would situate the museum so that a new Indiana State Museum could be provided for in the future. There is no thought, on anyone's part, to bond for a new state museum without the legislature's approval.*
>
> *I personally feel that a new state museum should be built. Their present plans for expansion, and some requests for expansion, amount to about what it might cost to build a new one. At the West Street location, I think that it would add to the overall significance of the office building complex. But, this decision is to be made later on.*
>
> *From my standpoint, I'll also assure you that the matter was not handled in a sneaky manner during the session. Solutions were discussed in leadership meeting, in the Senate majority caucus, on the floor of the Senate, and in the budget conference committee.*
>
> *I do hope that your comments, regarding legal action, are directed at the possibility of initially bonding for actual construction. I do think that buying the land is reasonable and will allow the museum people to plead their case to the legislature for further action.*
>
> *Sincerely,*

Representative Richardson replied:

October 10, 1985
The Honorable Lawrence Borst
Dear Larry:
I have always made it clear that I was not aware as to whether a new state museum was discussed in the Senate as being a part of the SOB bill. What I have said is that a museum was not discussed in any forum in the House; not in committee, not in caucus and not on the floor, as part of HB 1285.

I read the bill when it passed the House and I read it when it came back from the Senate, waiting for a reference to a state museum so that I could discuss its merits. No such reference appears, and I will maintain in my lawsuit that no authority exists for the SOB Commission to bond and build a state museum. You maintain that you were talked out of your attempts to specifically name a state museum in the bill—I interpret that as a purpose-ful attempt by persons to avoid discussion of the issue.

I have no objection to the construction of the Eitlejorg Museum with pri-vate money and no objections to situating it so that a state museum could be built adjacent to it, if properly approved by the legislature. I am convinced, however, that were it not for the publicity the legislature would never have been consulted again and the state museum would have been built.

Please understand that I do not maintain that I must prevail on the question of whether a new state museum should be built. I only insist that it be specifically approved by both houses. No one would have heard from me on this issue if you had prevailed in your efforts to list the state museum in HB 1285.

I hope that you understand why a House member would be offended by the procedure.

Very truly yours,

The war of the letters continued as I wrote to Richardson on January 7, 1986,

I haven't quite figured out if you are for a new museum if one is needed, or against a new museum. Makes no difference. Those in the museum busi-

ness think that it would be wiser to build a new one in a convenient setting than to spend the money to renovate the present building. The present structure makes a better city hall than a state museum. (The state museum had been located in the old Indianapolis City Hall).

I had also placed an appropriation of $150,000 in the new budget for planning and for preliminary schematics for the new museum. Gary Mayor Richard Hatcher about that time, inquired if the legislature could also consider funding a National Civil Rights Hall of Fame. My reply, "One museum at a time." Lee Theisen, the state museum director, used the appropriations to construct a cardboard mockup of what the new structure might look like.

HB 1258, sponsored by Representative Pat Kiely, was considered and passed in the 1986 legislative session. It authorized construction of the various buildings in the state office building complex, but did not include a museum. The legislature easily passed the bill supporting the governor and his building program. The only opposition centered around the museum.

Later in 1986, the SOB Commission was authorized to borrow thirty million dollars, with an interest rate of four and a half percent. The loan was to be paid back when initial bonding occurred. This money was to purchase various parcels of land within the proposed boundaries of the White River State Park, including a hardware manufacturer, a Hardee's Restaurant, the Convention Center Inn and the Acme-Evans mill, among others. Ken Kobe, the budget director, negotiated the loan and Orval Lundy pursued the land purchases.

A press release from the governor's office stated: "A model for the thirteen million dollar Eiteljorg Museum of the American Indian and Western Art was unveiled in Governor Orr's office on January 22, 1987. The museum was expected to open in 1988, and is to be located at the main entrance of the White River State Park on Washington Street. The new structure will house the Western art collected by Harrison Eiteljorg, an Indianapolis philanthropist. The artwork, which includes painting, sculptures, ceremonial objects and masks, reportedly was valued at forty million dollars. Works by Georgia O'Keefe and Frederic Remington would also be included." All of this did eventually happen, as the governor's release outlined.

Harrison Eiteljorg himself was a most interesting man. A fabulously successful entrepreneur, Harry had a wide variety of interests. Jim Morris, then president of Lilly Endowment, asked if I would accompany him and Harry to New York City to tour the old, elegant American Indian Museum in Harlem. Time and change had passed the museum by. Where once the location had been ideal, the museum was now in a high-risk crime area. The director had had his car stolen off the museum parking lot the week before we arrived. We were counseled to have the driver stay with the limo at all times.

We flew in Harry's private airplane, piloted by his fulltime pilot, landing somewhere with a limo waiting to take us into the city. Harry had proudly mentioned that he had just purchased an Indian tribal mask, good quality, fairly rare, for $16,000. He now possessed three of these Indian masks in his private collection. Once in the museum we were by chance led to a twenty-foot high room about half the size of a basketball court, completely full of Indian masks. Masks from floor to ceiling, all hanging by hooks on pegboards. And this was the storeroom, not the public viewing area. There were hundreds of masks. Harry's jaw dropped and this was the last we heard of his new purchase.

Nowhere in this country are there more Indian artifacts than in the collection we saw that day. Literally hundreds of authentic birch bark canoes, hundreds of tribal suits and dresses, millions of dollars worth of gold and silver, hand-made pottery and woven baskets. Morris began negotiations to bring this Indian museum to Indianapolis. For a time that was a possibility. Looking back, it was apparent that the relocation discussion with Indianapolis was being used as leverage by the museum people. The secret aim of the museum directors was to obtain further subsidies from the state of New York and from the city of New York. Eventually that strategy worked. Jim Morris, ever the optimist, returned his concentration to Mr. Eiteljorg.

The highlight of the visit for me was lunch. Harry was a member and a frequent diner at the "21" Club. I had heard of the restaurant for years and had seen it used as a background in the old William Powell movies. I remember that the hamburger I ate that day cost twenty-one dollars. I never did find out the price of the bottle of beer.

Harry was all for the Indian museum to be built and named after him, and to be used as a showplace for his large collection of native art. He was rather reluctant about contributing financially for construction of the new facility. I know that Jim Morris suggested that it might be appropriate to contribute a coal mine for the museum's endowment. I have no knowledge whether or not this did happen, but I do know that the museum is appropriately named for a great human being.

I did not give up on providing a new museum for the state and neither did Ray Richardson alter his dogged opposition. I placed an appropriation of two million dollars in the 1989 state budget for the planning of a new museum. This was accomplished during the conference committee on the budget. No authorization, just planning. Representative Richardson immediately contacted the budget agency, asking the agency to sit on any recommendation for the release of this money. He stated that the money should not be committed, as the House was opposed and would defeat any mention of a museum during the next session. He maintained that "Senator Borst is trying to force the legislature into approving a new state museum through the expenditure of the architectural and engineering fees."

Richardson continued his attacks on both the museum and White River State Park in general. During the summer of 1989, the Sunset Evaluation Committee wanted to restructure and to reassign the White River State Park Commission and, in fact, recommended the elimination of the commission. The negative actions by the Sunset Committee theoretically eliminated any further development of the park. Within the law establishing the Sunset Committee, there is a provision allowing a sunsetted agency to continue for another year if the governor approved.

Governor Bayh did approve but that was about all he approved of, whether this, or any other program that another (read Republican) administration had begun. Richardson should not have been so concerned. He found an ally in the governor.

The two million dollars was never allocated "because of other pressing financial needs," according to budget director Frank Sullivan. Advocates for a museum, including Dr. Dennis Nicholas and the lieutenant governor's wife, Judy O'Bannon, were not re-appointed to the museum board by Governor Bayh when their terms expired. In 1990 the House defeated a bill to reestablish the commission. After all, there had been no appointed director for the commission, and without a director to convene the board, there had been no meetings of the commission for over a year. Governor Bayh did appoint new members, but no director.

Over a period of months, with some not-so-gentle urging from the media and messages from some of the governor's politically contributing constituents, a director for the commission was appointed. Some planning began for the park but none for the museum. I then wrote a letter on October 24, 1994 to John Kish, executive director of the White River State Park Commission:

Dear John:

Seemingly, I write an annual letter to the Commission and send it to a different person. You should have on file in the Commission, a folder of Borst letters. I am still concerned with the direction of the Commission and what it hopes to accomplish.

I did attend one of the background meetings on the new IMAX Theater proposal that was conducted by the consultants. I was less than favorably impressed. I agree with some of the recent contention that their attendance and financial figures are also somewhat overstated. Common sense and simple division should tell us that some of the figures are not quite possible. Consultants being consultants are supposed to sell a rosy picture, but I do disagree with them; when they say that this would be the focal point of downtown Indianapolis.

Originally I could envision a lot of grass, and the banks of the White River being modified in such a manner that picnics would be in order. There should be a boat livery on the river. Amenities for family congregations should be built. I still do not think we necessarily must have some sort of gigantic centerpiece. If an original idea does come about, let it happen, rather than creating an idea that may or may not work out.

I would hope the state museum might be included in some of the land. I would also hope that someone might once again enter into a discussion with the people that own Deer Creek. I would hope that some sort of outdoor stage or terraced auditorium could be included.

Green grass, lots of space and places for families may not be the in thing in park planning. My best advice could be to allow the Children's Museum to do their thing and try not to compete with them in this area. Some day if you have an endowment as large as theirs, you might be able to afford to do such a thing.

Sincerely,

I had no idea that building a new museum was so little thought of. Or more likely, it was because Governor Bayh knew that I was associated with the promotion. The next correspondence was written following a public unveiling of the new park concept by the consultants. Tramways from downtown Indianapolis, huge fountains, a conglomeration of lights (supposedly visible by the orbiting astronauts), maybe every left-over idea that the consulting architect had left over from other projects.

December 30, 1994
Mr. John Kish, Executive Director
Dear John:
I enjoyed most of the presentation last Wednesday except somehow I missed the location of the new Indiana State Museum. Hopefully, there may be some room for it other than on a parking lot. I know of the present governor's distaste for the project but, two years from now there will be a new philosophy within that office. The legislature has shown its willingness to appropriate funds for the new Indiana State Museum and would undoubtedly allow moneys for construction.
I would still counsel you that a park is a park, and not necessarily a statement about life.
Sincerely,

Beautiful plans were presented. A place for a zoo. The canal was extended to the White River. Magnificent waterfalls. A huge central parking lot. But nowhere was to be found a site for a future state museum. Not really an oversight. A technical happening, I was told.

A change in the administration in 1996 brought a positive change in the attitude towards the thinking of actually building a new state museum. Judy O'Bannon exerted her influence and expertise in bringing about the new facility.

White River State Park is now a beautiful sight. Seemingly, the park has simply just evolved without following a formal plan. The park today looks much different than the original plans. Straightening out the canal has done wonders. The waterfall at the western end of the canal as it cascades into the White River is one of the hidden architectural gems in the state of Indiana. The zoo on the west bank of the White River is a popular attraction for the whole state, young and old. The re-routing of US 40 and the refurbishing of the Washington Street bridge that connects the two sides of the river is a work of art as a pedestrian walkway. The Congressional Medal of Honor display underwritten by the Indianapolis Power and Light Company, the headquarters of the NCAA with its Hall of Champions, the IMAX Theater, and the new Indiana State Museum next to the Eiteljorg Museum make for an attractive state park.

The park is on ongoing project. I would imagine that in the years to come, both sides of the river will be beautified in some manner from 16th Street south to Raymond Street. The Berveridge Paper Company's eyesore of a building has been demolished and, lo and behold, green grass and open spaces have taken its place. And the Indiana State Museum is the pride of the state—the best state museum in the nation.

chapter   16

The Dome

About the same time that the White River State Park was getting started, community leaders were envisioning a domed stadium nearby.

A three-man Stadium Study Task Force announced on September 4, 1980 that construction of a 60,000 seat, multipurpose stadium could be considered as financially sound with or without a National Football League franchise. William Carter, the chairman, suggested that the eighteen-story-high stadium should be built adjacent, and connected to the Indiana Convention Center, thus providing the center the expansion room it had been seeking.

It was thought that the new stadium at a cost of about $60 million could be financed by bonding and donations from the private sector, and financing would not be contingent on the use of property taxes. The bonds, interest and principle would be retired with the proceeds of a one percent tax on restaurant food and beverages purchased within Marion County.

P. E. MacAllister, chairman of the Capital Improvements Board, in his usual forthright style, sounded the call for action. "The convention center has to expand and we're open to suggestions," he said. "And if someone official says to proceed, then we'll pick up the ball. But we're looking for an official mandate from an officially mandated agency."

Indianapolis Mayor Bill Hudnut said that the facility could stand on its own, but did admit, "I might have egg on my face" if the city was not awarded a NFL franchise. Mayor Hudnut had written me in August of 1981 informing me, "The primary purpose of the 'Domed Stadium' project is to expand the Indiana Convention Center to allow our community to capture a larger share of the growing convention business market." Hudnut also pointed out, "Since there is a very real possibility that the National Football League will be expanding from twenty-eight to thirty teams in the near future, it seems prudent that we should set up a high-level committee to sell Indiana and Indianapolis as an expansion site to the NFL." I was then asked to serve on the newly formed committee which was chaired by Tom Moses, chairman of the Board of the Indianapolis Water Company.

I sponsored the legislation that enacted the Marion County food and beverage tax in the 1981 session. For a while the issue became a Marion-County-versus-the-rest-of-the-state issue. Hudnut and David Frick lobbied the legislature in a most effective manner. The only organized opposition was led and headed up by Warren Spangle, executive vice-president of the Indiana Restaurant Association. The association thought its members were being unnecessarily picked on. Because of the food tax, Laughner's Cafeteria put signs on its table denouncing the legislation. Charles Laughner sought me out at lunchtime to let me know that the legislation would drive him out of business. Some years later, Laughner's did go out of business, but it was not because of the Marion County food and beverage tax. Predictions were made that everyone on the Southside would travel to Johnson County to buy their hamburgers rather than spend an extra one percent in Marion County.

When the Colts did come to town, the Restaurant Association was rewarded with a whole row of seats, twenty rows up, on the fifty-yard line, behind the Colts bench.

To make the legislation more acceptable, a ticket tax was added, and wording was inserted into the bill that would limit the imposition of the food and beverage tax until the bonds were retired. The bonds were floated at a time of extremely high interest rates. They were backed by the Marion County property tax, were insured, and carried a tax-free interest of eleven percent. Needless to say, these bonds have been refinanced on several occasions since the original issuance, always and continually extending the life of the Marion County food and beverage tax.

In February of 1981, the Lilly Endowment gave a gift of twenty-five million dollars, and the Krannert Foundation added another five million dol-

lars towards the construction of the stadium. The estimated cost of the stadium had now risen to about sixty-five million dollars. The actual costs were
much higher. The original estimates were for a basic structure. Electronic
scoreboards and finished locker rooms were not included and needed to be
installed at a later date.

Building the dome was a sound and positive economic development
move for the city. The Colts use the facilities ten times a year, and church
groups probably use the building at least that many. Playing in the dome is a
highlight for many local and area high school football teams and for those
high school teams from around the state during state championship playoffs.
Peyton Manning, the Colts quarterback, and his foundation are responsible
for funding Indianapolis public high schools to play at least one game per
year on the artificial turf.

There was a push to use the stadium for professional baseball. The Indianapolis "Arrows" were formed and deposits on season tickets were solic-
ited. A major league old-timer's game, with a brief appearance by Joe Di-
Maggio, was attempted in the structure. But standing in the semi-finished
Dome, one did not have to be a surveyor or an engineer to realize that a ball
hit down one foul line would go about 380 feet, while down the other line
the distance would be less than 200 feet. Even with a "Green Monster" net,
the proportions were not right for baseball.

A contest was held to name the stadium. One can imagine the suggestions. The CIB with the final say, wisely, selected the name of Hoosier Dome.
The effort was a collective effort of many from around the state. Mayor
Hudnut felt that he was mostly responsible for bringing the Colts to Indianapolis and did not want to share the football team's name with the rest of the
state—so the team became the Indianapolis Colts. He was willing to allow for
the Hoosier Dome, but naming the team as the Indiana Colts was a no no.

chapter 17

The License Branch Reform

In the governor's residence shortly before midnight on election day in November 1984, Governor Robert Orr, seeking re-election, loudly announced to the Republicans assembled, "LARRY BORST, you have to do something about the license branches or John Mutz will not be elected governor in four years." That proclamation was the jump start for revamping the state's license branch system.

What was supposed to be an election that Orr would win handily became very tight late on election night. A six or seven point lead that had been forecast for Orr over the Democrat nominee, Senator Wayne Townsend, seemed to have evaporated. Senator Townsend had in the last ten days or so of the campaign settled on one issue: The "corrupt" license branch system under Republican leadership. Wayne's TV ads accused Republican county chairmen of making six figures from the sales of automobile licenses and plates. The election became so close that Wayne, to this day, says that he only needed another two days of TV time in order to have become the winner.

The Democrat Party had created the partisan system years before and the Republicans refined it. Keith Bulen was alleged to have established a corporation in Marion County that funneled license branch profits into the central party. When I first entered politics, the license branch in Perry Township was in a small insurance office owned by Martha Burnett who had the franchise. When Everett Newlon was ward chairman, he purchased an old house on Madison Avenue, renovated the house into an office and moved the branch there when he took over the Southside bureau. The public was not being adequately served and the argument that Townsend advanced as a campaign issue made some sense to the voting public.

In one of my many attempts to tilt at windmills, I had co-sponsored legislation in 1971 that would have placed all of the employees of the branches under a merit system and would have eliminated partisan control. The bill passed both chambers in the same form but with different effective dates. After both houses had passed the legislation, I was asked to appear in front of the members of the GOP state committee and was asked point blank by Keith Bulen, "Are you serious about the legislation?" Other questions from district chairmen made it obvious that I was experiencing a session in the "woodshed." The result was that I was not assigned to the now more politically favorable conference committee and the branch reform legislation that went into the conference committee, suddenly came out of the conference committee as a study committee for the coming year. The interim study committee was loaded with political friendlies and not very active. If a recommendation was ever made during 1971, I am sure that it would have been to have another study committee in 1972.

A few days following the November 1984 election, President Pro Tem Bob Garton wrote to the majority caucus that he had designated Senator Borst to review the license branch issue. The legislation that I had drawn up created a semi-independent governmental structure that would incorporate the license branches into the state system, as well as pay scale for employees, pensions and normal benefits. A governing five-member board would develop criteria determining the number and location of branches. There would have been an appropriation of five million dollars and the state take-over date would have been January 1, 1987. The legislation never had a chance to become law in 1985. Too many county chairmen of both political parties voiced their opposition to individual legislators.

At least the opposition was bi-partisan. Even though Governor Orr was for restructuring of the system, the GOP state chairman sent a letter to all of the Republican legislators urging them to defeat any move to turn control of the system over to the state.

The co-sponsor of SB 389, Senator Mike Rogers, arranged a closed-door meeting with Senators Townsend, Rogers, Borst, Gery and McCarty. The meeting lasted for over three hours and was cordial, productive and agreeable. It produced a version that passed out of the Senate Public Policy Committee by a vote of nine to two. None of the committee members had a copy of the bill as amended behind the closed doors and had to accept the outline as presented by Senator Rogers. Senator Bill Dunbar objected to not being able to see the completed bill, and Senator Les Duvall thought that there was no need to change the present system in such a substantial manner.

Representative Tom Coleman, chairman of the House Transportation Committee, declared any such legislation passed by the Senate to be "dead on arrival" in the House. He and Representatives Bill Soards, Earline Rogers and Bill Cochran believed that further study was the only course of action. Not to be deterred, SB 389 was passed on third reading in the Senate by a vote of thirty to nineteen. Senator John Augsburger, Jr. remarked that he thought that the additional employees and paper work would be difficult to manage. Senator Joe Harrison was turned down on a second reading amendment that would have gutted the bill. The governor's legislation passed the Senate with twelve Republicans and eighteen Democrats voting yea.

Despite a flurry of compromises from Orr and the state GOP apparatus, the 1985 session of the General Assembly raised the state tax on gasoline but did nothing constructive on license branch reform.

In September of 1985 Governor Orr still felt that license branch reform was in the best interests of the people in the state. Despite the negative feelings from the political organizations, his convictions were such that he wrote a rather lengthy letter to each of the legislators and to the state GOP chairman for distribution to the various GOP officials around the state. Few governors had ever taken such a bold and forthright stance on such a hotly discussed political issue as did Bob Orr.

For the 1986 session the previously Senate-passed bill was revised somewhat and a ten-branch pilot project was added for 1987 with full implementation to be by June 30, 1988. Representative Dan Stephan announced that the cost to the state for reform would be at least fifty million dollars, and later he promoted the idea of having a binding statewide referendum. The cost to the state to convert turned out to be less than three million dollars.

The aspect of the law whereby the net profits from the sale of the vanity license plates would be divided between the two political parties was retained.

These profits were being used for political purposes. Neither party wanted to give up that income, nor did either party desire that much reform.

For the Democrats, the negative part of the legislation was a section that I had inserted allowing the new commission to pay for office equipment that the bureau managers had purchased. This "buy-out" provision was only fair, but could have been thought of as a reward to some of those GOP county chairmen for giving up the branches.

The legislation did pass and was signed into law. Governor Orr appointed the commission which had its first public meeting in June of 1986.

The License Branch Shuffle

We are the Legislators tested and true,
We just came here working for you.
But we didn't come here lookin' for trouble.
We just came to do the License Branch Shuffle.

Now, my name is Dan,
I lead the troops.
They ain't that smart, but they still ain't dupes.
When they are in caucus, they still have their say,
But back on the floor, they vote my way.
Now, I didn't come here looking for trouble,
I just came to do the License Branch Shuffle.

My name is Mike,
And I'm here to say,
The Democrats will be in control some day.
To do nothin' would sure seem funny,
So let's give up the plates, but keep the money.
Now, I didn't come here looking for trouble,
I just came to do the License Branch Shuffle.

My name is Jerry,
And with a little luck,
Next year's plates will come from Sears and Roebuck.
Now I did come here looking for trouble,
Who gives a damn about the License Branch Shuffle.

Now, my name's Paul,
And here's my beef,
We have money for this, but not poor relief.
Now I didn't come here looking for trouble
But whatever you get, Lake County wants double.
Now I didn't come here looking for trouble,
I just came to do the License Branch Shuffle.

This is Wayne,
Your champ in this cause.
And in the news, I've exposed its flaws.
But in committee, if I don't show,
Just go on and vote me no.
Now, I didn't come here looking for trouble,
I just came to do the License Branch Shuffle.

This is South Bend Pat,
I'm here to say,
I've raised this issue on many a day.
If it's the year to meet its fate,
Don't take away our money from personalized plate.
Now, I didn't come here looking for trouble,
I just came to do the License Branch Shuffle.

—Written by a house member sometime in 1986.

War of Words—Orr vs. Bayh

A war of words enlivened the gubernatorial campaign of 1988. The incumbent Governor Bob Orr accused Democratic candidate Evan Bayh of airing a misleading television advertisement. He said the ad mentioning Bayh's role in the debate over license branch reform was "untrue, misleading and offensive" and should be withdrawn. Bayh countered that he had a part in the legislative action of license branch reform and accused Orr of simply trying to aid Republican candidate John Mutz. Orr countered by alleging Bayh was using "weasel words" to try to justify a misleading ad. Bayh then used the age card and claimed the governor "is somewhat confused about what the commercial says."

Orr had a news conference and blasted Bayh by saying, "Bayh is implying by what he says that he has been in the leadership role in license branch reform. He has not been at any time at the forefront or even been involved in license branch reform. I have." A further letter from Orr to Bayh said, "To suggest that you are responsible for reform when clearly you are not is simply wrong." Orr even spent $600 of his own money to tape the news conference and beam the remarks by satellite to stations across Indiana.

Bayh did admit he "didn't have any role in the 1986 legislation" backed by Orr. He did support a bill in the 1987 session that never was heard in committee. However, Bayh claimed that his "outspokenness" later in 1986 kept Republicans from reneging on their commitment to reform. Senator Lindel Hume also joined in, expressing outrage with Orr's actions.

The exchange of words may have helped Evan in his quest to become governor. His laying claim to have brought about license branch reform was a portent of things to come when he became governor. The Senate Republicans during the later years of his terms in office went about their business of providing for state government and allowed Bayh to claim credit for any new program or old program improvement.

chapter   18

Distress in Calumet Township

Difficulties in dealing with poor relief in Lake County were a recurring issue for the legislature in the 1980s—and before. The problems were not limited to Lake County, but it seemed to be perpetual there.

During the 1985 session, Dozier Allen, the Calumet Township trustee, revealed that the township poor relief fund was being grossly overspent. It is a common practice for a township to outspend its yearly budget, then head to a local bank and borrow funds to see it through the fiscal year. The township would then increase the next year's property tax levy enough to pay back the loan. In truth, this technique is used regularly throughout the state to hold property taxes down for a particular year. The township is hopeful that their assessed valuation will increase enough so that the tax rate does not increase appreciably.

Indiana poor relief is a mandated service for each of the more than a thousand townships throughout the state. Theoretically, each trustee must approach the matter in the same way. Still, many township trustees ignore poor relief. Lax and uneven standards by the trustees in the state energized a group of citizens to obtain a federal court ruling that ordered common procedures for all of the townships to follow. But the ruling has been routinely ignored by many of the trustees. Each trustee more or less shapes his or her own criteria to correspond with an individual philosophy on taking care of indigents. The general attitude of the local community towards the poor also influences the trustee. Most trustees act on the belief that poor relief is for the absolute destitute, the temporary down-and-out and, and by all means for only those citizens who live in that township.

Not Dozier Allen in Calumet Township. His criteria were not very strict. Dozier also would not limit relief to a bag of groceries or fifty gallons of oil for heating. He felt it was his job to take care of all necessities—food, rent, water, gas, telephone and almost all expenses for daily living.

Poor relief funding was discussed in 1985, but there was no resolution. Matters got to the point that Representative Charlie Brown, of Gary, called Representative Pat Kiely a "bleep" as the session ended. Representative Kiely's crime was that he would not give in to appropriating an outright grant of cash money to bail out Calumet Township. Whether Charlie Brown was convinced that Pat Kiely was really a "bleep" we shall never know, but at least they continued to speak to each other.

An interim study committee was authorized to conduct hearings and to bring about a solution for poor relief funding in Lake County. Representative Phyllis Pond was selected as chairman. Much detailed testimony was heard about Lake County and its poor. Gary Mayor Richard Hatcher asked the state to give money to Calumet Township to cover the township debts. Dozier Allen calculated that he would have a twenty-one million dollar deficit by the end of the year. Speaker J. Roberts Dailey called for compassion. He was concerned "whether they go to bed hungry in Gary, whether they have shirts on their backs, and whether their homes have heat."

The interim committee arrived at a loose consensus. Members recommended that the state institute a grant program to assist township trustees swamped by emergency relief expenses. The committee also agreed to support a change in state law that would allow a combination of state, county and township funds to be used for poor relief. Mayor Hatcher requested five million dollars of immediate aid "to prevent many residents of that area from starving and freezing." Governor Orr provided one and half million dollars of the amount, the rest to be raised locally.

Lake County attempted to secure temporary monies by offering to bond for fifteen million dollars. The problem was that no one wanted to buy the bonds. A citizen's march was organized in Lake County to descend on Indianapolis and Governor Orr, to "soften his heart." This, too, fell by the wayside. The designated leader, Mayor Hatcher, suddenly withdrew his support, saying that he was busy that day. Everybody then stayed home.

On October 16, 1985 I wrote to Governor Orr:

Dear Bob:

A couple of thoughts on the Lake County poor relief situation. Food and hunger are the main problems that need to be taken care of. I would be willing to appropriate some money out of the state general fund for feeding people and for food boxes. Surely there are some surplus government commodities available.

I would not give the money to the trustee. I would only give the charge to a state agency to contract with the private agencies in Lake County to prepare and serve lunches or whatever. Private agencies would be mainly churches, Gleaners, or what may already be formed. I would think that the volunteer sector in Lake County should be involved.

None of the money would go for shelter or energy.

This idea could accompany legislation that would impose a two year local option tax on Lake County. All proceeds would go for the support of county poor relief.

So far as back bills are concerned, the county must work that out through local funding. The state can be humanitarian and feed one and all. No qualifications. Only show up at designated places for a meal a day. It is a morass, but I think that state monies could be used for hunger.

Sincerely,

Trustee Allen had over 13,000 eligible families on the rolls. They were given vouchers to pay for electricity, natural gas and water bills, rent, food and medical bills. Vouchers were issued but payment to the vendors from the trustee to back up the vouchers was not forthcoming. The Gary-Hobart Water Company was owed more than $600,000. The school system had not received any payments for textbooks and for the free lunch program for over a year. More than 9,000 vendors were owed money by the Calumet trustee.

Governor Orr scrounged over one million dollars in the form of cash and advances for the township. A strange thing then happened. Dozier Allen rejected the help, citing something about fewer applicants, more stringent control, and it would be useless "because the township does not have any money anyway."

Enter the chairman of the House Ways and Means Committee, Representative Pat Kiely. He said that Allen had been careless in his administration

of poor relief. Kiely said that he would ask the 1986 session to authorize sending management and audit teams to Calumet Township as part of the cost of
the state's solving a twenty-six million dollar township debt to merchants. He
thought that the audit should at least cover the past five years of the trustee's
operations.

The Kiely proposal would establish a management team appointed by
the governor to take over the poor relief operation in Calumet Township.
This team would also review records and eligibilities and would suggest a
short and long-range funding plan. This team was to be paid out of the state
general fund which would be reimbursed by the county. Local authorities in
Lake County would have to accept any funding recommendations, or else
impose a local option tax on income in the county.

His legislation barely won approval in the Ways and Means Committee.
Several amendments were made and a seven million dollar appropriation was
added. Most of the proposed second reading amendments asked that the state
absorb all of the township's debts. None prevailed. HB 1185 was passed by
the House and was then assigned to the Senate Finance Committee.

In finance committee testimony Dozier Allen testified, "It is my hope
that the Democrats in Lake County will not make an effort to side track this
bill for political reasons when, in fact, they have been totally insensitive to the
needs of the poor in the past. HB 1185 calls for a state audit and while I believe it is not necessary, I am absolutely not resisting that it be conducted.
Since 1979, the Calumet Township Trustee and administration have been
under a criminal audit. First by the IRS from 1979 to 1984 and then by the
Indiana State Board of Accounts, from 1985 to 1986. I view another audit as
a necessary administrative procedure for those who support it, however, I do
not think it is necessary, and it would be extremely expensive to local taxpayers."

Representative Kiely made it his business to closely monitor the management teams that were sent into Calumet Township. The thorough audits
which were conducted revealed a lack of eligibility standards. Almost anyone
was eligible for poor relief, and once on the rolls, always on the rolls. Some
recipients did not need the township help while others could have received
the aid under several different names. Some individuals receiving a paycheck
as a member of the trustee's staff could not be located by the investigators.
Invoices were not in proper order. It was found that some vendors had made

more than one payment request for delivering the same service.

Eventually, the recipient roster was whittled down. The vendor list was brought up to date. The trustee staff was accounted for and stabilized and more businesslike procedures were put in place. The trustee could now live within its means. The county assumed the debt, and the county council did not need to impose the local option tax. Governor Orr even offered to use the residual four million dollars of the appropriated monies from HB 1185 to pay off township debts incurred by the smaller vendors. This would mean that all of the debts incurred by the township would be satisfied, except for the nearly seven million claim by Northern Indiana Public Service Company and the over three million loaned to the township by Lake County. Ken Kobe, as chairman of the Calumet Township Distressed Management Committee, had done his job well.

Allen wrote to Governor Orr on October 15, 1987:

> *I have continued to cooperate in spite of some grave reservations as to whether or not Calumet Township was ever distressed. I have some additional reservations about the constitutionality of 1185 and the process of denying recipients and on whether voters are disenfranchised.*
>
> *I do not know if accusations that wholesale corruption was occurring in Calumet Township was developed by large business interests in Gary and covertly passed to the media and to member of the General Assembly. The private accusations were responsible for the development of 1185 because they were accepted at face value. However, a closer examination has exposed the fact that neither myself nor members of the township staff have been involved in grand theft, larceny, fraud or bribery.*

Dozier Allen was appointed to the Governor's Blue Ribbon Committee on Tax Restructuring by Governor Frank O'Bannon in 1997. He was also awarded a Sagamore of the Wabash, the state's highest honor, by Governor O'Bannon. He was defeated in an attempt to be re-elected in the May primary of 2002. The *Gary Post-Tribune* reported that Allen is still being investigated by federal authorities. FBI agents resumed their probe in 2002 by checking into his office and his personal records.

Obscene Bumper Stickers

Late in 1988 I received a telephone call from Barry Hampton, a constituent of mine from Senate District 36. He said that he was sick and tired of having to drive behind automobiles that were adorned with obscene bumper stickers. He said he was very concerned that his two daughters were being exposed to the sticker's outright filth, innuendo and subliminal messages.

Could I introduce a bill outlawing such obscenity, he asked? I promised that I would have the matter researched.

To make the display of a word an offense, the word must be specifically included into the law. I knew that the Senate had tried to tackle obscenity in years past, and I was not prepared to introduce a bill with thirty or forty X-rated words, words more descriptive than the Lenny Bruce exclusions, written in bold type. So I had a broad-based bill written that amended the obscenity law to provide, as obscene, any descriptive word or saying on a sticker, decal and emblem. Simple little bill of ten lines.

Predictably, the ACLU made a big deal of it. Michael Gradison, executive director of the American Civil Liberties Union, said, "It's vague, overly broad and unconstitutional." He and others felt that the wording in the legislation meant that T-shirts and other items bearing logos that some people might find offensive also could be included in the definitions. Gradison said, "The General Assembly is so overloaded now we don't want to waste our energy on this garbage, but we'll try to stop this bill."

Quotes like that brought out the media. I hadn't told Mr. Hampton that I had written and introduced the bill dealing with obscene bumper stickers. I referred media questions to Mr. Hampton. He was great. When interviewed by both the print and electronic media he seemed in his element and was most convincing. He was quoted as saying, "I just don't think there's a place for it on the street. It's getting worse and worse. I just don't think our children should be exposed to it. At some point in time, we just have to say tough, even though there may be a freedom-of-expression argument."

The media did some of my homework for me and checked Florida's obscene bumper sticker law, and according to published newspapers reports learned that theirs had not worked out well. Florida columnists had written that deciding whether a bumper sticker is obscene is "all in the eye of the beholder." Many of the arrests and citations in Florida were dropped almost as quickly as they were filed, reported *The Miami Herald*.

In typical legislative fashion, the legislation received notoriety but no committee hearing and no other consideration. The number of letters in support of the legislation that I received would outnumber those that I might receive if I were in support of more money for education. The general public was in complete support of a ban of the stickers.

Such is the fashion in the legislature. My constituent was satisfied. Mr. Hampton had a good suggestion and it was acted on. The system did respond to a citizen's complaint.

Today it almost seems as if what were obscene sayings on bumper stickers in the eighties are now phrases uttered on prime time TV sit-coms most every evening.

chapter   19

Riverboat Casinos in Indiana

When talk of casino gambling in Indiana began, Lake County was in the forefront. The effort began in earnest in 1989 when two state representatives from Gary, Earline Rogers and Charlie Brown, pushed for a casino to be located in Gary. But the House voted against the proposal fifty-four to forty-six. That November the citizens of Gary went to the polls in a referendum and expressed their preference regarding casino gaming in Gary. Only thirty-two percent of the eligible voters voted but of those voting over sixty percent were in favor of casino gaming.

Re-introduced by Representative Rogers, the new bill directed the profits from the casinos be used to reduce the individual auto excise tax liability for individuals. Not having the necessary fifty-one votes, Rogers withdrew her legislation from consideration on third reading in the House. All types of discrimination charges were hurled about as an excuse for the bill's non-acceptance. The White River Park Commission continuation was caught in the crossfire and was killed on the House floor in retaliation for the demise of the casino legislation.

Over the years I have developed a friendship with a few of the CEO's of publicly held casino operations based in Las Vegas. During the summer or 1990 I had an occasion to visit Las Vegas and have long discussions with several of the people in casino management. These people had a long-range vision for the expansion of the gaming in the country.

Operators in Las Vegas know every rumor, every amendment and most every thought that is going on in the halls and rooms of the Indiana General Assembly. The reach for information is the same in all other states that allow legalized gaming. They knew of the efforts that were going on in behalf of Gary. They shared their several predictions regarding the future of gaming in Indiana.

The Vegas seers thought that riverboat casinos were just a passing fad. They could not imagine that any state in the Midwest would ever condone casino gaming on land or on sea. Riverboats were dismissed as only for "redneck" fifty-cent bettors. So much for visionary foresight. None of the 1990 Vegas prognostications ever came to pass.

What they dreamed of was a huge gaming complex somewhere within fifty miles of downtown Chicago, a sort of a domed affair with four or five casinos. Filling in the space between the casinos would be shops, hotels and restaurants. Under the center atrium would be acres of grass or fountains or parkland. This would be a destination resort within a day's drive of well over half of the population in the country.

It was felt at that time that a Gary address would be a detriment for the success of such a giant Midwestern gaming complex. The Vegas entrepreneurs thought that the cornfields of the western edge of Lake County would be ideal for building the resort. No need for Lake Michigan or mountains or any other natural attraction to draw customers.

Later that summer in a response to a reporter's question I stated, "I have the feeling that Gary may not be the Number One site if casino operators had their druthers." Naturally, there were headlines in Gary papers and denials by the casino industry. Be that as it may, there was no interest in Gary by the casino people in 1990.

Speaker Mike Phillips suggested that the casino effort now centered on Gary be expanded to allow casino riverboats on the Ohio River and permit gaming at French Lick. Senator Rogers (she was now a senator) agreed "to do whatever it takes to get the votes."

Up to this point the legislation as written had U.S. Steel as the number one beneficiary. Most of the profits would have gone for property tax reduction in the City of Gary and the surrounding Calumet Township. U.S. Steel was far and away the largest property taxpayer in Calumet Township, which would allow it to receive a gigantic windfall in tax relief. A small portion of the new money would be used for infrastructure for the city. Larger portions were earmarked for schools and retiring any present bonded debt, further reducing the dependence on property tax collections. The new money would have been "substitute" money for school budgets and not an enhanced amount for education.

The best feature of the establishment of multiple casinos would have been the creation of thousands of new jobs in northwest Indiana. John Walls, president of the Indiana Chamber of Commerce, and the Chamber itself endorsed legalized gaming for Gary as "a good way to bring money to a cash-poor city suffering from a dwindling population. Gary has all the problems of the universe on its back and the leadership there believes that nobody cares. I think you have to balance the immorality of gambling with the immorality of poverty and the breakdown of housing and infrastructure in a place like Gary."

The casino legislation offered in 1991 did add legalized gaming for French lick and West Baden Springs, with riverboats on the Ohio, as well as increasing the off-track betting facilities for Hoosier Park. This new version survived the House on a vote of fifty-one to forty-nine. Senator Rogers was most disturbed with my handling of the public hearing in the Senate Finance Committee, expressing her feelings about me in very emphatic terms. The senator believed that her citizens from Lake County were not given an unlimited amount of time to offer their testimony. I also voted against the bill in committee. The Senate Finance Committee rejected the legislation by a six to eight vote with one member absent.

Shortly after the 1991 session, Representative Brown wanted me to sit down with him and tell him and the Gary casino supporters how to construct a bill legalizing casino gaming that would pass the legislature. I personally would not have asked my leading opponent how to pass a bill; but then again, there is only one Charlie Brown. The legislature is a strange place in many ways. No one had ever asked me why I opposed casinos.

Legislative techniques

A failing of a great many legislators is that they assume they know the whys and wherefores of everything that occurs. That results in certain actions being taken based on false premises. I always like to know who my opposition is, and the motivation for the position they have taken. Maybe the legislator's attitude has come about because his or her county chairman is opposed to a program, and nothing can be done about that unless I talk with the county chairman. Maybe the stance taken is because of a morality issue. For heaven's sake, it may be that the legislator's wife or husband is absolutely opposed. Sometimes, when their reasons are known, their opposition can be attended to and the legislation can be altered to their satisfaction.

Whenever I begin to write complicated or contentious legislation, I will always sit down and list the individuals or lobbying groups who I am sure will oppose the idea at the heart of the legislation. I already know those who will support the legislation. The real key is to construct legislation so that you mute a significant portion of the opposition while not going so far as to offend the supporters. If the head count shows that the vote will not be close, then the authors have the freedom to make the proposed legislation the most responsible act that is possible. It is a matter of compromise.

An author of legislation needs to have an idea of the support he has in at least one house of the General Assembly. The mistake of some authors is being too dogmatic about the wisdom of their draftsmanship; some compromise is almost always necessary. Patience is a virtue, and legislation needs to survive one step at a time. The age-old adage of knowing that fifty percent of something is a lot better than 100 percent of nothing should be engraved in the mind of all legislators. Another piece of advice that I relay to new legislators is that perfection is tough to come by in this business. The secret is learning only to count to twenty-six or to fifty-one. Additional congratulations are not awarded to a bill's sponsor for securing more than just enough votes for passing legislation.

I did not respond to Representative Brown's request for almost a year. He reminded me several times that he had asked about how to pass a bill legalizing casinos in Gary. My response in April of 1992:

1. The project must be a Lake County project. Not only a Gary project.

2. U.S. Steel cannot be the dominant part of the picture.

3. The profits must be dedicated for the use of all of the entities in Lake County—not just for the reduction of property tax in Calumet Township.

4. I would think that you might want to improve education.

5. I would think that any profits should be looked after by someone other than by your elected officials.

6. Inducements must be offered the casino people to come to Indiana. They have so many options that they will be able to play one area against the next. Mayor Daley knows how to do this. I have not seen any effort in Lake County.

7. Financing of the needed infrastructure is a must. This is the first thing that they asked me last July. They are not going to pay for the land, interchanges and bridges. They know that Gary is broke. They want nothing to do with the slag pile. They want the cornfields in south and west Lake County. Airports make no difference. Interstates do. They will go to downtown Chicago if these things are not provided.

8. Lake County must impose a six-tenths percent local option income tax to generate the infrastructure money.

9. The Lake County delegation has to quit making excuses for failing to get this through. Ineptness cannot be excused away. You will never succeed as long as you call other legislators names and challenge their integrity. Someday, some from your delegation may come to a conclusion that some of the senators do vote their convictions and philosophy. You might also have the members of the Democrat Party stand up for your cause. It might help to have those from Gary, to quit calling out "racist" whenever anything goes wrong about this bill.

10. If you can't have Evan Bayh support your position, there may never be casinos in Indiana during his tenure. Evan will veto any casino legislation.

Charlie didn't release the letter to the media until March of the next year. *The Post-Tribune* headlined that Bayh holds the trump card and Gary must stop crying "racist." Switching the emphasis from land-based casinos to riverboat casinos on Lake Michigan and the inclusion of boats on the Ohio

River produced the winning combination for the authorization of casino type gaming in Indiana. Without the presence of Speaker Mike Phillips, the legislation would not have passed in the special session of June 1993. Once again the House had barely passed the bill and the Senate Finance Committee had rejected the legislation on a party line vote. The House bill never did have a Republican sponsor in the Senate.

Senator Garton and I were taken to task by many of the citizens of southwest Indiana. Vanderburgh County Republican County Chairman Joseph Harrison, a man whom I had never met, asked the GOP state chairman to recall our seats in the Senate, as well as directing a few personal barbs at our character. He also felt that both of us were an "embarrassment" to the Republican Party. Rex Early backed up the sentiment from Evansville, adding a choice comment of his own and that "Evansville is getting the shaft." Rex reasoned that the Republican members of the Senate were standing in the way of progress for Vanderburgh County.

What may have been worth noting about all of this was that Rex Early had been state GOP chairman just two months before this time. Oddly, it did not bother Rex that he was causing a split among the Republicans. The bill that did eventually legalize riverboats was a terrible piece of legislation written completely by and for the benefit of the gaming industry.

I was not actually offended by these major Republicans taking on other Republicans. I would have thought that they might have checked with someone regarding the state of the legislation and the strategy involved. We in the legislature were leery of such apparent outrages at this stage of the game. None of us knew who would benefit the most from such legislation. The franchises were up for grabs with the winning sides being able to cash in quite handsomely. Communication is only a phone call away, and neither Senator Garton nor I felt the complete facts were known to those who sought to so readily criticize.

I had two reasons for opposing casino legislation, whether land-based or boat-based. First, I had made a promise to thousands of ordinary citizens that I would support only the legalization of pari-mutuel horse betting. This promise came about in the sixties and seventies when horse racing was the only thing on the table. At dozens of meetings where I spoke the audience was concerned about horse racing opening the doors to more sophisticated gaming. For years I would assure them that would not happen. In all honesty,

I did not think early on that Indiana would go as overboard as they have since that time for all types of gaming. I cannot actually recall all of the groups to whom I made the promise, other than guessing, that the declarations made were more likely to have been in a church setting. Even though the promises were made years ago, the promises were made and I intended to live by them. The "orange shirts" from Orange County in the 2003 session could not fathom that kind of honesty and were disappointed that a politician would stand by his word.

The second reason was the origin of the proposed legislation. The gaming industry had written the bill and handed it to the legislative sponsors without any backup data. Hordes of well-paid lobbyists were patrolling the halls. Former legislators were in abundance. A cottage industry had been formed to promote gaming. The unemployment rate for jobs around the Statehouse was reduced by a large percentage and St. Elmo's was required to expand its staff because of the huge lobbying effort. Eleven boats meant eleven opportunities for ownership. Plenty of boats to go around, meaning that there would be plenty of lobbyists going around doing their thing.

The monetary return flagrantly favored the casino boat owner. The legislation was written so that the boats themselves would be minimally taxed at the local level. It was a tonnage tax in the same way fishing boats might be taxed. The new boats would have also escaped local assessment as real or even personal property. The state would be liable financially for providing the security and safety of the patrons both on and around the boats. The bill was written so that the gaming commission had to determine if the legislators really wanted the boats to sail or to simply stay docked at their mooring. A friendly commission almost let them become permanently land based. There was some doubt if the boats had to even come under the U. S. Coast Guard rules and regulations.

On the floor of the Senate I pointed out the confining geographical boundaries of the state of Indiana. The author of the bill thought that I was being obnoxious by wondering what was going to happen on the Ohio River when the Kentucky boundary was within a stone's throw of the Indiana shoreline. When I talked of the Indiana boundary in Lake Michigan I was thought to be an idiot, a person only interested in confusing the issue with obfuscation. As another speaker went on about the two-hour excursions up and down the Ohio, I questioned him, and finally realized that the legislator

I was questioning had never read that part of the bill we were about to cast a vote on.

I have had no problem with the authorization or operation of the present day boats. My problem has been with a multitude of statements from the floor of the Senate that swayed Senate votes for the passage of the bill. These were supposedly factual statements and alluded to promises that could not have come true then and have never since happened. Actually the boat owners themselves have lived up to all of their promises. An even greater investment than was promised has occurred in every instance. The promised number of new jobs created and diversity of hiring for these new jobs is also on target. Eight of the franchises are well above expectations. The two boats in close proximity on Lake Michigan in Lake County will one day be combined in some fashion and then will be successful.

During the following session, the talk among the casino lobbyists was that they would immediately push for dockside gaming. Under certain conditions, and with the addition of so-called "barges," this would allow the casinos to approximate the size of those in Las Vegas. I thought that enough was enough. I decided to go on the offensive this time. I prepared and introduced legislation that would have allowed a casino in Marion County and a riverboat license to be available for any county on the east or west fork of the White River and any county that bordered the Wabash River, thirty-five new gaming counties in all. The riverboat lobbyists decided to stick with what they had accomplished the year before. I was half serious when I prepared the bill. I can see in the future, on a local option basis, gaming extending to any county that thinks it might help out if a financial or economic crunch occurs.

The last time I visited Las Vegas, the inner circle of CEO's made a big demonstration of being offended by one of my amendments to the riverboat legislation. The amendment prohibited political campaign contributions to any incumbent Indiana public official or candidate for office from anyone associated with the gaming industry. The imagination is almost stretched to think of the Las Vegas types citing their First Amendment rights being abridged. I pointed out that I was saving them money. I also pointed out that the attorneys they paid so handsomely should be able to find a way around the Indiana campaign contribution prohibition. The proof of their ingenuity was shown in Indiana during the spring of 2002 when the gaming lobbyists with multiple clients were able to headline fundraisers for some of the more prestigious legislative candidates.

The owners of the riverboats were not completely satisfied by being able to establish a casino. The law was written in such a manner that each of the boats had to leave shore and to "sail," if for only a few feet from the shoreline, never out of sight of land. The sailing times and the gambling times were in two-hour increments. A late-arriving passenger might miss the boat and have to wait almost two hours for the next segment. The boat owners thought this arrangement to be onerous. The fact that the boats did sail, and the promises of leisurely cruises, is what convinced many of the legislators and caused the bill to become law.

Despite the fact that the owners had agreed to the "sailing" provision, these same people immediately began to besiege the gaming commission to allow the boats to remain at the dock at all times. The so-called "dockside gaming" became the goal of the boat owners. Rumors abounded that the commission would allow the riverboats to be permanently moored. I wrote the following letter to Alan Klineman:

> *May 17, 1994*
> *Mr. Alan Klineman, Chairman, Indiana Gaming Commission*
> *Dear Alan:*
> *My only knowledge of what the commission has said regarding dockside gambling is from the news media. I would say that the proponent's intent was that each and every boat should take a cruise. Acts of God would cancel out any dockside gambling.*
> *I personally pointed out the Corps of Engineer regulations, Coast Guard regulations, a Supreme Court decision on the Kentucky/Indiana boundary line, and the probability of no licensure at Patoka Lake. To each of these scenarios the answer was that "things" would be taken care of later or else there would be no gambling.*
> *I would hope that the commission, in it's wisdom, would suggest a violation of legislative intent. The proponents did not want dockside gambling, and hopefully they will not receive dockside gambling.*
> *Sincerely,*

Three weeks later I responded to Mr. Klineman's response to my first letter:

June 8, 1994

Mr. Alan Klineman, Chairman, Indiana Gaming Commission

Dear Alan:

Thanks for sending me a draft copy of the proposed rule on excursions. I have penciled in some comments throughout the text. My letter to you will be more general than specific.

The commission is responding exactly the way that the gambling industry desires. One must remember, the gambling industry wrote the legislation that did become law. The bill was purposefully written so that it could be open for revision and expansion of the as passed legislation.

The section that the commission seeks to explain by Rule was discussed on the floor of the Senate. It was then characterized as a loophole. The sponsors said "no." It was explained that if such things came to pass, as violating other state laws, or having a desired site on Lake Michigan, not securing permission on Patoka, then, there would be no gambling. No gambling until a succeeding legislature considered the matter.

If the Rule is promulgated, the gambling interests will be most thankful. The gambling interests, initially, could not put into the proposed legislation exactly what they really wanted. They knew from experience that it is easier to sway a commission, rather than a legislative body.

I personally feel that the proposed Rule establishes too much leeway for the boats. It is easy to see, how they might never have to go to "sea." Never have to fire up their diesels. As was said by the sponsors, if they cannot meet the criterion, then they cannot gamble that day.

The commission is attempting to write the law. Major revisions of already passed legislation seem to be the thing to do these days. The commission has an opportunity to ask for legislative clarification earlier this year and chose not to do so. I would hope that if any such major revisions are to be contemplated, delay for legislative input would be in order.

Some months ago, I made the announcement that the entire bill was loosely written, and should have many changes, in order to make it really work. I am still of that opinion. Hopefully, the commission and the Courts will not be the ones to effect those changes. The idea was born legislatively and should be nurtured legislatively.

Sincerely,

Chairman Klineman and the commission did not allow dockside gaming for any of the riverboats. But the legislature did allow for dockside gambling during the special session of 2002. In exchange for not having to "sail," the casino boats accepted a new way to tax the profits on the boats. All of the boats are still required to be "seaworthy" and to continue to be under the guidance of the Coast Guard. The boats are able to "sail" once again in case the Legislature changes its mind and rescinds dockside gaming.

Sometimes the work of a legislator required travel to exotic places, such as here to San Diego in August of 1993 to attend the NCSL.

chapter 20

Roadwork for Senate District 36

It's money and votes that impel legislators to siphon state funds for projects in their districts.

I sat on the Indiana State Budget Committee for several years. I have been a conferee on all of the biennial budgets passed by the General Assembly since 1971. I would sit there and listen to and watch the other legislators unashamedly fund a state hospital, a state park or a university simply because it was in their district. (I had no such conflicts because I have represented District 36 since I was first elected to the Senate in 1968 and there aren't any governmental facilities in the district. Senator Jim Merritt always corrects me by pointing out there are two U. S. Post Offices located in the district.) After a legislator succeeds in funding any entity in his district, he or she would make the front page of the hometown newspaper and would be hailed in glowing terms as taking care of his distinct.

I have also learned that it helps one's budgetary decision-making not to have graduated from one of the Indiana state-supported institutions of higher learning. The universities are merciless on legislator conferees who have graduated from their institutions. Every tactic imaginable is employed to convince the conferee to have a little extra money appropriated for a new exotic program or another construction project authorized for his alma mater. Purdue University is famous for supplying legislators representing

Tippecanoe County with a one-page printout listing the unfairness of Senate finance in okaying new buildings. They emphasize that IU is scheduled to receive appropriations in excess, in either dollars or numbers of new buildings authorized, of what was given to Purdue.

Purdue never wants money taken from IU, it wants money added to Purdue. I have even had Purdue officials tell me in the waning hours of a legislative session that they absolutely needed an appropriation for a building that even the Commission for Higher Education had never heard about. The pitch (threat) to me was that if they might receive an OK for an additional appropriation then they would not have their legislator complain in the caucus about the rest of the budget. Purdue especially enjoyed confusing freshmen legislators by including all of the construction costs at the IU Medical Center in Indianapolis in their side-by-side comparisons with IU. Such games are played at the highest level. Each of the universities plays the same games but with different variations. I decided a long time ago that I can pay for my own football tickets.

I have seen underachieving legislators who develop the attitude that unless they bring home the "pork," they are absolute failures. If I have heard it once, I have heard the plea fifty times of "give me something in the budget so I can go home and tell them that it's for the district." Members of Congress can serve for twenty years and never pass a bill or a resolution and be heroes to their constituency because of delivering pork.

The Lake County delegation annually compares the appropriations penciled in for Marion County with what they are scheduled to receive. A chairman of the House Ways and Means committee invariably would tell me what the total dollar appropriation was for Marion County the year before. The dollar disparity between Marion County and the county he represented became such an obsession that he even kept a running total of the differences dating backward for at least ten years.

At the beginning of the short session in 1988 I had a chance conversation with an official in the State Highway Department. He was lamenting the lack of gas tax money available to undertake several highway construction and reconstruction projects that the department deemed "ready to go." The plans supposedly were drawn, right of way mostly purchased, environmental studies completed; practically all of the procedures required before actual bid-letting had been done. Some years before, Representative Dick Bodine had based his campaign for governor on fixing up the "killer" highways in Indiana. He had a big chart with a lot of red lines up and down and across the state. Those that paid attention were impressed because Bodine's red lines went through about every county in the state.

I asked the official from the Highway Department for a list of these projects which could be under construction within a few months if the monies were available. He gave me a list of thirty fairly large projects and some smaller ones. I still remember that Indiana 1 was first on the list. It was also second on the list. It was explained that the section in Franklin County in southeast Indiana was a "must." The project was good but had been delayed and shuffled aside for a number of years. The second section of Indiana 1 to be reconstructed was miles north around the city of Bluffton. The other projects on the list were in various counties such as Allen, Hendricks and so on.

Senate District 36—my district—has no governmental buildings, but there are four important state highways running north and south through the district. Indiana 37, Indiana 135, US 31, Indiana 431. During the first years of Governor's Orr's administration, while there was a dearth of road construction in most areas of the state, it seemed as if most every dime of state and federal highway money was spent on Division Street in Orr's home county of Vanderburgh. The remainder, several hundred thousand dollars, Orr graciously allowed the state to spend on widening the northern portion of Indiana 431 (Madison Avenue) from two to four lanes.

The southern portions of Indiana 431 within District 36 had been reconstructed several years before by another administration. Representative Steve Ferguson had lobbied the legislature in 1969 for a two-cent increase in the gasoline tax to widen Indiana 37 from Indianapolis to Bloomington and on to Bedford. So District 36 had received some consideration and monies from the state and had not been totally ignored.

The second tier of projects listed by the Highway Department was more than interesting. What appeared in the list was the authorization and dollar amounts for the funding of the reconstruction of US 31 from Edgewood Avenue in Marion County south to Smith Valley Road in Johnson County. Also in the second tier was the beginning of the widening of Indiana 135. Money for two high-activity intersections to be improved was included. Visions of "pork" danced through my head.

Flipping to the next page of the list of road projects was the authorization for the complete widening of Indiana 135 from north of Thompson Road through Perry Township to Smith Valley Road in Greenwood. Everything a greedy legislator could want—thirty-eight million dollars. This was good news. As far back as 1983, the highway department had held public meetings in Perry Township, telling the taxpayers that construction was just around the corner. Even in 1986 the highway people promised that construction would begin in 1989. They then announced there would be a delay of a few years. With this as a background I felt that now was the time to be bold.

I wrote legislation that would enable the state of Indiana to bond for road construction, something that had never occurred before. The Indiana Transportation Finance Authority was formed and was given the ability to provide for maturing bonds of twelve to fifteen years to be used to build the roads that were on the list of the highway department. A one-cent gasoline tax increase would pay for the principal and interest of the bonds needed to finance the road construction.

The idea for bonding to build roads was good then and is still fiscally responsible. Shepherding this through the legislature was, and is, the best legislating that I have ever done. The one-cent tax was leveraged to provide for over $350 million of road construction. For the state to have tried to accumulate that much money in cash and then build the Highway Department's wish list project by project would have taken years with costs constantly escalating.

The governor became enthusiastic. Even though Bob Orr knew he would not be governor when the new roads came on line, he backed the idea because of the proposal's revolutionary bonding provisions. The idea did fit his philosophy of government for the needs of the people. The lieutenant governor, John Mutz, was running for governor and he lent his weight to the proposal. He could see himself awarding contracts and cutting ribbons and gathering votes. In fact, John knew that while campaigning he could go around the state and announce that a particular road would finally be built for the voters of such and such a county under his administration.

The State Highway Department came out of its bureaucratic shell and lobbied for the construction money. Highway contractors crowded the halls.

Some of the outsiders (and insiders) became carried away and developed lists of projects to be built that were not quite practical but did serve a purpose. I held tight to the original designated list and would remind the governor and the highway people from time to time that mine was the one that would be followed if the proposed legislation became law.

At the end of the session, some legislators were still reluctant to enact the legislation. Although bonding for university construction had first begun in the late seventies, bonding for highways was a new concept. The legislators, however, were basically wedded to a pay-as-you-go philosophy, and it was difficult for them to alter their way of thinking.

The argument that the primary road system in the state was in such a deplorable condition finally became convincing and over-riding. Each of the legislators could recite his or her own horror story regarding a road located in his or her district, which was totally inadequate. Securing road money is number one or number two on every legislator's list of "things to do" in each session. Sometimes the desire to obtain money for roads and highways exceeds the want for increases in public school funding.

Trying to explain to my caucus how the bonding officials determined the duration of the life of a bridge was difficult. Every facet of the road construction was itemized and referred to in the bond offering brochures. How did they determine that? I usually said that the people who sold and bought the bonds knew how to do such a computation, and if they said that such a thing could be done that was all that I cared about. The marketplace always made the final determination as to the legitimacy of the information. If the marketplace was happy, people bought the bonds.

At the last minute, during conference committee time, Senator Pat Miller said that she was still dubious about the procedure and would feel better if there would be only twenty percent of the bonds issued each year, and no bonding after 1993. The caucus seemed to think that this idea had merit and so supported her suggestion. I had faith in the procedure as proposed, but felt such a restriction might slow down construction. On the other hand, I needed the votes to pass the report and accepted the recommendation of the caucus without much argument. The other conferees agreed and both chambers adopted the conference committee report.

Governor Orr wasted no time signing the bill and telling the Highway Department that he wanted to see dirt flying as soon as possible.

John Mutz lauded the legislature for having the courage to act. Representative Pat Bauer painted the entire idea as politically motivated. "Republicans are trying to get through this election by mortgaging the future," he opined in the media. Pat Bauer became a convert and a proponent several years later when Governor O'Bannon sought to have a second highway bonding proposal much like the 1988 legislation,

The first bonding in June of 1988 raised sixty-three million dollars. This offering was made in Indiana fiscal year 1988. The second bonding was in September 1988 for sixty-four million dollars. Even though these offerings were made only three months apart, the enacted legislation was being legally followed. The second bonding occurred in fiscal year 1989. (The fiscal year for the state of Indiana is from July 1 to the next June 30.)

By adhering to the law, the third bond issue could not be offered until July of 1989. The third issuance was key to the pork for District 36. Widening of Indiana 135 was to be funded with the third issue.

John Mutz did not win the election in November 1988 to become governor. Evan Bayh won. Bonding for roads, or for anything, did not fit Evan's philosophy of how government should be financed. He told me that he had reservations about continuing the bonding program and might not use the rest of the increased gas tax for bonding. He felt that the money should go into the Motor Vehicle Highway Fund and be shared with the cities and towns. Evan also did not want to continue any of Bob Orr's programs.

In December of 1989 I wrote a pre-session newsletter to my constituents stating that the governor in all probability would hold up the construction of Indiana 135. The story made a newspaper headline on the southside of Indianapolis and in the *Franklin Journal*. I fed the fires, hoping to put pressure on the new governor to change his mind.

Age and longevity and knowing where a few of the skeletons are buried helps immensely in government and politics. I knew a gentleman who was a key advisor and a major fundraiser for the Bayh campaign and was also the owner of a huge amount of acreage along Indiana 135 north of Smith Valley Road. Indiana 135 went through mostly corn fields in 1988, and those purchasing land along the road were not about to farm the land. New owners were land speculators and developers waiting for the population to grow in White River Township. I contacted my friend making the prediction that unless there was a third bond issue with new road construction, his investment would be a long term one, and his land holdings would not appreciate for several more years. I also suggested that he impress on the governor that this road was the key to the development of the area. I did not have to spell it out to my friend that his land would be worth ten times more than he had paid for it when there was a five-lane road running alongside his property.

Valid and persuasive arguments are difficult to ignore. The third offering of bonds by the Indiana Transportation Finance Authority was announced June l, 1990. This offering raised nearly seventy-five and a half million dollars. The prospectus was printed with a cover letter written by Governor Bayh outlining that the bonding was necessary for the Indiana College Savings Bonds. This may have been the excuse by which Bayh could legitimately put aside his reluctance for bonding for highway construction. Several other projects from around the state were included in that financing issue.

My friend sold the land, dug up an area that was polluted by a fertilizer transmission pipeline and dumped the dirt in an adjacent wetland. Fines were forthcoming, but it didn't bother him much. Land for shopping centers can sell for far more per acre than the fines imposed.

The widening of Indiana 135 was a boon to southern Indianapolis and to northern Johnson County, with the new road helping that county to become Indiana's second fastest growing county in the nineties.

As I said, I think that enactment of the finance authority and the one-cent tax increase was the most difficult legislation to pass in my career. I know the positive effects of the legislation have made a tremendous amount of difference, not only in Senate District 36, but around the rest of the state as well.

Presidents

When President Ronald Reagan came to Indianapolis on February 10, 1982 to address the combined houses of the General Assembly, it was a great moment in the legislature's history.

I did not have the opportunity to meet President Reagan. My recollections of the speech were that he was trying to sell the idea of establishing Enterprise Zones where possible. These zones would be located in run-down areas and would provide jobs near to the persons who were unemployed. Tax breaks would be the incentive for factories to locate in the zones.

The second memory of the President's speech was of Sam Donaldson. My assigned seat was in the visitor's balcony in the House of Representatives, and Sam was five or six seats to my left and a row closer to the front railing. Donaldson made no pretense of giving his undivided attention to the President. He made one call after another on his cellular telephone and since Sam's voice on television is forceful and booming most of those seated in the balcony were distracted and entertained thoughts of throwing the man over the balcony railing. I presume that Donaldson was miffed at being assigned a seat far away from the President. He seemed also to be showing his contempt for being surrounded by lowly Hoosiers.

During President Reagan's re-election campaign, Keith Bulen extended an invitation for Reagan to attend a fundraising speaking engagement in Indianapolis. Keith invited a small group of his friends to one of the downtown hotels to a sit down visit with the President. The atmosphere was informal and relaxed. Cocktails were served and each of us had the privilege of addressing an individual comment or question to the president of the United States. Reagan sat on the far left of a sofa. I sat on a chair immediately next to the sofa arm. My chair caused me to sit six or eight inches higher than the president. I hate to admit it, but, looking down on the top of Reagan's head, I could not help but wonder if he really used "coloring" on his hair as had been reported. Terrible thought. My hair is white. His hair had not one white one. I decided that the color of his hair was totally natural.

Keith Bulen revered Ronald Reagan, believing in the president as a man whose principles guided him and the United States through some difficult times. Reagan armed this country and made our ability to defend the country the top priority. Russia tried to keep up and found out that socialism was not the answer. Reagan is now beginning to get his just dues for bringing about the fall of the Berlin Wall and the re-organization of the Soviet Union.

I have met former Presidents Bush the elder and Nixon, very casually. I have pictures taken with both men. I admit that I took down all of the political photos from my clinic office wall following Nixon's resignation. I missed President George W.'s appearance in Indianapolis in May of 2003 but had previously corresponded with him when he was governor of Texas.

The year that Lyndon Johnson was the Democrat candidate for the presidency he addressed a huge crowd on the north steps of Monument Circle in downtown Indianapolis. I was attending a strategy meeting with the Goldwater for president leaders on the third floor of the Columbia Club on the circle. The day was warm and sunny. The meeting windows were open. We all tried to ignore the rally and the speech by the president. The windows finally had to be closed so that we could better plot the defeat of the candidate less than fifty yards away.

chapter 21

"Good Enough Never Is"

Politicians, like ballplayers who retire and then come back for one last hurrah, often find they've made a mistake. It happened to Keith Bulen.

He had been a member of the Indiana House of Representatives in 1961 and 1963. He decided to give it another try in 1990.

He honestly felt that he would be able to impart a lot of good political advice to the younger members of the House if he served one more term. Unfortunately, the House was controlled by a Democrat majority and the idea of Keith's being "an older soothing uncle" did not materialize.

During the previous legislative campaign in 1988, Keith had taken it upon himself to guide the election efforts of the Republican candidates in the House. He took charge of finding candidates for open seats and candidates to oppose Democrat incumbents. He almost guaranteed a Republican majority for the 1989 session.

To accomplish all of this in 1988, he called upon what were left of the old battle-tested Republican Action Committee team members from the late sixties and early seventies. He had also found a contributor with deep pockets and spent hours checking candidate budgets and allocating funds. Meetings were held ad nauseum. Quotas and timetables were assigned. A buddy system was organized pairing an older legislator with a novice hopeful. What, at one time, had worked so well in a county did not work statewide in 1988. The lightning had escaped the bottle and could not be re-captured.

The political juices began to flow again, and having had a taste of campaign fever in 1988, when a legislative seat opened up in a three-person district on the far southside of Marion County, Keith announced his intentions of becoming a candidate for the legislature in 1990. There may have been some grumbling in the Perry Township Republican ranks when he announced, but no one else sought to become a challenger.

Each of the candidates in that legislative district was successful in the fall election. But with being in the minority in the 1991 session, and being treated as a freshman legislator by some of his younger caucus members who had never heard of his exploits with the RAC, for him the session did not turn out as expected.

I did make him one of my co-authors on the bill that legalized pari-mutuel in Indiana and he considered that to be his legislative crowning achievement. I was not invited by the governor to the bill signing, but Keith was. He kept the pen that Governor Bayh had used for the signing in a very conspicuous place in his home and pointed it out on each of my visits.

He enjoyed the two-year term but never became comfortable in that setting.

After moving to Valle Vista in Johnson County, he took on the persona of a fabled Italian Don. He gave up socializing but looked forward to visitations. He lived down Main Street, a short distance from Jonathan Byrd's Cafeteria in Greenwood. A favorite lady attendant there guarded one particular table in the cafeteria and saved it only for "Mr. Bulen." Bulen would go there for lunch several times a week and she would make sure that no one else sat at that particular table before his arrival. For those that wanted to talk with him, he loved to say, "OK let's have lunch. Be at Jonathan Byrd's at 11:20 AM." Reporters, senators, mayors, acolytes, it made no difference. This was now his style.

His new home in Greenwood was large enough (4,000 square feet) to accommodate and display all of the trophies that Abercrombie had amassed. Wall space was plentiful. Every available foot of space was covered with photos that he had saved throughout the years. Photos from high school, IU, posing with dignitaries, action shots—walls and walls of Bulen. Testimonials and Sagamore of the Wabash honors abounded. He even saved the Sagamore of the Wabash that Governor Whitcomb had given him at a private party in

Chicago. Keith had said he would never take one from Whitcomb, but Ed gave it to him unexpectedly. The date of the issuance of the Sagamore was for two years earlier. Evidently, both of these men wanted to avoid each other.

His new life style was written up in the national media by both John Apple and David Broder. Cafeteria power lunches and all.

Keith's grown daughters took up more and more of his time. He became something of a gourmet cook in preparing lunches for one daughter to take to work. Fancy things, far from baloney sandwiches. I would visit for lunch and he would go all out fixing a meal that was really great.

In remarks made at the Memorial Service after Keith's death, Mitch Daniels, Jr. who was the director of the budget for President George W. Bush, said, "Not by accident did the phrase 'Bulen operation' become a part of the local vocabulary. To those of you standing up today [in the funeral home], that's no accident either. Keith planned this event, and he always taught his advance men to pick a hall that was a little too small for the crowd you expected. When Keith pulled out the yellow legal pad, you knew it was going to be done right. I'm fond of the saying 'Good enough never is.' With Bulen, perfect was almost good enough.

"But after his tirades and the tongue-lashings, after the convention, or election or the banquet or the weekend was over, everyone involved knew he had been a part of something special, something first-rate and, almost always, something victorious.

"With Keith in charge, everybody got a task, a title, a ribbon, a name-badge, a committee assignment. Everybody understood that this campaign, and therefore the Republican Party, and therefore the fate of our city, our country, our state, and therefore the future of the United States and all of the Western civilization, depended, on them, by God. They all went away knowing they were somebody, they were important, they were part of something much bigger than themselves. So they damn well better come through. And, over and over, they did. Eagerly. Relentlessly. Overwhelmingly. Joyfully.

"Keith had class. Keith had class when I first knew him. Keith had class in all of the days that I knew him. Keith Bulen kept and maintained that class, no matter how difficult his final days were, to the very end."

Letter to Senator Richard Lugar — 1990

The Honorable Richard G. Lugar, presently a United States senator from Indiana, is a remarkable man and one of the more intelligent individuals on earth. I cannot say enough superlatives about Dick Lugar and his ability.

My introduction to Dick during the 1967 Marion County legislative campaign was very casual. Keith Bulen thrust him into the campaign structure and introduced him to me as an assistant issues person or some such designation.

Later I was able to participate in his selection as the Republican nominee for Mayor of Indianapolis. He and his wife, Char, were particular friends of our family during his tenure as mayor. He has continued to be a friend during his years in Washington, D.C.

Though his face is familiar in most of the capitols of the world, and though he has attained the rank of being considered as a statesman, Dick Lugar's background and interests are not much different than any of the rest of us.

The following letter was written to him on my birthday in 1990, reminding the senator of days and events gone by.

July 16, 1990

Dear Dick:

I am beginning to believe that it is a sign of aging when one begins remembering happy occasions out of the past.

Last evening, the family gathered for my birthday celebration. I had just replaced the outside basketball backboard and rim. One of the presents was a new basketball. Plain old basketball, not even endorsed by Larry Bird. Naturally, the evening gravitated to a shootaround with some one on one. Two sons, a son-in-law and two grandsons.

A couple of skinned knees brought back the memory of such a happening twenty-three years ago. A surprise birthday party commemo-

rating a fortieth. Such luminaries as Lugar, Mutz, Ruckelshaus, Bulen, et. al. were present.

If I recall, cigars were even in abundance. David Borst remembers that he accidentally caused a bloody nose to an eventual United States senator. I had forgotten, but for a seven year old at that time, it left an impression. Anyway, he still thinks about it. I guess that we all are destined to become famous for something or the other in our lives.

I am going to Honduras in August, just for the heck of it. If I become an incident, I shall call.

Sincerely,

Note: Lugar by 1967 had slowed down some on the basketball court. He had a nice set shot but couldn't go to his left.

chapter   22

Full-day Kindergarten

Frank O'Bannon's campaign for governor in 1996 and his re-election bid in 2000 emphasized his desire to institute mandatory full-day kindergarten in Indiana. No one denied that a full day was an enhancement for early education for the child, but the state school funding formula provided state support for only half a day. Lack of funding was the prime deterrent for full-day kindergarten. If the school corporation wanted to provide children in the area with a full day program, the individual corporation then had to find a method of financing the service. Twice as many teachers would be needed and twice as many classrooms would be required. On a voluntary basis, about forty of the school corporations in Indiana were full day, with Evansville as the largest school district to offer the program.

Along with the full-day, half-day discussion was the child's date-of-month controversy, which was a factor in determining the child's eligibility for attending the first grade. And while most states have a cut off date of September 1, Indiana's cut off date was in June. Any child born after the June date would have to wait until the following year to begin the first grade. Indiana had changed this date frequently over the years and now stood alone against the rest of the country. Indiana had the earliest cut off birth date of all of the states.

The selected date had nothing to do with education and had all to do with financing. Going to a September date would allow for an increase of twenty-five percent more children to be enrolled in the first grade. This would be a one-time occurrence but to some of the corporations it would represent a significant expense.

Originally I supported the full-day kindergarten program and opposed changing the cut off birth date. I had asked the superintendent of schools in the Metropolitan School District of Perry Township, Dr. Doug Williams, to survey all of the kindergarten and first grade teachers in the township as to whether or not they felt that a later birth date would be advantageous to the child's educational development. The results surprised me. Practically all of those surveyed opposed the September birth date. They felt that the June date should be retained and that changing the date to September would force children who were not mature enough to start school earlier than they should.

The governor and his wife spent many hours visiting elementary schools and espousing the benefit of early education. O'Bannon's number one campaign promise of 1996 was to fund full-day kindergarten. It was not addressed until the legislative session of 1999. Governor O'Bannon then made an all out push to include funding in the biennial budget for full-day kindergarten. O'Bannon flew around the state in 1999 trying to gather support for the appropriation. The amount needed for the two-year state support would have been a little over $210 million. Interestingly, the support that he generated from the public appearances was negligible. The budget crunch was so severe that the school people felt they would rather use any new money available for summer school programs or for other types of educational offerings.

The attitude of Bob Margraff and the Indiana State Teacher's Association, which he headed, had always been to make sure that there had been enough money appropriated for teacher's salary increases, and if there was any extra money left in the state general fund, then the ISTA would support state funding for full-day kindergarten. My conversations with Margraff came down to his protecting the money that was appropriated for the salaries of the teachers and had nothing to do with enhancement of education. Margraff, a former alter boy and graduate from St. Charles Academy, in Columbus, Ohio, did his job extraordinarily well.

Authorization and funding for full-day kindergarten made it through the budgetary process right up to conference committee time. On the second day of negotiations, during a break in budget negotiations, I was confounded when Representative Bauer told me that the issue of full-day kindergarten no longer needed to be considered and that the conferees should move along to other items of the budget.

My first question to Bauer was, "Is the governor in agreement?" Bauer responded "yes" and assured me that the governor was in agreement with not including the full-day provision into the new budget. Bauer said that one of the governor's reasons for now not considering the issue was that it would overwhelm the fiscal resources of the state during the coming budget cycle. My initial conversation with Bauer was private. My follow-up conversation with Senator Morris Mills was also private and he was as taken aback as I had been. When the full conference committee re-convened and this decision was announced, those representing the governor were more shocked than I had been. There was an immediate scurrying around and in not too many minutes another recess in the proceedings was called. I assume that Bauer was called to the governor's office to explain his actions in what appeared to be his unilaterally giving up state funding for full-day kindergarten. The matter was dropped when negotiations on the budget resumed. The subject became moot and has not been given more than a cursory look by the General Assembly since that time.

Bauer did condescend to move the birth date forward one month in a later conference committee session.

chapter   23

Tax Restructuring

The special session of the 2002 legislature was—special.

The state was under a court order to redo its age-old method of real property assessment. The biennial budget was over appropriated, normal amounts of money were not being collected, and the state was in an economic recession. Indiana had suffered the loss of over 100,000 jobs during the previous two years and commerce in Indiana was not competitive mainly because of an outdated corporate tax structure. Attempts to correct these three problems in the regular session were unsuccessful.

The governor and lieutenant governor had a fiscal plan. The House Democrats devised their own fiscal plan. The Senate Republicans presented a totally different fiscal program. There was a similarity between all three plans put forth but each emphasized one facet of the overall problem that the other did not. House Democrats wanted to correct the budget woes while the Senate Republicans were more interested in mitigating the effects of the new court-ordered reassessment. The governor's plan sought more money to spend and to provide for a huge general fund surplus while restructuring corporate taxes.

Even though discussions for property tax relief and corporate tax restructuring came to a head in the 2002 session, the genesis had occurred years before. Most recently in 1996 when Frank O'Bannon and his opponent Steve Goldsmith campaigned for the office of governor, both vowed to lower property taxes and to rearrange the unfair corporate tax structure. Governor O'Bannon, the winner, established a blue ribbon task force to study the various fiscal matters.

The task force met monthly from April of 1987 through November of 1988. In addition, ten public informational meetings were held throughout the state, all under the leadership of Dr. Kurt Zorn and Dr. John Huie.

O'Bannon had initially vowed to accept the recommendations of the task force and said he would support any and all changes that were offered. Later, when his pollsters realized that a tax increase might be recommended, O'Bannon recanted his pledge and said he would only "consider" the recommendations. This took all of the steam out of the proceedings with the final report being only a series of already known suggestions. Some were credible and some not so credible, but with no structural program for action. In the end, the only task force members willing to recommend a thorough overhaul of the Indiana system of taxation were the legislative members who represented each of the four caucuses, Bauer, Hume, Espich and Borst. The lay members had been appointed by the governor and were protecting their own turf without thought of future benefit to the state. A vote was never taken even for the "advisory only" report.

Even earlier than the O'Bannon administration and in the nineties, the Republican Senate had passed individual legislation that would have aided economic development in Indiana. Among the stipulations were the total elimination of the inventory assessment and taxation, enhanced credits for research and development, full state funding for public schools and phasing out of the corporate tax. None of the Senate-passed proposals became law.

This background of study and research set the stage for one more try in a special legislative session. Trying to project the new statewide assessment procedure was a most difficult task. The Indiana Supreme and Tax Courts had ordered assessments to be conducted with a "fair market value" technique. A Purdue University economist, Dr. Larry DeBoer, predicted that the assessments of residential property would increase dramatically, and some real property might easily double or triple in assessed value under the market value system. A doubling of the assessed value might not mean a doubling of homeowner taxes paid, but try telling that to the taxpayer. If there is one issue that individual legislators are sensitive to, that would be the complaint from voters about the property tax they have to pay. Reassessment became issue number one.

Faced with the possible anger of the constituents, legislators did not hesitate long in increasing the sales tax by one cent when they understood that all of the new money collected would be used for homeowner property tax relief. With the state assuming sixty percent of school general fund costs, the taxes on all real property would be lessened. Those paying the increased sales tax may not understand the program, but hopefully when reassessment is completed some real estate tax bills will be lower. The legislature in its wisdom did not immediately increase the sales tax on July 1 but waited until after the November election. The effective date for the new tax was December 1 and made Christmas shopping even merrier.

In a way, restructuring the corporate tax structure was an easier task. The holy grail of tax restructuring was to eliminate the inventory tax. Many schemes had been advanced through the years: local option, phase-downs, phase-ins, etc. The legislators finally decided just to get rid of the tax. Individual counties were given the option of opting out of the inventory tax at any time before the complete moratorium on inventory assessment in 2007. Taxes are collected on inventories at the same rate as taxes are collected on real property. Since all of the money goes for local governmental efforts, fourteen of the counties not having a lot of inventory to assess, opted out of the system for 2003. Instead of the auto dealers having a pre-inventory discount on their cars, dealers in Morgan County advertise as being in an "Inventory Free Zone," with prices lower than anywhere else.

To further Indiana's competitive place in economic development and job creation, the legislature eliminated the corporate gross tax and the supplemental corporate gross tax. To make these moratoriums and eliminations a fiscal wash, the adjusted corporate gross tax was increased. These legislative actions have made Indiana competitive once again in the marketplace.

The amount of new money necessary to balance the state's budget was a constant source of debate throughout the session. Some legislators wanted just enough to eke through the biennium. At the other extreme were those who wanted to re-establish a billion dollar state general fund surplus. All parties held to their philosophy until the waning hours of the second from the last day of the special session. There was a loose consensus that the tax on a package of cigarettes would be increased and that the riverboat casino gaming profits would be taxed at a higher rate. The governor essentially lowered his expectations of increased revenue and the Senate Republicans agreed to increase the tax on cigarettes more than they had originally planned.

With the final increase on cigarettes of forty cents a pack, for a total of fifty-five and a half cents, Indiana still taxes cigarettes less than surrounding states, excepting Kentucky. Ohio and Illinois are at about a dollar a pack and Kentucky is at three cents. This disparity is not good for the southern Indiana convenience stores and makes for crowded bridges as the Indiana people go back and forth across the river.

The riverboats were assessed an additional $300 million dollars with a new graduated tax structure. Graduations affect the boats that have been more successful than average by having them to pay increased amounts of their profits to the state. The legislature, in a trade-off mode, allowed for dockside gaming. To most legislators this provision was, in their minds, not extending gaming but was seen as more of a consumer-friendly feature. Dockside allows the patrons to come and go on the boats at their convenience. There are no two-hour gaming periods anymore. I had tried to have the gamers refer to this new method of entrance and egress as flexible boarding. It seemed to me that the average citizen conjured up the vision of people actually shooting craps and playing blackjack on the dock outside of the boat. The terms flexible boarding and freedom of access never did catch on.

Passage of the final package in the Senate was difficult. The most critical of the second reading amendments was defeated on the floor. Almost all of the senators thought that the end of the special session was in sight and began discussing when the governor would call the legislators back for another try. At this legislative low point, a dinner-time recess was called. I too thought that the legislative game was probably over. But, as I have said in retrospect, adjourning to Shula's and crying into three Guinness beers does wonders for the spirit. A type of rejuvenation.

When the Senate reconvened, I presented two successive amendments. The first raised the cigarette tax and the second defeated the hated brainstorm of mine that imposed a franchise tax on Indiana corporations. At least the board was cleared, and I could say that something progressive was acted upon. Minutes after these amendments were passed, the governor called and wanted to confer with Senator Garton and me. The two of us entered into negotiations with the governor and Lieutenant Governor Joe Kernan. Over the next hour several meetings were held, the final form for property tax relief, corporate tax restructuring, and enhancement of the state general fund was agreed on. Minor changes were made to the Senate package and the legislation was approved by a vote of thirty-three to fifteen.

The next day, Saturday, the House met to vote on the Senate version of the legislation. The vote would be to agree with the Senate changes to HB 1001ss and to not send the bill to a conference committee. Interest groups that had either been left out of HB 1001ss as it passed the Senate or were not accommodated as much as they wanted by the bill's provisions were walking the halls of the House in full strength. The House members were besieged on all sides by lobbyists, both for the bill's passage and for the bill's defeat. A lobbyist particularly friendly with a House member was hired by the day to exert his charms. The major law firms had positions on both sides. A House member might have been talking to lobbyists from the same firm but hearing two different stories. There was even one lobbyist present who had been hired by both sides (he left early but came back after the final vote).

There were two roll call votes taken in the House on HB 1001ss. For the uninitiated or casual observer, the first vote taken by Speaker Gregg did not make a whole lot of sense. A diehard proponent watching the proceedings must have thought about having a heart attack. For the experienced watcher the first vote by the House was a test vote. Neither House caucus wanted the legislation to fail. Everyone recognized that the legislation was well written and had been well thought out. This was legislative history in the making for the state of Indiana. Neither caucus wanted the onus of being a member of the political party that had killed legislation that was universally accepted by the governor, by business, by agriculture and even by labor at the last minute.

The lobbyists representing the gaming interests finally decided that this was not the legislation to defeat and ceased their attempts to kill the legislation.

The second House vote was conclusive. Property tax relief, corporate tax restructuring and budget enhancement awaited the governor's signature. The winners will be the citizens of the state. Legislation such as HB 1001ss cannot be evaluated in just the near future. Five to ten years from now the economists will look back to 2002 and rate the product of the session.

Two other winners were the speaker and the House minority leader, neither of who voted in favor of the legislation, but who somehow were selected by *Governing Magazine* as the co-winners of the national legislator of the year because of their progressive and outstanding leadership.

Gamers in 2002

There is not much to comment about regarding the extension of gaming during the 2002 regular session. Complete dockside gaming, no increase on the gross receipts tax on riverboats, legalization of hundreds of pull tab machines and casino gaming in Orange County was the agenda for the gamers. Money and arrogance were in abundance.

I had been assured by Senator Garton that I would be the conferee on all fiscal matters. Early in the regular session I made known that there would be no gaming legislation in any fiscal bill unless I had approved. Garton announced that he would not allow any gaming legislation to be combined with other legislation. The gamers were not awed by either announcement. I was told by two of the gamers in tandem that in the end I would be removed from all of the conference committees and would be publicly embarrassed, by design, because of their power and strategy. What the gamers did not take into account was that there were a number of Senate members who realized that there were other senators in the majority caucus who would, and could, stand up to the monetary onslaught of the riverboat and racetrack lobbyists. This resolve of the "silent majority" during the special session proved to be crucial.

The basic strategy of the gamers was to pass the expansion of gaming, especially the legalization of pull-tab machines, through the House and create a coalition of sixteen Democrats and however many Republicans it took to secure passage of their programs in the Senate. The number of Republicans needed would be less than half of those that made up the majority, ten out of thirty-two. The strategy didn't work.

Someone counted 106 individuals registered with the secretary of state as being interested in lobbying for gaming. The third floor bar in the Columbia Club seemed to be the headquarters of the prime gaming lobbyists. One visit to the bar for me was enough. Even my appearance was not enough to even slow down the appointment schedules of the head gamers from their supplicants. Maybe it only happened on that one day.

chapter   24

Abuse of Power

Frank O'Bannon

Heads of government such as presidents, governors or mayors are sometimes faced with most unusual situation, ones that call for drastic remedial actions. In rare cases, they sometimes bend a law a little, usually to benefit the public and that action may not harm anyone. By so doing, the problem is solved. Most of those involved know why it happened and accept the indiscretion.

Frank O'Bannon not only bent an Indiana law but he fractured the law. Governor O'Bannon cited an obscure bill that I had sponsored in 1981 during the OPEC oil crisis and proclaimed a sales tax collection holiday on each gallon of gasoline. He made his announcement in June 2000.

Governor O'Bannon declared the moratorium on a "fuel emergency," though there was none in Indiana. His logic seemed to be that the less you charged for a gallon of gasoline, the less gasoline the public would buy. The duration of the sales-tax-free gasoline would be for a period of sixty days, with an option of another sixty days, all without legislative approval.

What made this action so blatant was that his campaign for re-election was just beginning full force. I characterized all of this as a twelve-million-dollar, taxpayer funded, media buy for the O'Bannon for governor re-election campaign. I was also quoted as saying, "What they've done goes beyond a liberal interpretation of the law. They're screwing around with the public's money."

A portion of my letter to the editor of *The Indianapolis Star*:

> *I hope that the governor does have the general public in mind in creating this "energy emergency" that will eliminate only the sales tax portion on gasoline and diesel fuel, but not the state gallonage tax. I hope that his actions are not purely political. It would be a shame to realize that the state treasury was being used to further his political ambitions.*
>
> *As I write this letter, the price of gasoline on Madison Avenue is $1.56.9 per gallon.*
>
> *This means that a gallon of gas is twenty-one cents cheaper this week than it was last week.*
>
> *Somehow, someway, the governor, the legislature, Congress, the president, should be concerned with the extreme fluctuations with price and whether or not the producers and refiners are playing games with the people of Indiana.*

Evan Bayh

In 1990 I and other Republicans accused Governor Evan Bayh of using his power as governor to create a new technique in order to ignore legislative and legal intent. Bayh, we thought, made a unilateral decision that breached the prescribed process for spending profits from the state lottery.

Twenty-nine counties in Indiana that had been subjected to floods and tornadoes were declared disaster areas by President Bush. Bayh was seeking to divert funds from the lottery as matching money for infrastructure re-building. I agreed that the thought was worthwhile, but the technique left a lot to be desired. The amount involved would be about three million dollars but that was not the point.

Some of the problems associated with his actions were pointed out in a letter I wrote to him on June 20, 1990.

Dear Governor Bayh:

I have just been made aware of how you intend to capitalize on a certain portion of the proceeds from the state lottery without legislative approval. I understand the theory behind allowing the Lottery Commission to treat this donation as if it were advertising and promotion incentives or public relations.

Obviously, you are condoning a technique that could easily have a widespread ramification in the future. You are establishing a precedent that certainly could end up being an embarrassment to you or to the state of Indiana. With concurrence of the lottery director, any governor will be able to spend money in any manner that he or she may want under the guise as mentioned before. In theory, you, as governor, could spend the $100 million available in the Build Indiana Fund in any manner that you might want.

What seems so strange to me about this proposed technique is that there are several legitimate ways that the governor of the state of Indiana could pursue. I am sure the State Board of Finance would be willing to transfer some of the contingency fund money for this purpose. The legislature in 1991 could simply replenish the money through a special appropriation. This is the way that emergencies have been handled by governors in the past.

Your reasoning for approaching the matter in this manner stretches the imagination. You may not be skating on thin ice, but I would think that something somewhere is not correct or possibly legal.

I would imagine that the legislation creating the lottery will be addressed during the next session. Your administration had asked me to revise the legislation in certain ways, and now I see that your contemplated action is possible because of the amendatory language. Guaranteed percentage returned to the state of Indiana, within the legislation is almost assured.

Government is complicated enough without having to conjure up a new technique that one knows is not quite right. My advice, if it had been asked, would certainly have been to have proceeded the tried and true way.

Sincerely,

My advice was not sought nor was it considered. The director of the budget did allow that a precedent might have been set, but it was all for a worthy cause, he said.

chapter 25

The Build Indiana Fund

Sometimes spending state funds can be almost as difficult as collecting them. It was that way when profits from the state lottery began mounting.

I was aware that the lottery would generate significant profits for the state. Most states with state-run lotteries had dedicated a portion of the state levied taxes for education. In most cases this was simply a façade. The state would make a show of allocating a portion of the lottery proceeds for educational purposes, but when the budget finally was written, education had no more money than it ordinarily would have had. Monies would be moved around. Something of a shell game.

In most states, lottery taxes were being integrated and included in the spending flow. The base spending of the state increased annually, causing a continual reliance on the lottery taxes. Some states created scholarships for the university undergraduates. Others simply included these new monies in their general fund.

I was determined that the passage of the lottery legislation in Indiana would include at least two main components. First, that no portion of the new monies would be legislatively dedicated to any new program or for any ongoing state-supported effort in which the base of the state general fund would be increased. By building up the base of any general fund budget, one is obligated to repeatedly fund that portion, and usually to apply inflationary increases each year. I would stress that none of the new monies would be allocated by this legislation for specific programs including education.

The second component was that the money would be set aside in a protected fund, and only the legislature through budgetary appropriation could allocate. I did not think it wise to allow a governor to be able to somehow transfer any of the money without first going through the legislative branch.

In previous years, during the debate over the constitutional amendment authorizing a lottery, a large percentage of the public received the impression that all of the lottery profits were to be dedicated to elementary education. Even today, I receive correspondence wondering why schools need more money, when they are receiving plenty from the lottery. In the dozens and dozens of appearances that I've made in support of amending the constitution, I've stressed that the new taxes received would be encumbered and appropriated by the legislature. The legislature would have the option of enhancing education funding, but was not bound by any proposed legislation.

The signed legislation did contain a few dedicated appropriations. An appropriation was made in each budget cycle to both the Public Teachers Retirement Fund and the Police and Firemen Retirement Funds. The stability of each of these retirement funds was in jeopardy. The appropriation certainly did not make much of a dent in the liabilities of the funds, but the appearance and effort were worthwhile. Bond rating entities in New York that come to Indiana once a year and do interviews and surveys for the purpose of establishing Indiana state bond ratings would refer to this as an extremely positive attempt by Indiana to solve a deficiency. The appropriation gave the rating people the hope to cling to that was needed to assure themselves that Indiana would someday find a way in which to pay for its future pension obligations.

The integrity of the police and firemen pensions has always been a local concern. Payments to retirees are made by local governments. Still, the small amount of money dedicated was welcomed by the legislators. Less money needed for pension payments, less money needed from the property owners. Ergo, a property tax reduction. Sounds simple, but it works.

A second major concern was Federal Environmental Protection Agency edicts and their effects on the cities and towns: mainly the building of sanitary sewers and the treatment of raw sewage. Governmental units were under court order to provide for mandatory improvements. For a few years, the federal government supplied either block grants or matching grant money, matching the community's effort. Later the federal government reduced its involvement, which was then picked up by the state. Still later, the federal government eliminated matching money for this program and the local cities had to supply a greater portion of the cost. Some towns might build a sewer and treatment plant and charge the users over $100 dollars a month, with most of the charge going mainly for bond and interest repayment. Usage of part of the lottery revenues was for a dedicated yearly appropriation to pay for a portion of the new sewer expenses, and thus reduce the monthly charges for the ultimate users.

The final draft of the legislation, in addition to the lottery, created two other state supervised and licensed gaming subjects. Pari-mutuel horse racing was legalized, with various taxes being imposed. Bingo, raffles, etc. were defined in the statute, and the taxes to be collected were set out in the law. Within the over-all bill, a separate fund was authorized to collect the monies from each of the three gaming components. Once collected and deposited in the individual funds, these funds then would be emptied and co-mingled into a main fund. The legislature would be able to appropriate money from any of the funds at anytime.

The funds were named the Lottery Fund, the Bingo Fund, and the Horse Racing Fund. The ultimate fund was designated as the Indiana Infrastructure and Pension Relief Fund. This name adequately described what the proceeds of these gaming revenues were to be used for.

Nowhere in the legislation did the term Build Indiana Fund appear.

That name was supplied by Governor Evan Bayh or aides Fred Nation or Bill Moreau or someone in the public relations department on the statehouse second floor. Governor Bayh and his administration were famous for changing names. Bob Orr's A-Plus education program was dismantled, put back together with the same pieces, and was referred to as something new with a new name. The fund name change was the only alteration in the voluminous legislation that the governor's office did make. But I think the name change was positive. Build Indiana Fund (BIF) is a lot easier to say than Indiana Infrastructure and Pension Relief Fund.

Written into the legislation were procedures for the selection, funding and verification of expenditures for projects selected as recipients of the money. I had written both bills in the spring and summer of 1988. I thought that John Mutz would be the next governor. Still, both bills were written apolitically. I wanted to make sure that the governor, no matter what the political affiliation, had the supervisory and post-audit powers to carry out the philosophy of the legislation.

I did not want to create additional bureaucracy. I felt that the Budget Agency and the Director of the Budget Agency were the most qualified people in state government which could supervise the provision of the BIF. Frank Sullivan was appointed Director of the Budget Agency following the governor's election that fall. He followed the provisions of the BIF legislation to an exact T.

The legislation required the governor to appoint a bi-partisan panel of interested citizenry to serve as an advisory committee. In addition, four legislators were appointed to the committee, one from each of the House and Senate caucuses. The legislation stated that the chairman of the panel would be the director of the budget. In this way the panel would have an uneven number of members with the political makeup favoring the party that the governor represented.

The panel was convened following the implementation of the lottery. A small but significant amount of money was available in the fund after the first months of the lottery. That first amount was insignificant by today's standards, but still was enough to work with. Early on, the panel agreed on broad outlines as to what kind of projects might be considered for partial funding. Full funding for any project, no matter the cost, was out of the question. The panel felt that if the local entity did not think enough of the project to pay for a portion of the cost, the state would not regard it to be high on any priority list. Roads and streets and bridges were out. Township volunteer fire departments would have to seek donations from others. The bill, by design, omitted any reference to township government. Not-for-profit organizations were to be excluded.

Two-thirds of the requests had to do with either how to clean up sewage or how to obtain pure water for a community. Remodeling buildings was a strong second, with park improvement following. The panel developed a grading system, and with help from Sullivan and his staff, allocated the available monies in a most satisfactory manner.

Sullivan and his staff took if from there. The legislation also provided for reimbursement for any Indiana governmental time and expenditures when working with the Budget Agency in validating or doing any research having to do with the disbursement of Build Indiana funds. The agency in many cases did an on-site examination of a proposed project. As the projects got underway, the agency would only reimburse expenses on actual paid invoices, never on the premise that the state money was a down payment. The final payment never was made until all of the expenses were added up and the state's percentage share was determined. As a member of the panel I applauded the efforts of the Budget Agency to keep a tight rein on the designated projects.

In later years, some of the components of the BIF language were changed, but not the basic structure that secure applications, disburses monies and inspects the final form of the project.

The legislation, once implemented, worked very well the only time that the law was followed. The economy slowed and tax collections were down, so Governor Bayh detoured the BIF into the general fund. The Senate defeated several House attempts to permanently co-mingle the BIF money with the state general fund money. Governor Bayh later did take credit for supplemental funding for each and every school district in the state simply because a small amount of the BIF money was used in a small way for education.

In the meantime, Bayh thought the state was going to run out of money and asked in both a regular and in a special session to have a conglomeration of taxes increased. He was rebuffed in the Senate by his loyal opposition. Time proved the Senate correct. Indiana did not need additional money for its budget. Maybe the Republicans should have allowed Bayh to have received the tax increase he requested, because later "never having raised taxes" became his theme song and the cornerstone of a future campaign.

Later in the 1990s the conference committees on the budget began adding their own projects to be paid for by BIF. Some could be categorized as reasonable because such action freed up general fund monies. The chairman of Ways and Means, in his individual thinking, thought of all of the BIF money as "belonging" to the legislators. He would assign a dollar amount to each of the members of his caucus. Instead of going through a panel, each legislator would select a project or several projects, if they fell within the dollar amount that had been assigned. Could be for a township. Could be for a non-profit organization. Could be a fake group, so long as there was a mailing address.

It took no time until the members of the Senate heard about divvying up the BIF. "Me too" prevailed. In numbers, fire trucks seemed to top the requests. Fire trucks can be very expensive. Senator Morris Mills refused to take the time and go through the many requests and simply set aside one million dollars in the budget from the BIF for fire trucks—any community that had made a request needed to be on the ball, because the requests were honored on a first come, first served basis by the state budget agency.

In a blatant show of partisanship, the Republicans in the House were denied participation by the majority Democrats. What made it more galling was that the minority caucus in the Senate was provided for in dollar amounts, but to a lesser degree than were the members of the majority. To prevent a walkout by the Republican House minority, I struck a compromise with the chairman of Ways and Means. An extra authorization of BIF monies was inserted in the final version of the budget by the conference committee. All was well until later in the year when most of the conference committee members, now on the Budget Committee, were told by Chairman Bauer that no such agreement had been struck. The extra amount of BIF funds were liberally distributed to House Democrats while the minority members were left with little more than empty bags.

Splitting the proceeds of BIF proved that ultimate greed by legislators still exists. By now, the BIF was loaded with cash. Most of the revenues from the lottery had been used to reduce the excise tax liability of the owners of automobiles. I had written successful legislation that had reduced the excise tax by ten percent. The following session House Speaker Paul Mannweiler thought that this was such a good idea that he wanted to completely wipe out the tax. Fiscally this was impossible. We settled on the Senate version, which reduced the tax in all categories fifty percent and eliminated the tax altogether on older, smaller and less expensive cars. These actions used up most of the lottery income. The admission tax and adjusted gross tax from the riverboat revenues were coming into the state coffers in an ever-increasing rate. There was little profit from horse racing and even less from bingo. The three funds, representing the three gaming components, were now eliminated and any gaming money was accruing to the BIF.

For the state budget cycle of 2001–2003, the division of the BIF funds became even more contentious. Representative Bauer determined that the House members would receive forty-one million to divide amongst themselves. This was in addition to some money for Lake County and several others of the House Democrats. At this stage, representing the Senate, I said that the Senate should have forty-one million dollars to split up among their constituent communities. There was no objection. Somehow or another, it was decided that each of the majority members would receive an allotment of about $900,000, the minority members somewhat less. It was suggested to each of the senators that they should coordinate with their House members, representing the same geographic area, so there would be no overlapping projects selected. This cooperative coordination had rarely been done. There was more coordination between two or three geographically adjacent House members than occurred between House and Senate members. I sometimes wonder if the member of either body really knows much about his area counterpart from across the hall.

All of the projects took up many printed pages in the budget bill. Betty Cockrum, the budget director, threw up her hands and avowed that proper supervision of all of the projects would not be manageable. That said—there was to be no management. Which projects went before the Budget Committee for approval depended on whether or not you were a member or an advisor to the committees. Caucus stature helped. The list for approval was made up by the legislators with little input from the administration.

Jealousies among legislators reared its ugly head at times. The media began questioning some of the procedures and some of the projects. Questions were directed at township projects and especially towards those for non-for-profits.

Having been involved in the legislative process for the years that I have, I had a feeling that something was not quite right. Having watched members of the Senate compete for and question the BIF allocations, I could tell that a few corners might be cut. There is the feeling, if money is involved, basic human frailties come to the surface and are exposed. I did not want to see anyone in the legislature be accused of any improper actions. I wrote a letter and had it hand delivered to Governor O'Bannon before the start of the 2001 session.

January 8, 2001

The Honorable Frank O'Bannon
Governor, State of Indiana

Dear Frank:
There is still a procedure in the Indiana Code on how to allocate and
appropriate the Build Indiana Funds. These are the funds that are the profit
to the State of Indiana from various gaming activities.

The law was written and agreed upon by the legislature to expressly use
these gaming funds in such a manner that they would not be wasted, frit-
tered away, and to be used for the benefit of the infrastructure of the state of
Indiana.

The original technique did work. A committee is established, by present
law, to meet and receive applications, to investigate these applications, and
to authorize the chairman of the committee, who is the director of the state
budget agency, to approve these applications. The usage of the funds by this
committee and the approval of worthwhile projects did work. There was
also a follow-up to make sure the funds were used in the manner of which
they were asked.

I was a member of that original committee and participated in the pro-
ceedings. I was impressed in the manner in which deliberations were made.
I thoroughly recommend to you that this procedure be reinstated and fol-
lowed once again. The present manner of allocating Build Indiana funds by
the legislature is, at best, haphazard. It is most inefficient. The present tech-
nique lends itself to misuse, misappropriations and other sorts of mischief.
*   Sincerely,*

I sent copies of the letter to Garton, Bosma, Bauer, Buell, Espich, Simpson and Betty Cockrum and members of the Senate Finance Committee.

I feared that the governor and his budget director were being coerced into allocating the BIF in a way that was inappropriate. I wanted Governor O'Bannon to put his foot down, call a halt to the proceedings, refer to the law, and allocate the funds in a manner that was fair, equitable and above reproach. All of this fell on deaf ears. I can recall that there was only one conversation that was generated by the letter. And that was not with the governor.

Later in 2001, the investigations picked up. Media from all over the state tried to outdo each other. The political cartoons became tougher and more personal. The ACLU was heard from. I decided to try again, in case my January letter hadn't reached the inner sanctum:

July 2, 2001

The Honorable Frank O'Bannon
Governor, State of Indiana

Dear Frank:
I would think that the credibility of the individual legislative recommendations for Build Indiana funding could be easily ascertained. I would also think that the present law that was enacted in 1989 could be sufficient to be the basis of the review process for these Build Indiana recommendations.

As provided by law, the oversight committee should be activated by your office. I might also recommend that one of the lay members to be appointed by you could be Judge Frank Sullivan. Judge Sullivan, then budget director, implemented the present code in a most successful and non-contentious manner. This oversight committee would be charged to interpret the present code, especially as to funding and designated non-for-profit entities that might receive state funding. This was done before and could be a part of the procedure for the present recommendations.

Further, there is no question that additional personnel and additional time and effort need be taken to review application, to validating actual usage of money, to review invoices and to conduct on-site examinations. There should be enough monies within the Build Indiana appropriation to accomplish this task ...

Sincerely,

I wanted to make sure that more of the leadership knew of the present law and of this approach that could be taken. The letter was hand-delivered to the governor. Copies were sent to most everyone that I could think of.

Senator David Ford responded. Ford made a strong case for including township government and certain not-for-profits as being eligible for the BIF.

In the meantime, Senator Garton had appointed a Senate Task Force to investigate BIF procedures. I was to be the chairman and the members were Senators Johnson, Blade and Young. We actually had a meeting on August 28, 2001. I requested any information from Betty Cockrum and from Senator Bob Meeks, the Senate Republican appointee to the budget committee, regarding any communications to the senators about criteria for selecting BIF projects. There had been no communications or instructions from either the budget director or from Senator Meeks leaving the senators fairly flexible in their project selections.

The governor then did reply to one of my previous letters. I guess that the media was becoming more persistent. Some of the authorized and funded projects did not have the aura of invincibility. Or maybe I received the reply because I had circulated the previous letters to the media.

July 18, 2001
The Honorable Lawrence Borst
Indiana State Senate

Dear Senator Borst
Thank you for your letter of July 2, 2001, in which you made some suggestions with respect to the Build Indiana Fund (BIF) administrative procedures. As always, I appreciate your input on this important issue.

I hope you will find that the recommendations contained in the report from the state budget director, Betty Cockrum, and my decisions based upon those recommendations address some of the issues, that you have raised. Specifically, regarding the appropriations in the 2001 budget, we are addressing the funding of non-profit entities and providing additional personnel to review applications and establish procedures for tracking the use of money. However, we are not at this time calling for on-site examinations, without an additional appropriation from BIF for this purpose. We also did not want to assess the projects for the cost, nor did we feel we had statutory authority to do so. Therefore, we will be performing the oversight function for the BIF appropriations with existing personnel and existing budgets.

As for the BIF Review Committee, I have asked the legislature to look at

that committee to determine if its role had been properly defined. The com-
mittee is advisory only: it does not have an oversight role. If the legislature
wants to give the BIF Review Committee an oversight role, my staff and I
will certainly work with the authors and sponsors of such a bill. At this
time, however, I do not feel that it is timely to appoint the members of the
committee. The primary role of that committee is to assist in the recommen-
dation of items to be funded through the budget. Therefore, I believe that it
makes sense to wait until after the 2002 session to appoint that committee
for two reasons: First, as noted above, I hope the legislature will re-look at
the BIF Committee. Second, I want to direct the administrations time and
attention to implementing the current set of appropriations, before we start
working on the appropriations for 2003.

As always, I appreciate your counsel. Please continue to let me know your
views on the issues that face our state.

Sincerely,

Later, Speaker John Gregg issued a call to arms. *The Indianapolis Star* in
July reported the formation of the Senate Task Force, and the administration's interest, stating that "these reviews come in the wake of an investigation
by *The Indianapolis Star* which found that lawmakers are spending millions
of state dollars in contravention of the 1989 Build Indiana law. A commission, established by the law, is supposed to review all Build Indiana projects,
but it hasn't met in more than a decade. And the money is supposed to go
only to government units, but lawmakers give millions to non-profit groups
that are rarely audited by the state." This story also reported that "the FBI and
the Marion County prosecutor's office are conducting criminal investigations
into how this money was spent."

On August 28, 2001, the Senate Build Indiana Task Force issued the
following report:

The original reasoning, by Senator Garton, for establishing this task
force, has been significantly blurred by a multitude of decisions, subse-
quently made, by the governor and the State Budget Agency.

Early on, members of the Task Force, through individual telephone con-
versations, felt it imperative to ascertain if any guidelines or instructions
had been given to the Senate legislative members, to guide them in their rec-

ommendations for funding of individual BIF project. Communications, both written and verbal, were made to the offices of Governor O'Bannon and Senator Robert Meeks, subcommittee chairman for the budget of the Senate Finance Committee. Neither actually responded to the request, allowing the Task Force members to assume that the members of the Indiana Senate were not instructed in any way, to restrict their recommendations, for funding of BIF projects. Governor O'Bannon did respond with an outline of future activity in restricting BIF projects.

The president pro tem has declared that the enacting of the budget bill, does override the present law regarding BIF eligibilities and criteria. Therefore, with no stated criteria to individual senators, it is up to other entities to determine the validity of designating not-for-profits and township government as qualified recipients.

The Task Force notes that there have been several failed legislative attempts to amend the present law concerning the parameters of eligibility for BIF recipients. There is no developed consensus among the Task Force members as to recommended changes in the present law. There is general acceptance of the idea that all BIF projects, in some way, be post audited. Members of the Task Force cannot see any reason to exclude township government. Members of the Task Force generally think that any changes made in present law, should go through the legislative process and be strictly adhered to in the future.

So goes the saga of the Indiana infrastructure and Pension Relief Fund. The idea is still good. Thank goodness, I know of no legislators who got caught with their fingers in the cookie jar. Maybe a recipient or two. If there is not proper supervision and oversight in the future, some legislator will get caught up in the frenzy. The money should be limited. The applications should not be funneled through the legislators. Authorized funds should be paid only by the submission of an invoice. Authorized funds should be paid only in partial amounts with final settlement after an on-site inspection. Inclusion of not-for-profits should be open to legislative debate, and not automatic.

This whole scenario should be a good case study for future administrations—just follow the law that is on the books. Follow the law until the legislature makes changes.

chapter   26

Resolutions

The resolutions offered in a session must run in the hundreds—mostly those that honor something or someone. Not the kind that is debated at length, such as those designed to change the state constitution.

There are two simple types of resolutions that are offered on a daily basis—one a Joint Resolution that is offered in both chambers, the other, a Senate Resolution, is offered only in the Senate.

The most popular Joint Resolution is the one honoring a champion high school athletic team. Twelve basketball players, four coaches, a couple of managers, trainers, principal, superintendent and others that just happened to be there were all introduced. The senator in charge would usually fumble around and mispronounce the names, especially if the teams were from St. Joseph or Lake Counties, and might introduce the wrong player as the star of the team. He would compliment the group and then turn the introductions over to the coach. But Indiana now has class basketball and football. This means that each year, four championship basketball teams are introduced, and five for football. Introductions run on and on if two or more of the teams attend the legislature on the same day.

After the introduction, the president of the Senate asks for further discussion. Two types of senators then jump out of their seats seeking recognition from the president. One represents a portion of the school district that produced the championship team. The second is the one who represents the school that lost in the state final to the team appearing in the Senate. Normally the second speech ends with "wait till next year."

Football championship teams are awesome. Ben Davis and Penn high schools have won the big school titles the most, Ben Davis with seven titles and Penn five. Suddenly there are more football players lined up than Purdue or Ohio State have on scholarship. Dick Dullaghan, Ben Davis coach, must bring his J-V and ninth grade teams with him. There is not enough space for all of the kids even with the line of players beginning from one of the doors just inside of the Senate, continuing into the chamber, then snaking around the front of the Senate, and then running out the other Senate hallway door. The Ben Davis cheerleading squad also has more members than the Edinburgh High School football team. This football event occurs five times a year, though the numbers of players and cheerleaders diminish as we approach honoring the 1A small school champions.

Soccer and cross country have large contingents. It's amazing the number of girls on a volleyball team and that most of their champions come from a school in Delaware County, who have a coach by the name of Shondell. Baseball teams are not so often recognized because the baseball and legislative seasons usually do not overlap.

During recent sessions, the president pro tem has taken pity on the chamber and declared that only champions could come before the Senate. No runner-ups or third or fourth place finishers.

Lots of political people who have passed away are honored. If they had at one time been legislators, several senators will approach the microphone and offer small personal tidbits relating to an occurrence between them and the deceased. These resolutions I think are fine, relevant and always done in good taste; better even if the spouse or children of the person being honored is in the chambers.

Rarely are persons who are honored, are asked, or even allowed, to respond with more than a wave. The president pro tem will tell a senator that his resolution will be worked into the schedule but warns the senator of the tight agenda for the day and suggest that it would be best if the honoree remains mute. There is a good reason for such warnings. I can remember when the Indiana Classroom Teacher of the Year was asked if she wanted say something, which she did for twenty minutes, and most of it was to chastise the legislature for being so cheap in appropriating money for education.

The worst that the Senate has to endure, the absolute worst, is honoring a singer or musical instrument player and then have to sit and listen to a rendition that is meant to show off their proficiency. In these cases, I am willing to take the word of the resolution. What's next? Ben Davis suited up and wanting to scrimmage in the front of the Senate, or having the split end run a GO pattern up the middle aisle and catching a pass from an all-state quarterback.

One woman honoree was a virtuoso pianist, but to drive the point home a Steinway was produced and wheeled into the chambers and Chopin came with her.

Jugglers, quartets, mimes, standup comedians. All have been honored. About the time I become real cynical and irritable about the interruptions, someone, perhaps a high school kid, will tell me that being recognized by the Indiana State Senate was absolutely the greatest moment in their life. It makes me feel two inches high.

Legislators can become very personal in the resolutions they present. I offered one to the Senate commemorating my parent's fiftieth wedding anniversary, and ones for their sixtieth, seventieth, and seventy-fifth anniversaries. I was also able to present a resolution honoring my father, Lawrence M. Borst, Sr., on his one-hundredth birthday in 2003. Maybe it was out of respect for my dad, or maybe it was because I got a little choked up, but the senators rose to their feet and gave the resolution a standing ovation.

The legislature was in session on our own twenty-fifth wedding anniversary in 1973, but not on our fiftieth, so members were spared that ordeal in 1998. The day following the birth of Lawrence Andrew Borst to Beth and David Borst, I announced from the podium to all whom had known Beth when she worked for the Senate that there was good news and bad news. "The good news is that Beth gave birth to a fine boy and he and the mother were doing great. The bad news was that the world, ready or not, would have to deal with another Lawrence Borst."

The year 1985 was a good one for resolutions concerning sports. The Colts came to town and Bob and Jim Irsay came to the legislature to be honored by both chambers. This was a big deal for Indiana, Indianapolis and Mayor Bill Hudnut. I imagine that the Irsays were especially gratified to be honored after having just having just escaped the state of Maryland whose legislature had recently passed legislation that sought to prevent the Colts from leaving Baltimore. Barry Krauss, a Colt linebacker, was singled out to be honored later in the session.

Another resolution of 1985 that I was tickled to sponsor was the one honoring the Southport Little League baseball team that had finished third in the Little League World Series in August of 1984, a tremendous accomplishment for the kids from my own back yard. Then the Center Grove Little League team became the fourth place team in the Little League World Series in 1992. The Indiana Southern Stars won the National AAU girls fourteen and under basketball title in 1995 and was so honored. The Center Grove High School Lady Trojans won the Girls State High School Basketball Championship in 1995. The Southport High School girls had also been Indiana state high school basketball champions. Roncalli won the Class 3A state football championship in 1985, 1988, 1993, 1994, 1999, 2002 and were runners-up in 1983 and 1989. The teams did not always appear at the statehouse for recognition or else the whole process became too boring for them. Central Indiana high school football teams have won forty-one of these class championships and seem to have the tendency to take an afternoon off from schoolwork and come to the statehouse for recognition.

Senators Bob Garton, Mike Gery and Frank O'Bannon joined me in honoring the Purdue School of Veterinary Medicine in 1985 for simply being open for business for 25 years. I sometimes question if recognizing a Silver Anniversary should be on the list to be honored. Fifty years falls within championship feats, twenty-five is just being a participant.

Taking the idea of honoring someone or something to a new level, I received several copies of a "Proclamation" from Governor Orr in January of 1984. Evidently he and Secretary of State Ed Simcox conceived the idea that the governor could issue an executive order and label it as a "Proclamation," which both would sign and receive loads of recognition. The proclamation began, "To All Whom These Present May Come, Greetings:"

Governors vary in their awards. Sagamore of the Wabash was and still may be the better award of recent governors. Bowen did not give many, but, for a second or a third recognition to the same person he would add an Oak Leaf Cluster; with real oak leaves with a couple of acorns. Orr was more generous with his Sagamores. For Evan Bayh as governor, the half of the state that were Republicans were not eligible for the award, and every one in the other half received a Sagamore. Governor O'Bannon created something to be given to lesser lights, an Honorary Hoosier award. O'Bannon would also proclaim that a certain day was to be named for an honoree.

Lieutenant Governor Joe Kernan has his embossed award. Several of the past secretaries of state created their own certificates. I know of two state senators who have official looking "distinguished citizen" certificates available for distribution to likely voters from their districts. In any given year, if a citizen worked it right, he or she might be able to collect a dozen pieces of paper with proclamations or greetings from a variety of the Indiana officeholders.

Obviously I have not been very consistent in my beliefs of curtailing the resolutions. Weak moments and the survival instinct of politics often overwhelm any temporary thought of sticking to a pre-conceived philosophy of abstinence. I exhibited that weakness when I agreed to co-sponsor a resolution with Senator Mike Gery to honor the actress and entertainer Rita Moreno for "her glorious career on stage and screen." I don't recall how Mike came about writing this resolution. Ms. Moreno was probably appearing in a production at Clowes Hall. My ego getting the better of my good sense, I decided to be a sponsor, with the understanding that I would be able to meet and greet the subject. Alas, Ms. Moreno had more pressing business and was unable to attend. The body of the Senate was also disappointed but passed the resolution with great reluctance.

One honoree who did appear was Marine Corps Captain Sean Dardeen of Greenwood. Captain Dardeen was the Marine who appeared in the Marine recruiting television commercials. He attempted feats in the commercial that one would see in a movie like *Raiders of the Lost Ark*. All spit and polish in his Class A uniform. Doing all kinds of acrobatic feats with his sword. He ends up in the commercial, ramrod straight, with his sword pointing upwards in front of his chin and face. Sean gave a soft-sell pitch for Marine enlistments and kindly posed for photographs with any of the senators, pages, interns and staff. He was so good looking that it was a week before the secretarial pool came down to earth.

The most recent resolutions have taken on a more patriotic and somber note. Hailing the adventurous Lewis and Clark expedition, National Guard troops in the Mid-east, memorializing the valiant astronauts, 9/11 and those killed or injured in Iraq.

chapter 27

Tobacco Settlement

No matter how often the media castigates Indiana legislators for taking "junkets," using state money for transportation and drawing down per diem, legislators should never pass up an opportunity to improve their range and depth of knowledge. The medical and legal professions require their members to remain current on trends and new techniques by attending continuing education conferences. A legislator is no different.

I have gone to a veterinary conference thinking that I was the worst practicing veterinarian in the state of Indiana. After hanging around with other practitioners for a day or two, I came away with the realization that my veterinary practice was not doing too badly after all, but could use some tweaking. An Indiana legislator might get the impression that Indiana is somewhat backward in its approach to progressive ideas. Actual exposure to other legislators may give an entirely different perspective to the Indiana legislator.

I attended a winter meeting of the National Conference of State Legislators held in Washington D.C., in December of 1998. One of the topics was the settlement of tobacco health issues between forty-six of the states and the tobacco industry. Basically, the states would be required to pass model legislation promising not to sue the tobacco companies on any health issue and the tobacco industry would promise to pay each of the states a certain amount of money for perpetuity based on a complicated formula.

Indiana Attorney General Jeff Modisett who was one of the lead negotiators in the settlement case and I compared notes about what he knew and what I had learned about the settlement provisions in 1999. He had hopes of being the "tobacco settlement czar" for Indiana. But, the governor decided otherwise and ruled that all of the settlement money would be administered by his office and would be subject to the appropriation process of the General Assembly. I outlined to Modisett the type of legislation that I wanted to offer. He had definite ideas on how and where the settlement money should be spent. Ours ideas were compatible. Once enabling legislation was passed, Jeff wanted to be the detail man and head up the smoking cessation program in Indiana. His collected written matter on cessation programs was voluminous and he was well prepared for the task.

The program was on track until Jeff called and said, "I have some good news for you and some bad news. The good news is that I am leaving Indiana and the bad news is that I won't be able to work on the cessation and public health programs for Indiana." I considered this to be the worst of news. With his knowledgeable input the Indiana program would have been very successful.

Not enough was known about the details of the settlement to be of concern in the 1999 session. The tobacco settlement disclosures later estimated that Indiana would receive in excess of four and a half billion dollars over the next twenty-six years. An applied formula for yearly payments to the states included the number of cigarettes manufactured in the United States, the number of cigarettes imported to the United States, the number of cigarettes sold in this country, a three percent yearly increase of the rate of inflation and several other factors. If the smoking cessation programs were successful, then the tobacco companies would be able to lower their payments due to the reduced sales of cigarettes. But the tobacco companies then began a strategy of manufacturing more of their cigarettes overseas and importing the finished product back to this country to aid in their reduction of payments to the states. The yearly payment to Indiana was to be approximately $150 million.

What to do with the sudden riches was approached differently in the forty-six states. Wisconsin, for example, simply folded the payments into their general fund the first year and attempted to balance their budget. Small endowments for a variety of purposes were established in other states. Ohio had been under a court order to upgrade their public school facilities and applied a portion of the yearly payments to local school districts throughout the state. Most of the states appropriated their new found money to various projects that had nothing to do with curbing the habit of smoking cigarettes or even to health matters.

I thought that Indiana had the opportunity to be the model state for the country. I felt that the money had occurred because of tobacco-related health issues and that the money should logically be used for public health and related programs. Also a portion of the settlement money should be saved and escrowed into an endowment to be preserved over the lifetime of the payments. Twenty-six years down the road the endowment would have grown to over three billion dollars if we had set aside fifty percent of the yearly income. Using only the interest from the endowment would take care of a huge amount of the state's public health problems in the future.

I was told that the governor was going to announce the administration's plans for spending the money from the master settlement on November 10, 1999. I had never intentionally tried to pre-empt any governor's announcements before, but I knew that the first media report would establish the parameters of the effort. If the governor was first out with his plan, then what I wanted to do would not be accomplished. I had an idea of what the governor was going to propose but thought that my program was far superior.

Senator Pat Miller had already written legislation establishing an endowment of sorts. She had been chairperson of an interim health committee and the committee had come to no definite conclusion as what would be the best usage of the payments. She was kind enough to allow me to "hijack" her bill and then join me in holding a press conference on November 9, the day before the governor's announcement. Senator Miller and I spoke in generalities. We both wanted to establish an endowment and we both wanted to form a new board, free of political persuasion that would develop and administer a cessation program. We stressed that the public health effort should be basically directed at the younger generation. I apologized to Senator Miller for stealing her bill but timing was everything. She was the co-author of the legislation that survived to become the law in Indiana.

Governor O'Bannon had his press conference the next day. As I had guessed, his plan called for the state health commissioner to be the person who would develop all of the programs to be funded by the settlement money. The governor put in a strong plug for securitization of the Master Settlement Agreement future payments. It also was not a secret that bond counsels and attorneys close to the administration would have liked to see bonding (securitization) with the tobacco monies, maybe for the good of the state, maybe for the fees that would be generated through the bonding procedure. The question about bonding was, "What is done with the sudden wealth of cash?" "How do you hide it from the spenders?" The governor attempted to answer the first question in 2003 by suggesting its use for economic development, but had no specific use for the money in 2000. In recent years the state has somehow gone from a three billion dollar surplus to almost living hat in hand. Another billion or two through securitization in 2000 would have disappeared by 2003. Indiana is at least assured of steady payments for a few more years.

The governor's proposal was introduced in the House by Representative Charlie Brown, and I introduced the version that Senator Miller and I had written in the Senate. Public hearings were held in the House by the Health Committee and in the Senate by the Finance Committee. Both bills were complex. Both bills required a detailed explanation to the legislators. The 2000 session was the two-month session or so-called short session. Passage was not a sure thing.

Evidently, proper explanations were made because there was overwhelming bipartisan support for the respective plans that the House and Senate each passed on February 1. The House bill passed 84-14. SB 108 was approved by the Senate 49-1. Brown walked across the hall to watch the Senate debate and vote on. On completion of the vote I said to him, "my man, my man" and this bear of a man proceeded to give me a giant bear hug.

The basic structure of the new board that was to oversee the statewide cessation programs was very important to me. I wanted an autonomous group of people deciding how best to deliver the cessation effort. Up to that time, Indiana was fragmented in the delivery of anti-smoking programs. The Board of Health, Department of Mental Health, the superintendent of Public Instruction, and other state agencies were attempting to create competing programs. I was adamant that there be one unified approach.

Representative Brown and I both strongly agreed that this operation would be free from outside political influences.

The final version also created an endowment. The governor came to realize that such a "savings account" would be superior to securitization. Mike Gery, the governor's liaison, asked if more of the settlement money could be used for several programs that Governor O'Bannon had in mind. For one thing, I had not counted on the governor being so energetic in promoting his idea of aiding low-income senior citizens in purchasing prescription drugs. He flew around the state and lobbied the senior citizen organizations. He wanted to use twenty million dollars of the settlement money each year of this purpose. As a result, the endowment only received forty percent of the money rather than the contemplated fifty percent.

The senior citizen groups were the most vocal about telling the legislators that they should receive the bulk of the tobacco payments. They reasoned that their generations had smoked the most and the residual effects had caused their health to be frail. Senior citizen programs in place and on the drawing board were touted as the only ones that should be funded. I had an advantage. I was as old as or maybe older than the lobbyists and I could look them in the eye and inform them that this money was to go to the younger people. If we could do all of the necessary preventative health measures for the young, then we would not have the massive medical bills to pay when the younger generation became older.

The final obstacle to overcome at conference committee time was the push for a large portion of the Master Settlement money by the organized groups representing mental health. The Indiana Department of Mental Health earlier had been given the authority to supervise the treatment of addictive drug users. This authority could be broadly interpreted, and was construed to include nicotine. The motive of the mental health groups was not entirely for the cessation efforts, it was a way to obtain additional money for programs having nothing to do with on-going public health programs. Representative Brown and I held fast to allocating the money only for public health initiatives.

Brown and Representative Bill Crawford were advocates for the funding of minority health programs separate from the unified approach. They were given the opportunity to make their case before a legislative panel in an attempt to have a program that concentrated on minority health problems. The end result was a specially designed effort that did reach into the minority communities.

Most pieces of legislation of the magnitude of the Master Settlement

Agreement normally would involve the efforts of twenty or more legislators. There might be committees and sub-committees and egos that would need to be stroked. Discussions would go on and on. Bruised feelings are inevitable when so many participate. Basically, with this MSA bill, only two legislators, Brown and Borst, plus representatives from the governor's office were the ones that agreed to the final version. Evidently the rest of the body had faith in the proceedings because there was no interference from any of the other members of the General Assembly.

The Indiana Master Settlement legislation is the model for the rest of the country. Indiana is one of just a few of the states that did allocate all of the resources to public health problems. Since the 2000 session, other states have adopted several of the Indiana provisions.

The centerpiece of the legislation was the formation of the Indiana To-bacco Use Prevention and Cessation Trust Fund. An autonomous board was created that managed the fund. This board was appointed by the governor and was able to hire an executive director and to employ the staff necessary to advise and to assist the board. The board was given the express charge of de-veloping "a mission statement concerning prevention and reduction of the usage of tobacco and tobacco products in Indiana." Also, an equally impor-tant duty was to develop "a long-range state plan based on Best Practices for Tobacco Control Programs" as published by the Centers for Disease Control and Prevention.

The final appropriation of funds in SB 108 was thirty-five million dol-lars for Tobacco Cessation with two and a half million dollars of the amount to be directed toward minority concerns; twenty million dollars for prescrip-tion co-payment for low income senior citizens; fifteen million dollars for ex-pansion and maintenance of Community Health Clinics; ten million dollars one time for rehab of community health centers; nearly forty-seven million dollars for the Children's Health Insurance Program (CHIPS); and four and a half million dollars for the county boards of health.

An affirmative vote for the conference committee on SB 108 once again brought Representative Brown into the Senate chambers. This time he was the one who said, "My man, my man" and then proceeded to attach an ear-ring to the lobe of my left ear, and saluted me as his "new brother." Success has its moments.

NOTE: Available research shows that public cessation programs do reduce the percentage of smokers in the general population. The drop-off of new smokers is not huge but is discernible. Data from Massachusetts, Florida and California programs indicate that a sufficiently funded anti-smoking public media program can be beneficial.

NOTE: Because of the uniqueness of the Indiana MSA program of dedicating the monies to health concerns, *Governing Magazine* featured Representative Brown and me in one of their issues, even though we both voted for the legislation.

chapter 28

Gentlemen, It Has Been My Pleasure

My wife, Eldoris, and I were in Las Vegas with another couple in 1961. We had just taken in a stage show featuring Betty Grable, her legs, and six twenty-one-year-old-males at the Desert Inn. I had won a little money, and while the others went to their rooms, I stayed around to try my luck at the crap table. I had no idea on how to bet craps then and I have no idea today. I know "come" and "crap" bets and that's about it.

While I was standing at the table, a handsome well dressed man in his thirties came to the table with a gorgeous blonde on his arm. He signed a chit for a tray of $100 chips. He ordered a Scotch and tried his luck. The blonde tried her luck. When the dice came around to me, I warned him "that I was a crap shooter and he better bet against me." He didn't and lost more. He signed a second chit for another tray of chips. And then a third.

I was betting five dollars and he was betting five hundred. The blonde was betting whatever he gave her. He doubled up for a few passes. The chips dwindled and most were gone. He had gone through $30,000 in less than thirty minutes.

He backed away from the table, took a sip from his drink, and centered his tie. The blonde adjusted her mink stole, attached herself to his left arm and prepared to leave.

The man found two chips in his coat pocket, stepped back to the table, flipped the chips in the air and onto the table and said, "Gentlemen, it has been my pleasure."

Never have I ever been so impressed by the carriage and delivery of that gentleman. The buzz from the pit boss was that he was some young guy from up around San Francisco that had done "something" in computers. He came in monthly with a blonde who was more gorgeous than the previous one. His luck at the tables was always bad.

Talk about cool. A Cary Grant type of cool. A James Bond attitude. At that minute, the man had it all and I was there to see the performance.

I have always thought that I would like to have his phrase, "Gentlemen, it has been my pleasure" engraved on my tombstone. I thought, too, that it would make a good title for a book.

I have been more than fortunate in my life. I, more or less, flow along with the stream and take, and enjoy, what comes along in life. Without the cast of thousands in my life aiding me as I wander through life's pitfalls, and if I have accomplished anything, I could not have done so without the help and guidance that I have received from all of those people that I have been in contact with sometime in the past. I have enjoyed it all, and truly, **"It has been my pleasure."**

I enjoyed presenting a bill on the floor of the Indiana Senate.

I'm happy at the passage of the pari-mutuel program.

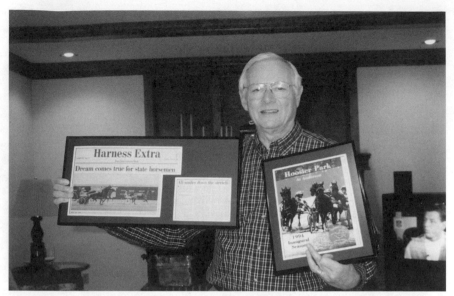

Pari-mutuel becomes a reality for Hoosiers in November of 1995.

Record attendance at program

Hoosier harness horsemen enjoyed an evening of excitement at the annual Indiana Standardbred Association awards banquet. Over 280 horsemen and guests from all parts of Indiana gathered in Anderson to celebrate an excellent first full year for harness racing at Hoosier Park and as an association.

The Standardbred Hall of Fame inducted three new members. Hall of Fame Board members Margie Hill, Gary Wilcox and Carl Colbert presented the awards.

Senator Lawrence Borst of Indianapolis was inducted for his long-time dedication and commitment to pass parimutuel wagering through the state legislature.

Greyhound, the horse no one paid attention to when he was young, was inducted for the notoriety he gave to the Indiana harness racing industry. He was trained most of his life in Indiana.

Margot Taylor dedicated her life to building the Indiana standardbred industry in all areas. She was a driver, trainer, owner, promoter and anything else she could fit in to build harness racing in the Hoosier state. Her husband Dick Taylor and daughter Ellen, along with many members of the family accepted the award.

Ellen Taylor, Executive Director of the Harness Youth Foundation, presented the awards for the outstanding harness racing youth of the year to Jeff Dever, son of Randy and Linda Dever and Justin Kieninger, son of Jack and Jeri Kieninger.

Indiana Standardbred Association President, Hank Blackwell, presented the prized headliner awards to Phyllis Edwards, Secretary of Indiana Standardbred Association and Mary Bell, Executive Vice President of the Indiana Standardbred Association for their contributions in promotion Hoosier harness rac-

ing.

"Mary and Phyllis didn't miss a night at Hoosier Park working the promotional table this past year," Blackwell said. "We are grateful for their hard work."

Fred Noe, Executive Vice-president of the United States Trotting Association, represented the organization at the banquet and was impressed with the enthusiasm he found.

"I'd like to take a piece of the excitement I see in Indiana everywhere I go," he said. "I'll walk away from this banquet with a sense of pride and accomplishment."

The record setting attendance at the banquet signaled a new era of growth and prosperity in Indiana harness racing. The evening marked a most successful and prosperous year.

Senator Larry Borst receives the Hall of Fame Award from Margaret Hill.

More awards
next page. . .

Receiving the Hall of Fame award for the late Margot Taylor were Dick and Ellen Taylor, friends and family.

In my Senate finance office everything Buckeye has been eliminated, except for Ohio State football.

At an October 22, 1996 rally for Governor nominee Goldsmith, Eldoris and I enjoy talking with the nominee, Mayor Steve Goldsmith.

Courtesy Tom Strattman of AP.

A typical conference committee explaining the Senate's position on a bill. (l-r) Sen. Lawrence Borst, Reps. William Cochran, Verne Tichner and Pat Bauer.

The legislative process also requires on-site inspections such as this trip to a coal strip mine in southern Indiana.

Legislators need to keep up-to-date on all aspects of Indiana facilities and personnel.

I'm dressed in the silks of Trotter Range *and ready to work out a horse. A legislator's time is not spent entirely in smoked-filled rooms.*

Senator Pat Miller explains one of her many bills to me.

Josie and Bob Orr and Oliver say "hello" to Eldoris and me.

Senate President Pro Tem Robert Garton and I hold a press conference in February of 1989.

Veterinary Medicine will always have a special place in my heart and so I was pleased to share this moment with Governor Bob Orr.

I sometimes think the trappings of political life can go a little overboard.

I was always grateful for all the marvelous team players that worked with me through the years as we geared up for the big race.